D0855769

SIXTH
EDITION

The
Modern
Conductor

A college text on conducting based on the
technical principles of Nicolai Malko as set
forth in his *The Conductor and His Baton*

Elizabeth A. H. Green

Professor Emeritus
The University of Michigan

 PRENTICE HALL, Upper Saddle River, New Jersey 07458

Library of Congress Cataloging-in-Publication Data

GREEN, ELIZABETH A. H.
   The modern conductor: a college text on conducting based on the
technical principles of Nicolai Malko as set forth in his The
conductor and his baton/Elizabeth A. H. Green.—6th ed.
      p.   cm.
   Includes bibliographical references and index.
   ISBN 0-13-251481-8
   1. Conducting.   I. Malko, Nicolai, 1883–1961. Conductor and his
baton.   II. Title.
MT85.G785   1997
781.45—dc20   96-28810
                                                                         CIP
                                                                         MN

Acquisitions editor: Bud Therien
Editorial/production supervision and interior design: Carole R. Crouse
Copy editor: Carole R. Crouse
Buyer: Bob Anderson
Editorial assistant: Lee Mamunes
Cover image: Janita Hauk, conductor of the
   Charlotte Symphony Orchestra, Port Charlotte, Florida.
   Photograph by Yun-Shen Wang.

This book was set in 10.5/12 New Baskerville
by Thompson Type and was printed and bound
by R. R. Donnelley & Sons Company. The cover was
printed by The Lehigh Press, Inc.

 © 1997, 1992, 1987, 1981, 1969, 1961 by Prentice-Hall, Inc.
Simon & Schuster/A Viacom Company
Upper Saddle River, New Jersey 07458

Printed in the United States of America

10 9 8 7 6 5 4 3 2 1

ISBN 0-13-251481-8

PRENTICE-HALL INTERNATIONAL (UK) LIMITED, *London*
PRENTICE-HALL OF AUSTRALIA PTY. LIMITED, *Sydney*
PRENTICE-HALL CANADA INC., *Toronto*
PRENTICE-HALL HISPANOAMERICANA, S.A., *Mexico*
PRENTICE-HALL OF INDIA PRIVATE LIMITED, *New Delhi*
PRENTICE-HALL OF JAPAN, INC., *Tokyo*
SIMON & SCHUSTER ASIA PTE. LTD., *Singapore*
EDITORA PRENTICE-HALL DO BRASIL, LTDA., *Rio de Janeiro*

Elizabeth A. H. Green died on September 24, 1995, in Ann Arbor, Michigan, having just celebrated her eighty-ninth birthday surrounded by friends, former students, and colleagues. Elizabeth had achieved both national and international recognition for her work in violin pedagogy and conducting. But most of all, she was known for her deep personal commitment to her students. Her retirement was filled with clinics, guest-lecturing, and teaching former students and "grandstudents." She inspired each of us—her students, colleagues, and friends—to have the courage to pursue our deepest hopes and dreams. Her spirit, vitality, and mentorship will remain with us always.

Elizabeth A. H. Green completed the sixth edition of *The Modern Conductor* just before her death. Several special friends agreed to follow the manuscript to print. Appreciation is extended to Dr. Catherine Nadon-Gabrion, who coordinated this effort. In addition, Lloyd Biggle, Jr., E. Daniel Long, and H. Robert Reynolds gave countless hours of assistance in providing quality assurance that this book accurately reflects the pedagogy of Elizabeth Green. We proudly dedicate this effort to our teacher and friend.

Contents

Part One: TECHNIQUE

EUGENE ORMANDY

The Art of Conducting

The art of conducting, one of the most complex and demanding activities in the realm of music, comprises both the visual public performance and the constant application of technique. Although they are inseparable in performance, they can be analyzed in the light of the unique problems which each presents. Similarly, the conductor himself functions on three levels, each dependent upon the other, all culminating in the performance itself.

Personal Study. On the first level, his period of study, the conductor prepares himself both technically and artistically. On this level he must be musician, historian, stylist, orchestrator, and listener. He must study the score so that he "hears" it in his mind. As he does this he evaluates the music and makes a beginning toward balancing the many strands of musical line. He must understand the historical context in which a particular work is conceived, and bring to bear upon the growing interpretive edifice a thorough knowledge of the stylistic requirements inherent in the work. To study such a masterwork as Beethoven's *Eroica* Symphony without some knowledge of the composer's response to the ideals of the French Revolution and Napoleon's unique political position in 1806 is to study music in a vacuum. Needless to say, it was not created in a vacuum. Among the elements of stylistic validity are tempi and dynamics. A Mozart allegro differs by far from a Tchaikovsky allegro. Similarly, a forte in Haydn is an entirely different matter from a Wagner forte.

A thorough knowledge of the orchestral colors and timbres enables the studying conductor to "hear" the orchestral sound while he studies. When

Reprinted from Encyclopedia International *by permission of the publishers, Lexicon Publications, New York.*

conducting older composers he must sometimes compensate for the technical inadequacies of the times by delicately rewriting certain passages in terms of today's more complete orchestras and more highly skilled players. Present-day performances of such works as the Fifth Symphony of Beethoven, the Great C Major Symphony of Schubert, the symphonies of Schumann, to mention but a few, are rarely given without many instrumental changes. Even so "pure" a conductor as Toscanini did not deny the composer the benefit of today's heightened instrumental resources.

Finally, while he studies, the conductor must "listen" objectively to the work, pacing its progress, spacing its climaxes, deriving a general aural concept of the musical architecture, and evaluating its merit as it will be heard by the public. He must recall Richard Strauss's dictum: "Remember that you are making music not for your own pleasure but for the joy of your listeners."

Rehearsal. The second level upon which the conductor functions is the rehearsal, in which he prepares the orchestra both technically and artistically. It is on this level that he acts as a guide to the orchestra, building up in their minds a concept of the work parallel to his own, for the eventual public performance requires an enlightened and sensitive orchestra playing not "under" a conductor, but rather "with" him.

During the rehearsals he must clarify all problems of metrics and tempi, elucidating his own pacing of the work. He must temper all dynamic markings so that the instrumental "sound" is balanced in all its components. The older composers always wrote the same dynamics vertically for each simultaneous part, straight down the page in their scores. It was only composer-conductors like Mahler or Wagner, who realized the pitfalls of dynamics incautiously marked.

As he rehearses, the conductor, surrounded by the physical sound of the work, checks his own concept of the music, comparing it with the actual music. In those particular instances where the two do not fit, he must alter one or the other. It is essential that the two, the concept and the actuality, run amicably along. In addition, there are instances, such as the lengthy oboe solo in Strauss's *Don Juan,* where the prudent conductor who is fortunate enough to possess a highly sensitive oboe player permits him to "have his head," acting almost as an accompanist rather than a leader.

Performance. It is in performance that the conductor operates upon the highest and most demanding level. Here the work is finished technically; the orchestra is fully prepared for all of its demands; the conductor, his study and preparation behind him, now immerses himself in the music, identifying himself with it both emotionally and mentally. But it is at this crucial time that the most difficult function of the conductor comes into full play. He must, while identifying himself with the music, keep a constant watch upon the progress of the work, allowing a portion of his analytical mind to constantly evaluate the sound and pace of the performance. He must be prepared to instantaneously make any adjustments, large or small, in the actual performance required for the fullest realization of his inner concept. Many factors make this necessary: a different hall, a player's momentary inattention, the effect of several thousand persons upon the acoustics, even the understandable enthusiasm of performance which might affect the tempo. At such a moment the experience of a conductor tells, for the young conductor, new to such emergencies, tends to do one thing at a time. Music does not permit this, for it flows in time, and all adjustments must be superimposed upon the uninterrupted continuum.

In the extent to which he succeeds on any or all of these levels lies the measure of the conductor's merit, both as a musician and as an artist. In his study he can separate the art from the technique, but in performance he must strive fully and constantly for a total artistic experience. Otherwise he can never fulfill his high calling: creating the reality of the work itself.

Preface

This sixth edition of *The Modern Conductor* continues the preferred format of the fifth edition. The writing is to the point, it is often addressed directly to the student, and the use of **highlighted words** enables the reader to locate quickly the information being sought. Certain "drills" are inserted into the text as before.

It has been most gratifying to see the gradual acceptance, by the teaching profession, of the Nicolai Malko pedagogic principles as presented in the first edition back in 1961. The efficacy of Malko's eleven "physical exercises" (the development of independence in the left hand and the ability, manually, to speak a language clearly understood by the players) has been made apparent by the professional successes of young conductors who have devoted serious practice to the development of their manual technique as well as to their musical skills.

The current brain research has given us valuable knowledge concerning the amazing activity taking place in the infinitesimal neurons. We have the means of accomplishing our goals. Our hands will learn whatever we teach them. As our skills mature, the time ultimately arrives when our musical thoughts appear in our gestures, but only if the training has taken place. Practicing the exercises strengthens the "neural pathway" from brain to hands.

Conducting is a *time-space* activity. *It is impossible to change the size of a gesture without first changing the speed of the physical motion between beats.*

This facet of conducting technique has been largely neglected pedagogically, but Malko made the skill available in his eleventh exercise, the summation of the conductor's ability to show the musical qualities of the interpretation. An example? That single moment when the illusion occurs of "stretching the beat," still arriving on time with the following beat: that one tenuto gesture between two beats, moving momentarily slower, thereby covering less space. See Appendix F, item 11, page 277.

In *The Modern Conductor* there are several technical distinctions to which special attention should be directed:

1. For the triplet division on each major beat in beating $\frac{12}{8}$, most books show the triplet division of **beat One** as moving to the left, toward beat Two. There is a better way. Since the triplet is part of the *major* beat (1, 2, 3, or 4), it should move, following beat One, just as it does after the other major beats—namely, in the *same direction as the major beat*. Let beat One move downward for its subdivisions, slightly to the right if necessary. Then **beat Two** is easily identified, uncluttered by the small extra beats following beat One. It is much clearer for the players. See page 33, Figure 22b.

2. For the "dead gesture," emphasis is laid on motion in a perfectly straight, unemotional, and "lifeless" line. No curves. It takes real control but is effective when perfected. It describes absolute silence. See page 59.

3. The term **staccato** means a STOP, a separation, between notes. Too often we see the staccato indicated as a heavy, demanding accent (rigid arm and hand) *without any stop* but continuing enthusiastically, with high rebound into the next beat. *The STOP must show in the baton if the musicians are to respond to it.* See pages 46–47 and Figure 28 (page 47).

4. To *control* responses that must come after the beat instead of coinciding with the beat, the conductor must have absolute mastery of the stops in the baton. This is one of the most valuable "tricks of the trade." It is rewritten herein. Alert observation shows its use by outstanding conductors. See pages 52–58.

5. There are two instances requiring specialized handling of the opening measure of certain compositions: when a legato prep-beat **must** be connected to the downbeat, and when there **must** be a stop between the preparation and the downbeat itself. See page 63, eleven lines beginning with the **sentence in bold type.**

6. For ease of handling and reading the FIVE pattern beaten in TWO, see page 113 and Figure 42, the high rebound after One for 3 + 2; low rebound when Two comes first, thus leaving the long upward line for the Three. **Note:** This is quoted in new texts coming out, but proper acknowledgment is not being made. It IS, as are the preceding items, a Malko technique, originated by him.

Malko, the great Russian conductor, developed his analyses of the conducting gestures during his years as Administrative Director and Chief Conductor of the Leningrad Philharmonic Orchestra and concurrently as Professor of Conducting and Chairman of the Conducting Department at the prestigious Glinka [National] Conservatory of Music in Leningrad.

Quoting Malko: "When I had to teach it, then I had really to know." Maestro Yevgeny Mravinski, who conducted the Leningrad Philharmonic on their first United States concert tour (1959–60?), fondly acknowledged Malko as his teacher.

Tragically, Malko died in 1961, one month before the first copy of *The Modern Conductor* came from the presses. He had carefully critiqued the manuscript but did not live to see the book itself. The contract was, and still is, on a 50/50 basis at my instigation. Mrs. Malko has placed their share of the royalties into The Malko Foundation (New York) to be donated to *The Nicolai Malko* [memorial] *International Competition for Young Conductors,* held triennially in Copenhagen, Denmark, under the auspices of the Danish National Radio Symphony Orchestra with Royal Patronage. Malko was knighted by the King of Denmark, honoring him for his work with the Danish orchestra.

Once again special appreciation is expressed to the following list of influential conductors for their continuing interest in these methods: H. Robert Reynolds, Director of Bands, Chairman of the Conducting Department, The University of Michigan; Donald Schleicher, now faculty of the University of Illinois at Champaign; Dr. Larry Livingston, Dean, School of Music, The University of Southern California; and Conductor Henry Charles Smith, former Principal Trombone of the Philadelphia Orchestra and now retired from the faculty of Arizona State University (Tempe). Thanks also to Dr. Jamie Hafner, University of Toledo; to Gabriel Villasurda, Interlochen Arts Camp conducting faculty and Punahou School, Honolulu, Hawaii; to Dr. Marcia Lareau, Conductor of the Pueblo (Colorado) Symphony and faculty at the University there; and to these choral musicians: Professor Emeritus Thomas Hilbish, University of Michigan; and Dr. Deborah Smith, Associate Professor, University of Southern Illinois at Edwardsville.

Finally, accolades to our brilliant editors at Prentice Hall, whose patience has been inexhaustible: Norwell "Bud" Therien, publisher; his able assistant, Lee Mamunes; and production editor Carole Crouse.

Elizabeth A. H. Green

Credo

Music lives only when the notes fly off the page and soar into glorious sound.

The performer, the conductor, releases them from bondage through his or her feeling for their message, through the power of the imagination, and by means of the physical technique one devotedly acquires.

We build the technique *only* to ensure that *our music* can achieve its unforgettable moments, evanescent as they are, before once more returning to its prison of impatient silence.

The most profoundly inspiring performances of a lifetime were those where the performer's technique was so superb that we forgot it existed. Music spoke its own language in its own way, uninfluenced by human frailty.

CHAPTER

1

So You Want to Be a Conductor?

Have you committed yourself to success? Yes? Then this is your chapter. It was written for you. The rest of the book is like any other textbook—full of information for those who desire it. It tells you how.

Your mind, your hands-arms complex, your musicianship: These are your tools for carving out your future as a conductor; or, if you prefer, they are your weapons to fight your way to the top. They must be in good condition. Rusty tools or weapons that jam are not of much value in this world.

The following quotation from Robert Beverly Hale was addressed to artists who paint, but it suits us just as well in our profession.

> Your style will develop through the decisions you make. . . . These decisions will all be influenced by the qualities of your mind, by your selflessness or selfishness, by your curiosity or lethargy, by your dignity or vulgarity, by your honesty or insincerity. . . . Never forget that the good critics can look right through the canvas into the eyes of the artist beyond.*

So how does one learn to conduct? Conducting, like everything else, starts in the brain—your storehouse of knowledge.

Your brain has some 30 *billion* nerve cells called neurons. They are one of the attributes of a normal human brain. When you start to learn something new, these smart little neurons connect themselves up in new patterns. They make pathways. The more you reinforce a pattern by repetition (practice!), the

*In *Drawing Lessons from the Great Masters*. Used by permission of Watson-Guptill Publishers, Inc., New York, N.Y. © 1964.

more powerful it becomes. After a while it works automatically, and it is at your service thereafter.

Your hands-arms are your technique in conducting. They speak a very skillful language. You have stored that language in the neural patterns you have created in your brain by your practice. Your clear-speaking **gestures are your vocabulary.** Be canny about what you store up there. Accuracy in the beginning pays enormous dividends in the future.

The commands issued by your mind travel through a **neural pathway** that links your mind to the hands-arms complex. The more you use this pathway, the quicker the trip becomes. Eventually it becomes instantaneous. The hands perform automatically what is in your mind. When the process arrives at this degree of efficiency, it is ready for use on the conductor's podium.

It is wise to build your technique away from the podium, for as soon as the music starts, in rehearsal or performance, the full powers of your mind switch over to the music, and your hands are left to their own skilled (or unskilled) devices. Take time to build your hand-arm technique. Set those first neuron patterns and neural pathways correctly and then reinforce them with the kind of practice that secures their accuracy.

Pay attention to what your hands-arms are saying. Look at them when you practice. Use a mirror if necessary. Are they speaking clearly to your musicians, or are they flapping around in uninhibited emotional ecstasy? Well, you get the picture!

Now, about your musicianship. In one short, spicy sentence, musicianship is **what your ear hears** *while you are conducting.*

What are you judging as you rehearse? Is it the togetherness of the ensemble? Are you pitch-conscious? Did you notice that missing F-sharp in the trumpet? He played F-natural. (Of course, it was a misprint.)

Did you hear the tone quality of your ensemble? Did you really hear the melody in the clarinets, or was it actually drowned out by a rambunctious snaredrummer who thought he was still on the football field?

As a conductor, you will find that your biggest hurdle is to adjust the balance among the several parts—to "rewrite" the printed dynamics until they fit your orchestra, your band, your chorus. And then you have to convince your players that **"the music is in the sound, not in the printing."*** The quote is from Charles Owen, who was Principal Percussionist of the United States Marine Band and thereafter of the Philadelphia Orchestra, 1954–72.

After all, the conductor is the only one who stands where he or she can hear the whole ensemble at once. It is up to him or her to make it intelligible to the audience.

So now, proceed to face the horrors of learning to control your hands!

Note: As you read the text, perform the small drills as you encounter them. When you come to those marked **"Training Exercise,"** take them seriously.

---

*From *The Dynamic Orchestra*, Green, © 1987, by Prentice-Hall, Inc., a division of Simon & Schuster, Englewood Cliffs, N.J. Used by Permission.

They are the building blocks of future independence in your two hands and a means for getting your hands to respond to the musical ideas you have created in your imagination.

Sharpening Your Tools

Life with the baton will be easier if you do several things now. To start, practice bending the thumb on your *right hand.* (No! Sorry! The left hand won't do. The baton is held in the right hand.) Notice that your thumb has only two joints: one at the base where it joins the hand and the other halfway up to the nail. We shall call the latter the mid-joint. Exercise the mid-joint diligently, bending and unbending.

Swing the bent thumb over to place its tip on the palm of the hand just below the little finger. This activates the base-joint and should produce an open circle between thumb and palm of hand. This open circle helps to relax the hand when it holds the baton.

Play around with your thumb this way whenever you happen to think of it during the day.

This next exercise is helpful to both hands. Drill each hand separately. **Each has its own particular technique later on.**

Place the right arm with the palm of the hand flat on a table or on the arm of your chair. Without moving your arm, swing the hand upward as far as it will go and bring it back down. Drill this a bit. Then gradually increase the speed, still using the *maximum height* of the upward motion. Go fast. Still faster!

In your effort to increase speed, do you find tension building in your shoulder and upper arm?

Relax! The way to build speed is to cut down on the distance moved. So try the same exercise and gradually lessen the height as you speed up, thus bringing the hand closer and closer to the tabletop. Practice this sequence. Curve the fingers and tap with good rhythm.

What are you accomplishing in all of this? You are **strengthening a neural pathway from the command in your brain to a specific skill in your hands and wrists.**

Repeat with the left hand.

Technical application: **For faster tempos, be ready to condense the size of the beat.**

For this next experiment, reset your arm so that the hand hangs over the edge of the table or over the end of the armrest. Raise the hand up to the level of your arm and wrist. Suddenly relax the muscles, allowing the hand to collapse downward from the wrist. Move slowly as you bring it back up to the level again. Repeat this several times. Then, still using the relaxed drop of the hand, move slower and slower on the upward recovery gesture.

Do you have any difficulty with smoothness of motion on the very slow tempos? Does the hand want to quiver a bit? Do not panic! The smoothness will come as your control gradually improves.

Instead of building speed, this exercise starts you on the road to control. Repeat these two hand-wrist exercises using the left hand. *Slow motions build control.*

Slow motions can hypnotize an audience; fast motions excite.

When Evgeny Svetlanov (Moscow Symphony) ended a slow piece with a long diminuendo-ritard, he held the audience spellbound. We were scarcely able to breathe, so tremendous was our fascinated silence. His left hand, palm toward the players, slowly descended—the sound growing weaker and weaker. In fact, it had vanished completely as his hand passed his thigh. But the descent continued, slowly, slowly until his arm hung straight down. When it could go no farther, he consciously relaxed the muscles and his hand went limp. We saw the music die right there on the stage.

What an effect! What control! And what a storm of applause when we could finally bring ourselves to break that mesmerizing silence!

The preceding story gives you an idea of the power of a trained left hand, moving independently from the right hand.

Independence in the two hands is simply a matter of training, step by step. Success in each of the following training exercises builds on the mastery of the exercise that preceded it.

Clarence B. Evans, Principal Viola of the Chicago Symphony (1926–39), once said, "Master it first. Because until you have mastered it you have no right to judge it." It is good advice.

We begin now to build your permanent technique.

As conducting skills mature, the ability to command relaxation is of vital importance. Most tension starts in the shrugged shoulder. Anxiety causes shoulder tension. Also, when you are suddenly startled, your shoulders instantly shrug before you can think. It is a self-preservation instinct. We must learn, right from the beginning, to recognize tension when it exists and to command it to relax.

Relaxation: The Starting Point

Introduction to Relaxation and Tension

1. Stand with arms hanging loosely at the sides, palms to the rear.

2. With feet firmly planted, pivot the body rapidly left-right, left-right several times. The arms swing freely around the body. If completely relaxed, the right arm will impinge on the left side of the body and the left arm on the right side.

3. Stop the body motion, and let the arms continue their relaxed swinging as long as they can. Do not interfere with their motion. As they approach the end, they move only infinitesimally and finally stop of their own accord.

Note: In the first stages of practice, your arms will stop very soon. But as you repeat this exercise during a week's time, the relaxed motion will go on longer and longer. This is good progress.

Now let us explore **tension.**

1. Glue your arms tight to your sides from shoulders to wrists. Rigid! Palms face rear.

2. Flap hands forward and backward as violently as you can, moving from the wrists. Keep arms rigid. You will tire very soon. Stop as soon as the arms begin to ache.

You have now set up some neural connections between relaxation and tension. (Which is more comfortable?)

Unskilled Mischief Makers: The Arms

You may never have noticed this, but all motions of the arms are naturally circular in character, regardless of which joint bends.

Lift your right arm up, straight out in front of you, level with your shoulder and with the palm facing the floor. Bend your elbow, and your hand moves horizontally in a curved path over to your left shoulder.

Repeat with the left arm, and the hand arrives on the right shoulder.

Further, as the stretched arm bends upward from the elbow, the fingers point to the ceiling and slightly over the shoulder.

When a baton is in the hand, these several motions leave it stranded, pointing at the audience instead of at the players! Obviously the curved pattern must be replaced by straight-line motion.

The Two Basic Training Exercises

We introduce you now to the two most important exercises of all—the two from which all others spring. These are the first of the Nicolai Malko series. The importance of conquering these two cannot be overemphasized. (In my own classes, we checked them en masse each time the class met for the first two or three weeks before proceeding to the next pair in the series.) Please read carefully the following "how-to" description. Note particularly the emphasis on the wrist.

Training Exercise 1: The Horizontal Straight Line

Cross your hands on your diaphragm, palms toward the body, right-hand fingertips opposite left wrist, elbow to elbow forming a straight, horizontal line. Run the hands outward on a *straight* line, right hand to the right, left hand to the left. Go only about two-thirds as far as your limit of reach. (If you go farther, the shoulder joint begins to add curved motion.)

As you move outward, the fingers point constantly toward each other and the hands form a right angle with the arm. At the terminus of the motion, stop!

Turn the hands so that the palms face frontward, and slowly retrace the straight line back to the starting point. On this return trip, keep the fingers pointing outward as nearly as possible until the wrists touch at the diaphragm.

Be sure that the hands retain their starting position all the way to the end of the line, when you will send them a definite order to reverse their position. *Guard against shrugging.*

SHORT-SUMMARY QUICK REVIEW (HORIZONTAL)

1. Cross hands on diaphragm,
2. Hands point IN.
3. Move outward in straight line.
4. Stop: Order palms to face front.

----

5. Palms face outward all the way.
6. Return on straight line to diaphragm.
7. Reset hands and repeat.

No shrugging. Elbows not resting on rib cage. Arms hanging freely from the shoulder.

Training Exercise 2: The Vertical Line

Let the arms hang full length at the sides, palms facing backward. Gradually raise the arms in a perpendicularly straight line to eyebrow level. Maintain the hanging position (fingers downward) of the hands throughout. At the top of the line, flip the hands upward, palms to the front. Bring arms downward to the starting point, retaining the position of the hands (fingers upward) as nearly as possible. Gradually the arms will acquire the feel of the vertical-plane motion, noncircular in character. Wrist flexibility will also have begun its development.

SHORT-SUMMARY QUICK REVIEW (VERTICAL)

1. Arms hang full length at side.
2. Palms toward the rear.
3. Raise arms vertically, hands hanging down.
4. Stop at top.

----

5. Palms to front, fingers point straight up.
6. Down in straight line to lowest point.
7. Hands point up all the way.
8. Reset hands and repeat.

No shoulder shrugging. Relax shoulders throughout.

The danger here is that the hands will start to change their position before you reach the terminus of either gesture. Guard against this. It often happens. Remember that you are establishing **mental control over your motions.** Be accurate!

Ten minutes a day, every day, is all that you will need for ultimate success with this manual aspect of your technique.

Exercises for Practice: Training the Ear

1. Drill your sense of "inner hearing" by playing any note on the piano and then, without singing that note, imagining the sound of the next higher half step and singing that pitch. Do the same with the lower half step; then use whole tones. When the correct pitch forms in your imagination, it will come out of your throat. Your vocal cords can produce only what you have first imagined in your brain. They cannot be activated in any other way.

2. Now, when exercise 1 becomes easy, play pitches on the piano that are outside your singing range, thus expanding your ability to identify with the extremes of range in the orchestral/band instruments. Sing the imagined pitch in your own vocal range.

3. Finally, sing major and minor thirds, perfect fourths, and so on above and below the given piano note. Softly, hum the scale notes between the intervals, using the played pitch as the keynote of the scale. This will not work until you are secure in imagining half steps and whole tones. Later on, you will find that you can "hear" the scale tones without resorting to the audible humming. You will be able to solve any troublesome contemporary interval accurately.

Recommended Reference Readings

Complete facts of publication for the references given at the end of each chapter may be found in the Bibliography.

BLACKMAN, CHARLES, *Behind the Baton*. The first chapters, pp. 17–40. Very readable. The why and wherefore of conducting. The book includes a section written by professional orchestral players.

DAVISON, ARCHIBALD T., *Choral Conducting*. Chapter 1, pp. 3–10. A fine set of ideals for the choral conductor.

Note: Publication information for the following recommended videotapes may be found on the pages indicated.

Great conductors of the past in action: *The Art of Conducting*, p. 137.

Showing superb interpretational technique: Carlos Kleiber, dir., p. 169.

Depth of understanding of what the music itself wishes to say: *Celibidache Conducts Bruchner*, p. 241.

2 The Conductor: Basic Time-Beating

Standing in front of an orchestra, a band, or a chorus and beating time does not make one a conductor.

☆ But to bring forth thrilling music from a group of singers or players, to inspire them (through one's own personal magnetism) to excel, to train them (through one's own musicianship) to become musicians themselves, personally to feel the power of music so deeply that the audience is lifted to new heights emotionally—or gently persuaded, through music, to forget momentarily the dust of earth and to spend a little time in another world—yes, *that* can be called conducting.

☆ Fine conductors are, first of all, fine musicians. They are sincere and inspiring leaders. They have integrity where the music is concerned. They know the score thoroughly and can convey its meaning to the players through superbly trained hands. They have developed a sense of pitch, not only to be able to sing any part of the score, but also to be able to hear it in the mind (the inner ear) so loudly that when the actual rendition does not come up to the standard fixed in the musical imagination, they will set about attaining that ideal during the rehearsal. They *know* theory, harmony, counterpoint, musical history, form, and analysis. They have reached a professional performance level themselves on some one instrument (or with the voice), and they are eternally interested to learn more and more about the problems of each instrument of the ensemble. They have, somewhere along the way, taken a thorough course in orchestration; and all transpositions have become second nature to them.

The best conductors are innately endowed with musicality—a term that need not be defined because those who have it know what it means and those who do not will never understand it through definition. Finally, conductors must have a mind trained to work as fast as lightning and a thousand times more continuously.

The art of conducting is the highest, most complete synthesis of all facets of the musical activity, and it should be so regarded by anyone dedicated to the profession of the baton.

Time-Beating in THREE; in FOUR

Time-beating is the basic skill of the right hand. But it is necessary for the left hand to develop at least some proficiency in this aspect of the technique. In the beginning, train each hand individually. Later on, the hands may be combined, but the left hand has its own language.

We begin with the easiest pattern: time-beating in THREE. Note that we use all CAPITAL LETTERS when referring to the number of beats in the whole measure. We capitalize only the first letter when we wish to designate any single beat within the measure as One, Two, and so on.

In all time-beating, **beat One** *is a* **vertical line** *straight down.* It indicates the beginning of the measure—the passing of a barline. At the bottom of the vertical line, try to feel the tap and rebound of the hand in the wrist as it states the beat-point. Holding the baton, you have the illusion of actually tapping the beat with the tip of the stick.

Figure 1 gives the diagram for time-beating in THREE. Right hand = down, right, up. (Left hand = down, left, up.) Try it a few times with each hand and then read on.

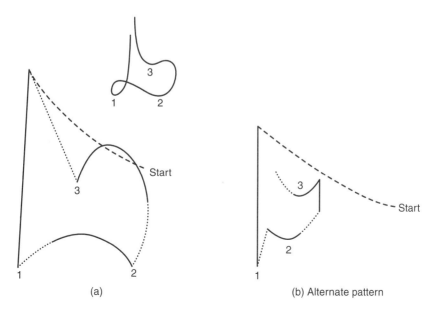

Figure 1. Time-beating in THREE.

Your arm moves through the pattern, and your hand, using its motion in the wrist, taps each beat as it occurs. The tap is very small, very clear. This indication of the precise instant of the rhythmic pulse is called the **ictus.** The steady reiteration of the beat-points is called the **takt.**

Notice that after your hand taps the ictus, it springs back slightly. This is termed the **"rebound" or "reflex."** It appears on the diagrams as a dotted line and acts as a kind of springboard for the arm as it moves on toward the next beat.

Drill the right hand in the THREE pattern.

Drill the left hand in the THREE pattern.

Proceed to the following Problems.

PROBLEMS, Series 1: Time-beating in THREE

Set a good rhythm. Keep the rhythm going as you change hands. Repeat each problem several times without stopping. Relax momentarily between problems.

1. Beat	3	measures,	Right Hand,	in	THREE,	followed by
	3	"	Left Hand	"	"	
2. Beat	2	"	Right Hand	"	"	followed by
	3	"	Left Hand	"	"	
3. Beat	3	"	Left Hand	"	"	followed by
	1	"	Right Hand	"	"	
4. Beat	2	"	Right Hand	"	"	followed by
	1	"	Left Hand	"	"	
5. Beat	6	"	Both Hands	"	"	followed by
	2	"	Right Hand	"	"	
6. Beat	1	"	Both Hands	"	"	followed by
	2	"	Left Hand	"	"	
7. Beat	2	"	Right Hand	"	"	followed by
	3	"	Both Hands	"	"	
8. Beat	2	"	Left Hand	"	"	followed by
	3	"	Both Hands	"	"	
9. Beat	1	"	Right Hand, in THREE, followed by			
	3	"	Left Hand, in THREE,	"		
	2	"	Both Hands, in THREE,	"		
	1	"	Right Hand, in THREE,	"		
	1	"	Left Hand, in THREE			

10. Now alternate 1 measure in Right Hand to 1 measure in Left Hand. Insert 1 measure of Both Hands here and there.

Figure 2 gives the pattern for time-beating in FOUR. Right hand = down, LEFT, right, up. (Left hand = down, RIGHT, left, up.) The two hands cross in front of the conductor on the second beat in FOUR.

Danger: The third beat is the troublesome one here. Note the "equidistance" in Figure 2. When the third-beat ictus is too near the place for the first-beat ictus, the pattern tends to **look** unbalanced and unrhythmic (Figure 3). Further, a curtailed third beat neglects the players on the conductor's right. Let them know they are part of the ensemble, too.

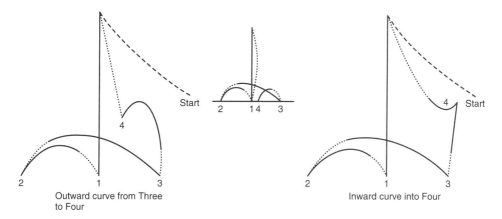

Figure 2. Time-beating in FOUR.

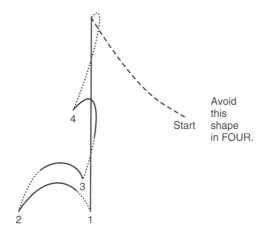

Figure 3. Unbalanced design pattern in FOUR.

Drill the right hand.
Drill the left hand.
Proceed to the Problems. Handle them the way you did the first set.

PROBLEMS, Series 2: Time-beating in FOUR

1. 2 measures, R.H. / 2 measures, L.H. Repeat.
2. 3 measures, L.H. / 1 measure, R.H.   ″
3. 1 measure, R.H. / 1 measure, L.H.   ″
4. 3 measures, R.H. / 1 measure, L.H.   ″

In the following drills, place the inactive hand on your diaphragm.

5. 3 measures, R.H. / 3 measures, L.H.

6. 3 measures, L.H. / 2 measures, R.H.

7. 6 measures, Both Hands / 1 measure, L.H.
   3 measures, Both Hands / 2 measures, R.H.

8. 2 measures, Both Hands, 1 measure, L.H.
   2 measures, Both Hands, 1 measure, R.H.

9. R.H. 2mm./ L.H. 2mm./ R.H. 3mm./ L.H. 1m./ B.H. 2mm./ R.H. 1m./ B.H. 2mm./ L.H. 2mm./ B.H. 3mm., end.

10. Repeat this series, 1 through 9, making all right-hand gestures large (*forte*), and all left-hand gestures small (*piano*). Then go through again, making the left-hand gestures large and the right-hand gestures small. This is a drill for changes in dynamics in your two hands. Use sometimes large, sometimes small for both hands when they are called for.

The final set of Problems deals with changing from THREE to FOUR and vice versa—a mental challenge!

PROBLEMS, Series 3

1. 3mm. R.H. in FOUR/ 3mm. L.H. in THREE.

2. 2mm. L.H. in THREE/ 2mm. R.H. in FOUR.

3. 2mm. B.H. in FOUR/ 2mm. R.H. in THREE.

4. 2mm. L.H. in THREE/ 3mm. B.H. in FOUR.

5. 1m. R.H. in FOUR/ 2mm. B.H. in THREE.

6. 2mm. B.H. in FOUR/ 3mm. R.H. in FOUR.

7. 2mm. L.H. in FOUR/ 3mm. B.H. in THREE.

8. Using 1 through 7, add dynamic changes as you wish. Let your mind decide.

9. Start on the Fourth beat in FOUR (the up motion) in the Right Hand, and continue with 2 measures in FOUR.

10. Start on the Fourth beat in FOUR, R.H.; make the downbeat One, and then bring the Left Hand into play on the second beat and continue with the FOUR pattern in Both Hands.

Having conquered all of these, you are well on your way.
Try humming "America" as you beat THREE.
Then try something like "The Battle Hymn of the Republic" or even "Pop! Goes the Weasel" beating in FOUR. Loosen up! Let your imagination roam!

Starting the Sound: The Preparatory Beat

Your first problem will be starting the sound. It takes courage, plus what is called **impulse of will.** When the impulse of will is anemic, everything is lost. There is no conducting. When the impulse of will is strong and the technique is weak, the conductor is eternally confronted with feelings of frustration. Muscles tend to tense up, and he or she tries to substitute mental and emotional drive for physical technique. When the impulse of will is strong and the technique is secure, the ensemble truly has a leader who can unify the musicianship of all into one secure interpretation. Such a conductor has the finely developed technical skill and the confident drive to convey by gestures exactly what he or she wants.

To start the sound, the conductor has to signal his or her intentions regarding speed, dynamic, and style. This is done in a special motion, called the **preparatory beat,** that precedes the first playing beat.

The speed with which this beat is executed shows the coming tempo. It must, therefore, be absolutely accurate rhythmically. When the baton starts to move (in the preparatory gesture), the *rhythm of the piece begins.* This means, then, that **the preparatory beat must take the time of exactly one beat of the time-beating gestures to follow.** In very slow tempos, the half-beat often suffices.

The size of the preparatory beat usually gears itself to the loudness of the coming dynamic. In general, the larger the preparatory beat, the bigger the sound to follow.

The style of the preparatory beat (legato, staccato, tenuto, light, heavy, sustained, ponderous) should set the mood of the music.

The slant of the preparatory beat should be upward. A downward curve in the preparatory beat can be mistaken by some of the players for a command to play—with unhappy results.

The preparatory beat says "Look out! Here it comes." The next beat says, in no uncertain terms, "Play!" or "Sing!" The beat that commands the sound to come forth should have a downward trajectory, plus impulse of will.

The preparatory beat moves upward and in a direction opposite to that of the "playing" beat. Samples are shown by the broken lines in Figure 4. For example, if the piece is to start on the fourth (last) beat of a measure in $\frac{4}{4}$ meter, the direction of the preparatory beat would be from left to right (third beat of the measure) but in a slightly upward direction. When the piece starts on Two, make the preparatory beat (One) downward but very small, and then enlarge the lead into Two (Figure 4b).

Note: Young conductors are often prone to making a long, slow preparatory beat followed by the real tempo of the music. This results in a ragged performance of the first measure. Reiterating, *the preparatory beat must be in the tempo of the piece.*

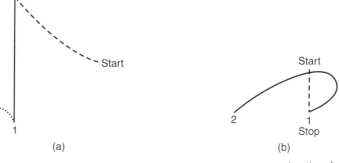

(a)   (b)

(continued on next page)

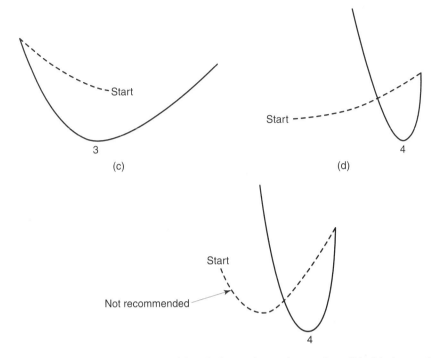

Figure 4. The preparatory beat: (a) with the music starting on One; (b) with the music starting on Two; (c) with the music starting on Three; (d) with the music starting on Four; (e) common error, too much drop in the preparatory beat, causes accidents.

Stopping the Sound: The Cutoff Gesture

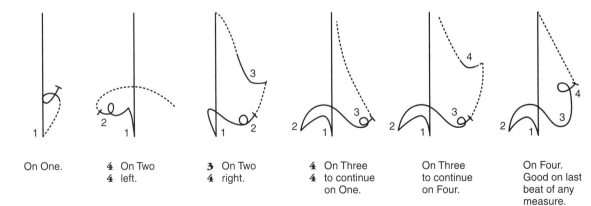

Figure 5. Stopping the sound: The cutoff gesture.

MUSIC FOR PERFORMANCE

The excerpts in Examples 1–4 have been adapted from the *Fifteen Sonatas, Op. 1, for Flute and Figured Bass,* by George Frideric Handel. They deal here with two important fundamentals, the melody line and the bass line.

Set the tempo in your mind before raising your hands to conduct. What kind of a "mood" do you want to set with this music? Take a moment to think. After all, the musicians cannot start until YOU are ready.

Example 1. Sonata No. V. Fourth movement, beginning, Bourrée.

* Use the *8va* for instrumental performances.

Example 2. Sonata No. XI. First movement, beginning.

Example 3. Sonata No. VII. Third movement.

Example 4. Sonata No. IX. Fifth movement, beginning.

Example 5A. (BAND) Skillfully adapted by Composer Robert Jager in reduced score for use here.

"The Debtor's Welcome" from Colonial Airs and Dances *(GB851) by R. Jager. © Copyright 1988 Neil A. Kjos Music Company. Used with Permission, 1995.*

Example 5B: Drill Study. Conquer the baton time-beating. Then **add left hand** to indicate the chords on **One** and **Three.** Use a simple downbeat gesture for **each chord.**

Recommended Reference Readings

BLACKMAN, CHARLES, *Behind the Baton.* See especially the chapter on "The Function of the Conductor."

FARKAS, PHILIP, *The Art of Musicianship.* Section 4, pp. 17–20: "Tempo."

3 The Baton

The baton is the conductor's **technical** instrument as distinguished from a **sounding** instrument, the orchestra, band, or chorus. The manual technique should be mastered both with and without the baton, and the both hands should become skilled. Whether or not to use the stick should be the inspiration of the moment, not the result of insecurity in working either way.

The baton in its present form is the end result of hundreds of years of experimentation in the leading of massed musical performances. The earliest conducting was done with gestures of the hands alone, describing melodic contour, pitches, lengths of notes and phrases. Later the leader sat at the organ or piano (often with the figured-bass part) and made signs now and then to the singers and players. Progressing since then from the thumping-out of an audible beat, to the silent waving of the concertmaster's bow, and finally to the use of the baton and patterned rhythmic designs, conducting has grown into a well-refined form of sign language. And the baton has emerged (especially for the instrumental ensembles) as the *most efficient means of conveying a precise message to the players*. The tip of the stick gives the clearest possible definition of the **ictus,** the precise point at which any beat in the rhythmic pulse called the **takt** begins, and the cleanest outline of the beat pattern as such. A skilled baton technique is a great time-saver in rehearsals.

To be read easily, the conductor's gestures should be projected to the tip of the stick. The projection to the tip takes place through the medium of a slightly flexible wrist. Gestures initiated from the elbow but accompanied by an inflexible wrist can be clear, but they are rigid in appearance and do not depict the *musical* aspect of the sound.

Ease with the Baton

The manner in which the baton is held can contribute greatly to the subsequent development of a facile and comfortable technique. Over the years a certain basic grip of the hand on the stick has emerged, subscribed to by such internationally recognized conductors as Sir Thomas Beecham, Wilhelm Furtwängler, Nicolai Malko, Pierre Monteux, Yevgeny Alexandrovich Mravinsky of the Leningrad Philharmonic, Charles Munch, Eugene Ormandy, Herbert von Karajan, Bruno Walter, and George Szell.

The baton is held in the **right hand.** No exceptions are allowed. See page 24.

The basic grip is a fundamental way of holding the stick (Figure 6). As such it should be made the point of departure. This grip, however, is not an eternal attribute. It is often interchanged with the "light grip" (Figures 7 and 11) during the performance to show some particular quality dictated by the music itself. George Szell, for example, often resorted to the light grip in his greatly admired interpretations of Mozart.

When the baton is used, it is of utmost importance that it be held so that the tip is clearly visible to all members of the performing group. There is a current tendency to grasp it so that it points too much toward the left. This handicaps the players on the conductor's right and is caused by the faulty grip shown in Figures 14 and 15.

1. The stick is held, fundamentally, between the *tip* of the thumb and the *side* of the index finger. The stick contacts the finger somewhere between the middle joint of the finger and the nail. Just where the contact is made depends upon the relative length of the individual's thumb and finger. It varies among the great conductors. Experimentation will result in a proper and comfortable adjustment. (See Figure 6.) Use the baton in the right hand.

2. It is most important that **the thumb bend outward at its knuckle.** This bent knuckle contributes to a more relaxed wrist* and relieves a certain amount of muscular tension in the wrist and lower arm. (See Figures 6, 7, and 8.) An open space should form between the thumb and the side of the first finger. (See Figure 11.)

3. The heel of the stick rests in the fleshy hollow near the base of the thumb. (See Figure 7.) This spot shows up well as a dark shadow in Figure 13.

4. The ring finger lightly contacts the heel of the baton, completing a three-point grip: tip of thumb, side of first finger, and ball of ring finger. This grip is both flexible and secure.

5. In time-beating with the baton, the palm of the hand should face the floor. (See Figure 9.) This permits the hand to move freely up and down in the wrist joint. In

---

*The wrist, as such, is only a link between the hand and the arm. When the hand is curved upward, the wrist appears to be low; when the hand hangs downward, the wrist appears to be high. What actually happens is simply an adjustment of angle between hand and arm.

performing the time-beating patterns, the student should feel as if he or she is tapping each beat with the *tip* of the stick.

6. The tip of the baton should point forward, not leftward. (See Figures 9 and 10.) Keep the heel of the stick near the base of the thumb.

7. The light grip is shown in Figure 11. It is used for delicate passages in the music but lacks intensity in the *fortes* of a broader character such as in Wagner and Brahms. Both grips should become functional, instantly interchangeable, and used interpretatively as the music demands. Figures 6, 8, and 9 give the basic grip.

Avoid the following:

8. When the first finger presses on top of the stick (Figure 12), a certain stiffness shows in the other fingers, and this is inclined to transfer itself to the wrist. Further, such a placing of the first finger often results in a "low" wrist that becomes quite inflexible. Thereafter, the beat-point, instead of being projected to the tip of the stick, actually lies beneath the wrist itself. In passing, notice the rigidity of the ring finger and the little finger in Figure 12.

9. When the heel of the stick does not contact the palm of the hand, but is allowed to "float," the wrist flexibility tends to become exaggerated; the tip becomes uncontrollably free and precision is lost. (See Figure 13.)

10. One should guard constantly against letting the heel of the baton slide to a position under the base of the little finger. (See Figures 14 and 16.) Such a position causes the stick to point far left and presents it broadside to the players in the center of the ensemble. Readjust as described in item 3 above.

11. When the stick slides under the little finger, it sometimes protrudes beyond the palm of the hand, resulting in "two conductors." (See Figure 15.) When the tip is downward on the beat-point, the heel is upward—a difficult situation for the players on the conductor's right.

12. The leftward pointing of the stick (Figure 15) can be corrected by holding the hand thumb upward when conducting (Figure 16). But now the wrist cannot bend in its natural up-down direction and therefore cannot deliver the conductor's intentions to the tip of the baton. A real tenuto gesture becomes almost impossible.

13. In an effort to make the baton "line up with the arm," certain overly conscientious students have sometimes put an ungainly turn toward the right with the hand in the wrist joint. (See Figure 17.) This is unnatural, feels uncomfortable, and looks clumsy. Make a straight line from the elbow to the base-joint of the middle finger and adjust the stick properly under the thumb.

Visibility of the Baton

The natural motions of the arm are circular in character. Any bending of the elbow or the wrist causes the fingers to describe a section of a circle. In spite of this, the baton should not be allowed to make circles around the conductor's body, nor should it make arclike vertical lines in its up-and-down motions, swinging back over the shoulder or dropping below the music stand. The tip of the stick should move in a perpendicular plane opposite the conductor's body and should be clearly visible to all members of the ensemble.

Recommended

Figure 6. The basic grip. Note the bent thumb.

Figure 7. The light grip.

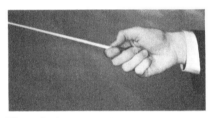

Figure 8. Contact of the ring finger.

Figure 9. The basic grip: palm toward floor. Little finger relaxed.

Figure 10. Baton pointing forward.

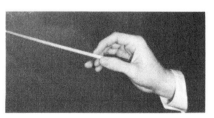

Figure 11. The light grip. Second finger replaces first.

Not Recommended

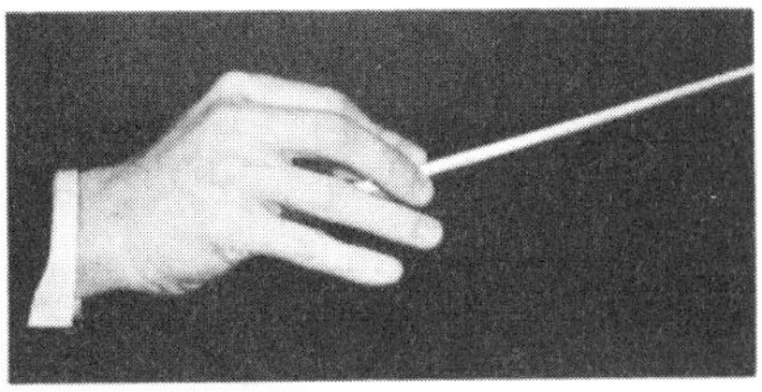

Figure 12. First finger on top. Ring and little fingers stiff.

Figure 13. Heel of stick not contacting palm of hand. Thumb stiff and flat.

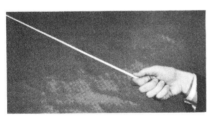

Figure 14. Heel of stick under little finger.

Figure 15. Heel of stick protruding beyond hand. Baton points left.

Figure 16. Inefficient wrist position, palm not facing floor.

Figure 17. Strained wrist position: Heel of stick is under little finger.

A word of comfort to the **left-handed student:** Each hand has its own language to speak. One hand or the other will be more "talented." But all conductors must train both hands. Remember that whereas the time-beating is in the right hand, many of the expressive controls are in the left hand. The hands must be independent.

What Type of Baton to Choose?

What type of baton to use? Although personal preference colors one's decision, there are several factors that should be considered. First, is the baton clearly visible, without strain, to the players who are farthest from the conductor? Second, does the stick have a feel of good *balance* in the hand? Third, is the heel of the stick so constructed that the standard grip is easily acquired? The answer seems to indicate a stick that is about twelve inches long, made of light wood (holly wood is often used), and properly tapered for effective balance, and that has a pear-shaped handle of a size that fits the particular hand and allows the thumb and first finger to contact the shaft. A white baton is easiest seen by the performers.

Exercises for Practice: The Baton

1. Practice holding the baton with the basic grip while you are reading a book or studying. This will help the hand to acquire a feeling of ease and familiarity with the stick. Be sure that you check accurately on the directions as given in the text. It is a waste of time to form an incorrect habit.

2. Practice flicking imaginary drops of water from the tip of the stick. This produces a "crack-the-whip" motion in the wrist and hand and begins the motion needed later on for a good staccato gesture.

3. Study the time-beating patterns for three and four beats per measure (pages 9 and 11). Perform them with an easy, natural freedom in the arm. Check on the appearance of the time-beating by looking in a mirror. Is the beat-point clearly defined? Can the performers see the stick clearly? Does the tip of the stick make a good connective arc between beat-points?

4. Without the baton, try to acquire the feel of bouncing a ball by tapping it with the tips of the fingers. Then repeat with baton in hand.

Note: One last word. Too much flexibility in the wrist is as bad as none at all. Keep the wrist motion small.

CHAPTER

4 TWO, ONE, SIX, FIVE, and Subdivided Beats

The building of our manual technique is a very personal thing. We do it for ourselves. But we must also remember the altruistic aspect of our technique, namely, that what we build has to be readable by the players in our ensemble. A sloppy technique brutalizes the performers, delays the rehearsal, and frustrates the conductor.

Thinking Like a Conductor

The Problems of Chapter 2 were a first step in learning to think like a conductor. During one's time on the podium, the **ear** must be alert to what is actually **sounding.** But the **mind** must be able to **project ahead.** It was Leonard Bernstein who called attention to the fact that whatever the conductor does, it must be done in time for the musicians to respond to it.

Our first two series of Problems drilled the hands mechanically. Repetition was required but with a minimum of thought. Behind the scenes, the brain was learning to switch its commands instantly from one hand to the other. In each case, the message had to arrive in time for the correct hand to respond without upsetting the steady rhythm of the beats. Series 3 required more concentration.

If you neglected the Problems in Chapter 2, you should retrace your steps and do them now. They work their own magic, and *the mental training is as important as the manual training.* So let us proceed.

Time-Beating

In TWO

Straight down, swing upward to the right, and retrace back to the top (Figure 18). The ictus is at the lowest point in each direction. (The expressive variations are found in Figure 53, page 153.) See Example 6.

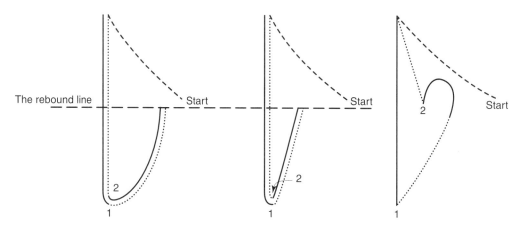

Figure 18. Time-beating in TWO.

Danger: If the upward rebound after One climbs too high, beat Two will appear to be another One. A player, glancing up suddenly, cannot tell which is which. *For clarity, the rebound of One should not go higher than halfway up the length of the downbeat.*

Example 6. William Schuman, *The George Washington Bridge.* © 1951 (Renewed) by G. Schirmer, Inc. International Copyright Secured. Used by Permission.

In ONE-to-the-bar

The direction is straight down–straight up. Here the rebound springs all the way back to the top. This is the only pattern in which this action should occur. See Figure 19 and Example 7.

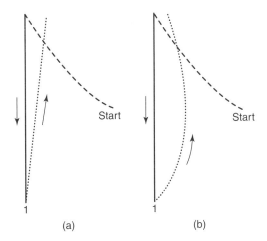

Figure 19. Time-beating in ONE.

Note: Since all measures in all patterns start with a down gesture and end with an up gesture, it is better to indicate full measures of rest by completing the down-up gesture and stopping at the top. That way the entire measure is accounted for. When the pause is at the ictus, it makes the rebound resemble a preparatory beat for the following entrance—unnecessary when no one is to play.

Note: The stop at the top is also easier seen from the stage in operatic performances.

Example 7. Dvořák, *Slavonic Dance*, Op. 46, No. 1, in C major (measures 18–29). (Tacet instruments not shown.)

In SIX

This is the first of the "multibeat" patterns. Patterns from Figure 20a and 20c are preferred. Figure 20a shows a four-beat pattern enlarged to a SIX. Figure 20c springs from an enlarged two-beat pattern.

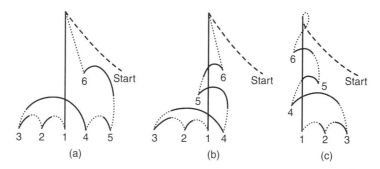

Figure 20. Time-beating in SIX.

Divided Patterns

When the music is very slow and florid, so that the conductor must show the half-beats (the "and" beats), this can be done by the addition of a second small beat attached to the main beat. Figure 21 shows the "and" beats for the THREE and FOUR time-beating patterns. The small beats move in a direction opposite to that of the following main beat.

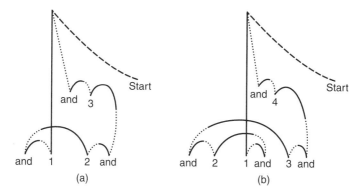

Figure 21. Showing the "and" beat.

THREE in a "divided" pattern becomes a type of SIX, and FOUR, divided, takes care of measures in EIGHT. These divisions are customary in the slowest tempos, Adagio and Largo. *The divided-THREE should not be confused with the true SIX,* and vice versa. A SIX is 3 + 3. A divided-THREE is 2 + 2 + 2. In Example 8, Tchaikovsky cleverly uses both. His signature is a SIX.

Example 8. Tchaikovsky, Symphony No. 5 in E minor, Op. 64. First movement (measures 97–100).

MUSIC FOR PERFORMANCE

Example 9. Beethoven, Trio for Double Reeds, Op. 87 (measures 1–18). Use the divided-THREE for practice. Small subdivisions! Set the mood in your mind and listen as you conduct. Use lower notes for C instruments or for singing.

*Use lower notes for singing and for nontransposing instruments

The Triple Division

A THREE-beat pattern with **two** subdivisions added to each beat becomes a **NINE-beat measure;** a FOUR-beat pattern with the added pulses handles the **TWELVE**-beat notation. See Examples 10 and 11 and **Figure 22.** When using the divided-beat patterns, it is often sufficient to use a small subdivision as a preparatory gesture at the beginning of the piece.

Example 10. Prokofiev, Symphony No. 5, Op. 100. Third movement (measure 128).
© Copyright 1946 by MCA MUSIC, a division of MCA Inc., New York, New York. Reprinted by permission. All rights reserved.

Example 11. Debussy, *Prélude à l'après-midi d'un faune* (measure 31). By permission of Jean Jobert, Editeur, Paris. Société des Editions Jobert, 76 rue Quincampoix 75003 Paris.

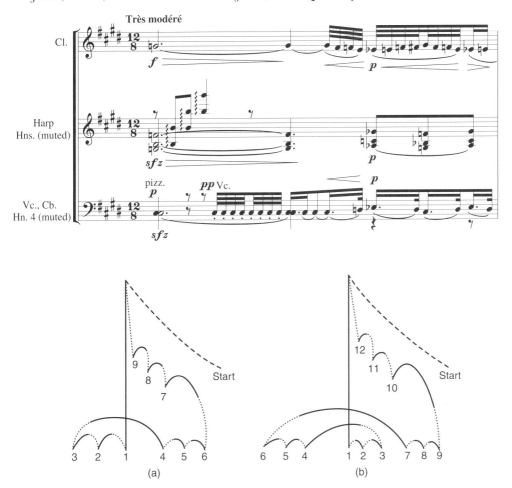

Figure 22. Time-beating in NINE and TWELVE.

Note: In the TWELVE-beat pattern, notice the placing of the subdivisions to the right of the ictus of One. When they are allowed to move left, we find five subdivisions in a row, going in the same direction. The result is confusion for the players! For clarity, *the small subdivisions should move in a direction opposite to that of the next main (large) gesture.* After One, they can also move **down.**

Setting a Tempo

As the beat patterns and the music become more complicated, the choice of a proper tempo also presents problems. The convincing musical tempo should not be affected by the difficulty of the notation. Beware! Check to see that you do not unconsciously conduct everything at the tempo of your own heartbeat. It can happen—and too often does!

In FIVE—The Unbalanced Beat

Here we see the unbalanced or "mixed subdivisions" beats. One half of the measure may add one pulse to each beat; the other half, two subdivisions per beat. The takt is steady throughout.

Simple time-beating in FIVE takes one of the following forms: 3 + 2 (One-and-and/Two-and) or 2 + 3 (One-and-Two-and-and). The downbeat line, One, divides the pattern, and **the long, horizontal line, crossing from left to right, shows where the second half of the measure begins.** See Figure 23 and Examples 12 and 13. See also "FIVES," pages 112–113.

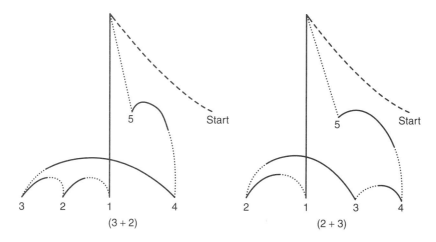

Figure 23. Time-beating in FIVE (contemporary patterns).

Example 12. Stravinsky, *The Rite of Spring.* (a) Sacrificial Dance: The Chosen One (measure 155). (b) Mysterious Circle of the Adolescents (measure 6). Copyright 1921 by Edition Russe de Musique. Renewed 1958. Copyright and Renewal assigned to Boosey & Hawkes, Inc. Revised Edition Copyright 1948 by Boosey & Hawkes, Inc. Reprinted by permission.

Example 13. Barber, *Medea's Meditation and Dance of Vengeance*, Op. 23A (measure 104). © 1956 (Renewed) by G. Schirmer, Inc. Used by Permission. Rhythm only here.

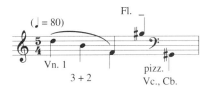

Caution: When the composer writes a 3 + 2 measure followed by a 2 + 3 in the next measure (and vice versa), the conductor should show the change in the baton. See Example 62, page 113.

There is an older form of FIVE (traditional) that is gradually becoming obsolete. It comprises a large THREE pattern with a small TWO pattern attached, higher up in space. In TWO-plus-THREE, the TWO is large. Such designs are encumbered with two downbeats in the same measure. The change of size in the two patterns is confusing visually and dynamically (Figure 24).

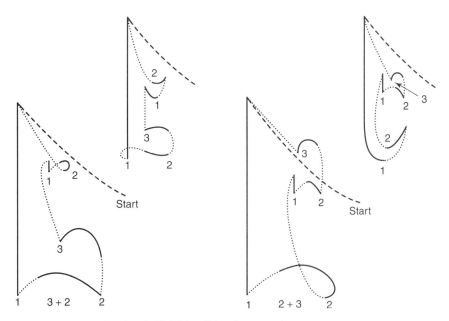

Figure 24. Time-beating in FIVE (traditional patterns).

The traditional pattern was current at the time that Tchaikovsky wrote his famous "Five-Beat Waltz" (Example 14).

Example 14. Tchaikovsky, Symphony No. 6 in B minor, Op. 74. Second movement, beginning.

When the composer places a barline between the two-beat and three-beat measures, and they alternate consecutively throughout, then the normal patterns are used as notated (Example 15).

Example 15. Stravinsky, *The Rite of Spring*. Evocation of the Ancestors (measures 28–31). Copyright 1921 by Edition Russe de Musique. Renewed 1958. Copyright and Renewal assigned to Boosey & Hawkes, Inc. Revised Edition copyright 1948 by Boosey & Hawkes, Inc. Reprinted by permission.

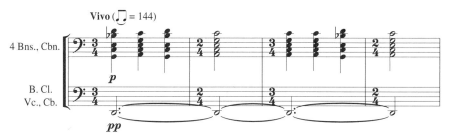

Drill: Now try the following series. The takt (speed of the beats) remains a constant throughout.

Time-beating in

    (a) 4 2 3 1 4 1 2 5 3 2 1 4 2
    (b) 4 1 2 1 3 1 2 1 4 2 1 4 3 1 2
    (c) 4 1 3 2 5 1 2 4 3 2 4 1 5 1 3
    (d) 3 2 4 1 3 1 2 4 2 1 3 2 3 1 4
    (e) 3 4 5 2 4 3 1 2 6 1 2 4 2 5 1 3
    (f) 6 2 4 2 6 5 1 4 6 2 1 4 3 6 2
    (g) 2 1 3 6 4 3 1 6 2 5 4 1 3 6 1

Try divided beats as follows (the takt is the eighth note throughout): divided $\frac{4}{4}$, $\frac{9}{8}$, divided $\frac{4}{4}$, $\frac{12}{8}$, divided $\frac{3}{4}$, $\frac{9}{8}$, divided $\frac{4}{4}$, $\frac{6}{8}$, $\frac{12}{8}$, divided $\frac{3}{4}$, $\frac{9}{8}$. See that the small beats go in the correct direction and that the downbeat, One, is clearly recognizable.

Other Styles of Time-Beating

As conductor or player, you should be able to recognize the time-beating patterns shown in Figure 25. In (a), all beats touch the baseline. In (b), all icti are placed at the bottom of One. In (c), beats Two and Three are raised, forming a cross. In (d), all connecting arcs are downward. In (e)—the pattern used in this book—arcs are upward; the least-accented beat (Four), being higher in space, eliminates the fast rebound of style (a), leading to One.

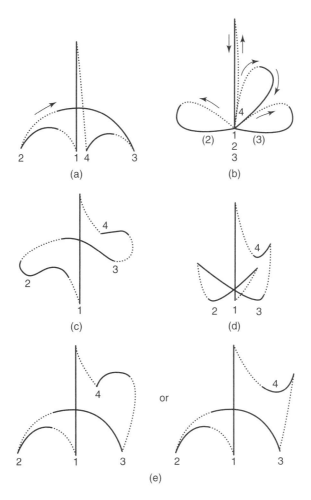

Figure 25. Styles of time-beating.

Regardless of which type of beating is preferred, three things are universally important: a good sense of rhythm, a lack of tension in the arm muscles, and a readable beat (especially for the first beat of the measure).

Exercises for Practice: Divided Beats

1. Three measures in $\frac{3}{4}$ slowly, to $\frac{9}{8}$ in NINE. ♪ = ♪

2. Two measures in $\frac{12}{8}$ to two measures in $\frac{4}{4}$. ♪ = ♪

3. Two measures in $\frac{2}{4}$ to two measures in divided $\frac{4}{4}$.

4. Two measures of $\frac{9}{8}$ in NINE, to one measure in $\frac{2}{4}$.

5. Two measures in SIX to one measure in $\frac{3}{4}$ showing the "ands." ♪ = ♪

6. In the following examples: (a) Keep the takt regular throughout. (b) Change the takt and beat out the NINES and SIXES.

Two measures in TWO and one measure in THREE. (Notice that each of the following notations will require *this same type of time-beating.*)

Repertoire for Practice: Third Suite *by Robert Jager. Time-beating changes in consecutive measures. Columbia Lady Music, Inc. 1967.*

Note: Repeat exercises 1–10 with the left hand, then with both hands together. Pay attention to the reversal of direction in the small beats in the left hand.

MUSIC FOR PERFORMANCE

Example 16. Haydn, Symphony No. 104 in D major *(London)*. Finale (measures 1–18).
Time-beating in TWO. Set the tempo in your mind before raising your hands to conduct.
Control the *piano* dynamic.

Example 17 is excellent for getting the feel of contouring the beats to match the melody. Note the tiny beat Five in measures 2 and 4. It is almost on top of beat Four. See page 46, Figure 27.

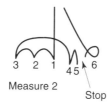

Example 17. Schubert, Symphony No. 5 in B-flat major. Second movement (measures 1–8). Time-beating in SIX. Legato. Listen to the phrasing.

At this point, refer to Appendix F, page 276. Add Exercise 4 to your practice routines.

Recommended Reference Readings

BLACKMAN, CHARLES, *Behind the Baton.* See especially the chapter on "The Function of the Conductor."

EARHART, WILL, *The Eloquent Baton.* Chapters 2–5, pp. 4–38: time-beating patterns; and Chapters 9–10, pp. 68–84: "Nine, Twelve, Five, and Seven Beat" and "Divided Beats."

FARKAS, PHILIP, *The Art of Musicianship.* Section 4, pp. 17–20: "Tempo."

5 The Expressive Gestures

In this chapter you will meet some of the most fascinating aspects of conducting. Mastery of the expressive gestures will gradually enable you to obtain musical effects from your players just by using your skilled manual technique. "Showing" rather than "stopping to tell" saves an appreciable amount of rehearsal time—and boredom for the players.

By now you should have established an acceptable legato beat and the ability to produce a good consistent rhythmic drive. So let us explore, adding some new ideas, new techniques, and a slightly different way of thinking about your conducting.

Here is a diagram of a four-beat measure:

1----2----3----4----

When your baton shows the ictus of any beat, the players begin playing that beat. This means, then, that once you have indicated a beat-point, no power on earth can get the players to change, within that single beat, what they have already begun to do.

Therefore, *except in the tenuto gesture* (page 49), *your baton is no longer responsible for that beat.* Instead, it can use the time after the ictus to show what is to happen on the next beat. What you show between beats is your **Declaration of Intent.** The preparatory beat at the beginning of the piece is a very vital declaration of intent.

The Line of Connection

You are now confronted with the line of connection from ictus to ictus. Thus far you have used a legato connection, an upward (outward) arc that descends to a clearly recognizable and unmistakable ictus at its lowest point.

After the rebound from a beat-point, it is also possible to swing into a downward (inward) arc as a connecting line. See page 37, Figure 25d, and page 11, Figure 2, "The Inward Curve into Four." When this form is used for all connections in all beats, the conductor and the players must be dead sure as to exactly where the ictus is located: at the lowest moment of the arc? at the highest peak where one arc connects with the next? Whatever is decided, it should be consistent.

The Interplay of Time and Space

Your speed of motion in the line of connection controls the size of your gesture. Obviously, a fast motion, at a given metronome setting, will move farther than a slow motion. **The size of your gesture is a by-product of your speed of motion.** What has to be developed, then, is your ability to control your speed of motion from ictus to ictus without upsetting the basic rhythmic drive. If you can get from your mind to your hands with precise accuracy, it is not so difficult to get from your hands to your players. What they see is what you get!

Let these several ideas percolate in your mind for a few days, but do not strain to apply them at this time.

The Expressive Gestures: Active, Passive

The expressive gestures may be divided into two categories: the **Active Gestures** and the **Passive Gestures.** The Active Gestures are your "control" gestures. They are endowed with great Impulse of Will on the part of the conductor, and they request an active response from the players. The Passive Gestures request silence. They show the passing of time when the players do not play.

ACTIVE

Demanding a response from the players. Characterized by Impulse of Will.

1. Legato
2. Staccato
3. Tenuto
4. Gesture of Syncopation (controls reactions that must come **after** the beat instead of **ON** the beat.)

PASSIVE

Requesting only silence from the players. Characterized by lack of Impulse of Will.

1. Dead gestures
2. Preparatory beats

The ACTIVE GESTURES: Legato, Staccato, Tenuto

Legato Gestures

The legato gestures are those that show the *smooth, flowing connection from ictus to ictus*. The beat-point is defined, in the long line of the legato, by a gentle tap, delivered to the tip of the baton.

Make a distinction here. The purpose of the arm is to move the hand into position to make the tap showing the exact instant of the beat. The wrist is flexible. Tapping is *not* a function of the whole lower arm.

The legato gestures lend themselves easily to variation in size. The larger gestures are usually associated with the louder passages, although it is possible to perform large gestures so gently that the texture of the resulting sound will be as fine as a delicate silk veil and correspondingly soft.

The customary small gestures for *piano* passages are centered in the hand and wrist, the tip of the baton preserving clearly the beat pattern (Example 18). Use smaller gestures for the triple *piano* with added intensity.

Example 18. Schubert, Symphony No. 8 in B minor, Op. posth. *(Unfinished)*. Second movement (measures 92–95).

Legato gestures may be varied in size within the measure to show dynamic or phrasal contour, the larger gesture coinciding with the climax of the phrase. See Example 89, by Haydn, where the fourth measure is often conducted as an echo of the third measure, the contouring remaining similar but the size being adjusted. Figure 26 diagrams this contour. The sweep of the "and" of Three, in the Haydn example done lightly, brings with it a reaction of a longer, lighter bow in the first violins—a case, again, of texture. Dynamic control is aided by the left hand.

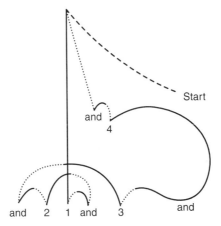

Figure 26. Variation of gesture size in the legato.

When great smoothness is desired and the rhythm is safe, the ictus-point may be smoothed out as shown in Figure 27.

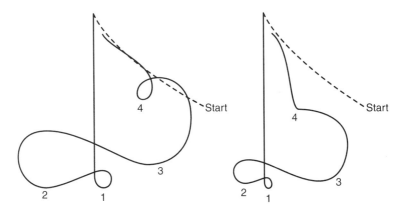

Figure 27. The curved ictus in legato.

Staccato Gestures

The staccato gestures are characterized by the *momentary stop* of all motion in the stick, hand, arm *immediately after the reflex*. The student can acquire the feel of this gesture in the wrist if he or she will practice flicking imaginary drops of water off the end of the baton. The flick is performed by the sudden motion of the hand in the wrist joint, ending in an abrupt stop at the end of the rebound.

In practicing, wait (no motion) after each staccato gesture, until the momentary rigidity of the arm muscles relaxes. Then make a preparatory arc into the next staccato. The important thing is the *control of the stop* (Figure 28).

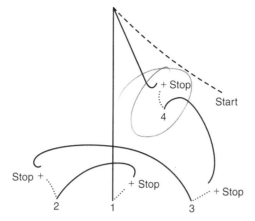

Figure 28. The staccato gesture.

There is no true staccato if motion continues in any part of the hand or arm. The stop must be as clean as the staccato sound the conductor expects from the players.

Danger: Particularly difficult is the stop at the top of the last beat of any measure.

The staccato gesture should be used whenever there is a possibility that the performers will fail to observe the composer's important staccato dots. (Beethoven was most conscientious in marking his staccatos. Observe them!)

In general, the more sudden the stop in the baton, the shorter the resultant sound from the performers. When the music shows continuous florid passages, unslurred and marked staccato, it is best to use the legato gestures, conducting the **line** of the music rather than its style. In slow tempos, with notes of longer duration, the baton can show the length of the staccato note and stop after the reflex. Interpretatively, **there are a thousand varieties of staccato, and we choose the one that fits the passage.** What remarkable "character" the staccato imparts!

Note: The staccato sound is inevitable when spiccato bowing is used (see Appendix C) and when fast passages are tongued in the winds.

In Example 19 we see a typical passage requiring the staccato gesture in the baton.

Example 19. Schubert, Symphony No. 8 in B minor, Op. posth. (*Unfinished*). First movement (measure 77).

A type of heavy staccato gesture is sometimes used to indicate accentuation of certain notes in the score. An excellent place for the heavy staccato is shown in Example 20.

Example 20. Schubert, *Rosamunde.* Overture (Allegro vivace, measure 25).

Note: The control of the stop is your most difficult bit of technique. If you find you cannot control it efficiently, try this: Set the metronome at 60. Make a staccato gesture on the first click. Say to yourself "stop!" as you make the gesture. Freeze and wait until you have heard the next click. After the click, prepare the next staccato and say "stop!" again. (When you think only "staccato," it does not send a definite message to your hand telling it exactly what to do. "Stop!" does.) When this drill becomes very easy, increase the beat to 80, then to 96. Later, as things speed up, use 60 with a staccato on each beat, then 80, and finally 96. Thereafter, apply the staccato to the $\frac{4}{4}$ time-beating pattern.

Training Exercise 3

This is your first big step in gaining independence in the two arms. This exercise builds on your mastery of Training Exercise 2 (page 6): the up-down motions in the two arms. If Training Exercise 2 has not been conquered, Training Exercise 3 will be frustrating—perhaps even impossible!

1. The two arms now move in opposite directions, using the motions of Exercise 2. Left arm comes down while right arm goes up.

2. Start with right arm hanging straight down from the shoulder, palm facing rear, fingers pointing down. Left hand is at forehead level, palm facing front, fingers pointing straight up.

3. Left arm moves downward while right arm moves upward in the straight lines of Training Exercise 2.

4. At the end of the motion, reverse hands—left facing rear, right facing front, and move back to starting point. Drill!

5. Later, speed up the gestures, making them staccato. Wait momentarily at the end of each direction.

Danger: Be sure that neither hand changes its position during the long up-down motions. Check that the arm moving downward goes all the way, not stopping at the waist.

Training Exercise 4

The second step in independent action of the two arms combines Training Exercise 1 (pages 5 and 6) with Training Exercise 2 (page 6).

1. While the right arm performs the up-down gesture, the left arm performs the straight-line horizontal motion. Drill!

2. Reverse arms—left arm in the up-down motion, right arm on the horizontal motion. Drill!

Danger: You may find, at first, that the up-down arm begins to pick up some sideways motion from the horizontal arm, and that the latter tends to rise or fall a bit in response to the up-down arm. Guard the straight lines. Remember, you are building control even more than you are building the straight lines. Insist on perfection from your arms-hands. Keep shoulders relaxed, unshrugged.

As you proceed now to the tenuto gesture, notice how the up motion can become the means of intensifying the sustaining of the tenuto beat and the horizontal motion can be used in moving from Two to Three in the $\frac{4}{4}$ tenuto pattern.

Tenuto Gestures

The tenuto gestures might also be called the **very heavy legato gestures.** They signify great cohesion in the musical line: introspection, intensity.

The motion is slow and controlled. The gesture covers less space than the legato. The tip of the baton feel heavy and the hand pulls it away from the ictus instead of rebounding. Hand hangs below wrist level.

One can acquire the feel of this gesture by pointing the baton straight down toward the floor, pulling upward with the hand while the left hand pulls downward on the tip. The tenuto is a feeling in the hand and wrist. In a well-executed (and readable) tenuto, the tip of the baton is well below the level of the wrist. The curves between beat-points are controlled as if being drawn on paper.

Care should be taken not to release intensity as the baton changes direction between beats, especially the last beat of one measure and the first beat of the next. Each beat is "placed," carried through and sustained into the following beat.

The tenuto gesture is used whenever the composer writes "*ten.*" over any note, often where the wind player would use the "du" tonguing, where the legato-articulated slur occurs in string music (written with a line under each note plus a slur, *louré* bowing), and wherever the sustaining power of the tone is of vital importance. See Example 21, second and fourth measures, second full beat.

Example 21. Haydn, Symphony No. 94 in G major *(Surprise)*. Second movement (measures 1–4).

In Example 22, the *pianissimo* might start with legato gestures, move into a soft tenuto in the second and third measures, and return to the legato as the third measure goes into the fourth. Such conducting would help the players to feel the legato line and to sustain adequately the last note of the first slur, so that this note would not be clipped in execution. In performing the given gestures, the conductor must guard his or her tempo.

Example 22. Schubert, Symphony No. 8 in B minor, Op. posth. *(Unfinished)*. First movement (measures 352–355).

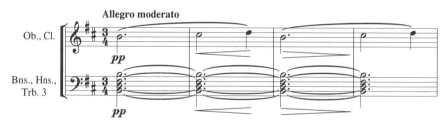

There is also a second way of performing the tenuto gesture. The hand bends upward from the wrist and pushes outward, with the lower palm stating exactly the length of the note. This is invaluable as a replacement for the cutoff on soft endings. At the end of the gesture, the hand retracts instantly. The conductor "stops conducting." The sudden retraction acts as a cutoff. See the last quarter note, Example 23.

PROBLEMS, Series 4: Staccato-Legato Changes

1. **The Easy Change: Staccato to Legato.** Six measures in ONE, staccato; six measures in ONE, legato. Keep tempo *slow*. Control the stop at the top of One in the staccato.

How? Count your measures aloud, 1,2,3,4,5, and when you come to 6 say "Six-and" rhythmically. After the stop, use the "and" of that beat to show a legato preparation for the coming downbeat—a declaration of intent.

2. **The Difficult Change: Legato to Staccato.** Slow tempo. Six measures in ONE legato, plus six measures in ONE staccato. At the top of the last legato beat, on the "and," show a sudden **staccato** preparatory gesture and come down on One, staccato.

Example 23. Schubert, Symphony No. 8 in B minor, Op. posth. *(Unfinished)*. First movement (last two measures).

Use the upward flick of the hand in the wrist (page 3) for the prep-beat. The staccatos will cover less distance than the longer legato line. Guard against speeding up the tempo on the staccatos.

3. In the following exercises, three factors change in the middle of each exercise: the number of measures, the number of beats per measure, and the style. These are a challenge to the mind, and they will help to activate the ability to think ahead. Do not be discouraged if they are difficult at first. As you practice, the mental aspect will improve, and as it improves, you will feel a real technique coming into your hands. Remember to watch your gestures in the mirror as you practice. Repeat each study without stopping, several times or until it becomes easy.

4. Two measures in TWO staccato and one measure in THREE tenuto.

5. Three measures in THREE legato and two measures in TWO staccato.

6. Three measures in TWO tenuto and two measures in ONE staccato.

7. Two measures in FOUR legato and three measures in TWO tenuto.

8. Two measures in FOUR legato and one measure in SIX staccato. Prepare and repeat.

9. Two measures in TWO legato and three measures in ONE tenuto. The measures remain the same in length.

10. Two measures in THREE tenuto and two measures in TWO staccato.

The ACTIVE GESTURES (After-the-Beat Responses): The Gesture of Syncopation (GoS)

Nicolai Malko gave this gesture its name. The gesture of <u>syncopation is the **ges-</u><u>ture used to control an entrance or some other response that must come</u> *after* <u>the beat instead of on the beat.</u> The nomenclature comes from the fact that syncopations start *after* the beat.

In Example 24, the gesture of syncopation is indicated by an X.

Example 24. Tchaikovsky, *Romeo and Juliet Overture-Fantasia.* Double bar, Allegro giusto (measures 111–113).

Gesture of Syncopation on Three

When the musicians must react after the beat (instead of on the beat), the beat itself must have its own distinctive character that cannot be mistaken for any other type of gesture.

Description of the Gesture of Syncopation (GoS)

Essentially, the gesture of syncopation is a *staccato gesture.* **The gesture of syncopation has no preparatory motion. Its "preparation" is a dead stop in the baton, on the beat-point, one entire beat ahead of the GoS beat.** The gesture states only the ictus of the beat with its subsequent stop. See Figure 29A, page 53.

Practicing the GoS

To acquire the gesture, choose a *slow* tempo. Pay good attention to the stops. Look at your hand. There should be no motion until the GoS occurs: *no preparatory motion;* just the GoS itself.

After the hand stops on the preceding beat, it stands perfectly still until the exact moment for the GoS beat. Then, suddenly, the hand makes an in-stantaneous <u>sharp twist toward the right,</u> similar to turning a key to *unlock* a door. This IS the gesture of syncopation. *It occurs exactly ON the beat.* Any uncon-trolled motion before the gesture itself spoils its effectiveness.

The unprepared suddenness forces the afterbeat response from the musi-cians, and it is so clear that every player has seen that beat at the same instant.

It helps to say to yourself "ump-pah" as you perform the gesture. You are the "ump" and the players are the "pah." Following the "pah," the baton moves instantly toward the following beat. This motion occurs during the "and" of the GoS beat. It is indicated by the broken line in the diagrams (Figure 29).

So easy to demonstrate—so difficult to diagram! As you practice the gesture, as shown in Figure 29, bear in mind that a beat-point states only the very beginning of a beat. The GoS is indicated by an X.

A. GoS on Four:

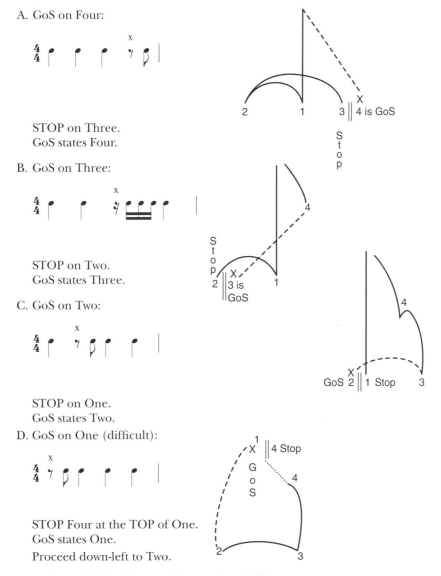

STOP on Three.
GoS states Four.

B. GoS on Three:

STOP on Two.
GoS states Three.

C. GoS on Two:

STOP on One.
GoS states Two.

D. GoS on One (difficult):

STOP Four at the TOP of One.
GoS states One.
Proceed down-left to Two.

Figure 29. The Gesture of Syncopation (GoS).

Note: The difference between a GoS and a staccato is that the staccato has a preparatory motion, whereas the GoS is preceded by a dead stop. Both gestures stop after the reflex. Care must be taken when the GoS comes on One. To stop the baton at the top of the rebound at the end of the preceding measure seems to present real difficulties for those learning to master either gesture.

Examples 25 and 26 offer additional musical excerpts requiring the use of the gesture of syncopation.

Example 25.

(a)

(b)

(c)   **Presto**

(d)   **Allegro**

(e)   **Adagio**

Stop on first dot.
GoS on the second dot.

Example 26. Nelhybel, Vacslav, *Overture for Symphonic Band* (measures 149–152). Woodwinds only quoted. © 1985 J. Christopher Music. Used by permission of the Publisher. Sole representative, Theodore Presser Company.

In slower tempos, a leisurely push forward with the heel of the hand (the lower palm), starting after a stop and exactly on the takt, will produce the desired entrance on the second half of the slow beat. The length of the "push" is exactly the length of the half-beat. Then stop and prepare the next beat (Example 27).

Example 27. Tchaikovsky, *Romeo and Juliet Overture-Fantasia* (measure 40).

Specialized Uses of the GoS

One of the most helpful uses of the GoS is its **control of precision after tied-over notes.** The more sudden the gesture, the quicker the response. Time it carefully—not before the beat.

Note: Musicians are trained to replace the terminal note of the tie with a rest when the tempo is fast. This is imperative in the string sections. It ensures good ensemble. See Example 25b.

Compositions Starting on an Afterbeat   When the first note of a composition is an afterbeat, the GoS is in its element. A small downward flick of the fingers of the left hand states **one beat before the first written beat.** The right hand follows **rhythmically** with the **sudden GoS** on the initial beat of the composition. **The time between the left hand and the right hand is exactly one beat.** There is **no preparatory motion in either hand.**

Explain the left-hand pre-beat to your ensemble and demonstrate it for security. See Figure 30.

Instrumentation: All brasses, low saxes, snare drum. Others tacet.

Figure 30. Holst, *Second Suite in F: Song of the Blacksmith.* Beginning. One line of rhythm. © Copyright 1922 by Boosey & Co. Ltd. Copyright Renewed. Reprinted by permission of Boosey & Hawkes, Inc.

Using the left-hand–right-hand technique solves the problem nicely. But if you want absolute security, then the technique would be this: GoS for three beats, legato on Four-One, GoS on Two, legato on Three-stop. The passage repeats.

New Tempo Starts on an Afterbeat   In Example 28, the musicians have to begin playing in a new tempo on the end of a beat that is preceded by sustained silence. Showing only the entry beat is highly dangerous. It is impossible to divide anything into equal parts before one knows what the unit is in its totality. To ensure excellent rendition of the opening notes of the Allegro, the conductor may resort to the *left-hand–right-hand technique* discussed in the previous paragraphs. This enables the players to proceed securely, with good ensemble.

Caution: The baton must stand perfectly still during the flick of the left hand. If it makes any motion whatsoever before the exact instant of the GoS, the result will probably be a ragged entrance.

Example 28. Weber, *Oberon*. Overture (measures 22–23).

The Beethoven example quoted in Example 29 is pertinent here. The flick of the left hand can show the cutoff of the fermata at the same time that it states beat One in tempo Allegro. The baton then performs the gesture of syncopation on the sixteenth rest and the music is off to a good start.

Example 29. Beethoven, Symphony No. 1 in C major, Op. 21. Finale (measures 5–8).

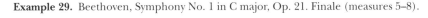

Note: Some editions do not show the caesura before the sixteenth rest; others do. If the conductor has made a long fermata, very soft, he or she may wish also to prolong the silence a bit. In this case, the fermata is cut off completely, and thereafter the left-hand–right-hand technique takes over as described above.

When the time-beating is in ONE, as shown in the Beethoven First Symphony, third movement, the left-hand gesture states one full measure that is not in the score. The right-hand gesture of syncopation flicks UP on One, since the players are coming in on an upbeat (the last one-third of the measure). The conductor's downbeat then meets them on One of the first full measure (Figure 31). There is **no motion in either hand between the two gestures.**

Figure 31.

The PASSIVE GESTURES: "Dead" Gestures

The "dead" gestures are those that are used when the conductor wishes to show the passing of rests (silent beats) or the presence of any single tutti rest. See the tutti rests at the beginning of the second measure of Example 30.

Example 30. Mozart, *Così fan tutte.* Overture (measures 11–12).

The connotation of this dead gesture is "Do not play. Be patient and I shall show you when." It must be lacking in impulse of will so that no one shall respond actively to it.

To perform the dead gesture, the **conductor shows *only the direction* of the beats by absolutely expressionless straight-line motion in the baton.** The gestures are *small,* and no ictus is defined as such in the beat pattern. Figure 32a shows four beats of "dead" gesture; 32b shows One-Two as playing gestures, Three-Four "dead"; 32c shows One-Two-Three "dead," then a preparatory loop warns that Four will be "active," requiring an entrance into the music. Like the gesture of syncopation, *a dead gesture has no preparatory beat.* Death does not breathe.

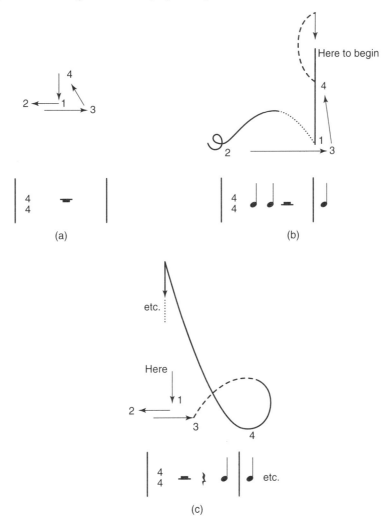

Figure 32. The dead gesture.

Any slight rebounding or curving of the line from ictus to ictus will show impulse of will or "personality" and will make the gesture appear active instead of passive. In performing the dead gesture, the conductor's hand should become completely devoid of expression—as if he or she has disowned it. The straight-line motion shows the passing of beats in accordance with the takt and does so in the quietest manner possible. The marvelous quality of silence is not to be disturbed. This gesture can become hypnotic in quality, holding the audience breathless.

When the dead gesture is used to show the passing of several measures of tutti rest (such as those that occur when accompanying a soloist), only the first beat of each measure is given. A dropping of the stick downward with an immediate return to the top is all that is needed. Such a single down-up gesture is also used to designate a measure marked G.P. (Grand Pause). This beat should be shown, to account for the measure that may come in the middle of a series of vacant measures for performers who are counting rests.

When **tutti rests** occur within a measure, they are generally beaten as dead gestures coincident with the takt. However, in recitatives, one may outline these missing beats unrhythmically, then pause in position for the next sounding gesture. (See page 223 for the Recitative.)

In **closing chords interspersed with rests,** the silent beats within the measure are generally not conducted. The baton simply stands still while the time goes by. However, if there is a whole measure of silence, it should be indicated by a small dead One (Example 31). A preparatory gesture precedes each on-the-beat chord.

Example 31. Beethoven, Symphony No. 5 in C minor, Op. 67. Finale (last seven measures).

Refining the Preparatory Beat

Since the preparatory beat requires no sound from the performers, it can be classified, as far as they are concerned, under the heading of passive gestures. However, the preparatory beat is active for the conductor. It is a "declaration of intent" leading to a command to "Play!" **Caution:** Limit the time you hold the hands in the "ready position."

The preparatory beat after a fermata, a completely silent measure, or a sustained whole note is similar in character to that at the beginning of the piece. It should again set tempo, dynamic, and style.

In time-beating of One-to-the-bar, the preparatory beat states one full measure of the music. Make it an upward rhythmic motion that says "Ready," followed by a downward One that says "Play!"

The dead gesture is also used for the tied-over quarter note. Distinguish between the examples in Figure 33.

Figure 33.

The preparatory beat in Adagio need not necessarily take the time of one full beat. Often the half-beat is sufficient, especially when the divided beat is being used.

A specialized type of preparatory beat may be used on a composition that starts with a *double forte*. The baton is positioned high in space. It descends suddenly and returns immediately to the starting point, and the performers attack at the top of the beat. Charles Munch of Boston Symphony Orchestra fame was seen to use this type of brilliant *forte* beginning.

An **unrhythmic preparatory beat with a "breathing gesture"** preceding it may be used when the first measure is composed of a *forte* or *double forte* tutti whole note or a fermata. (A sustained tone is rhythmically static; therefore a rhythmic preparatory beat is not essential.) See Figure 34. To perform the breathing gesture, the hands assume a ready position slightly away from the body. The hands then move horizontally to center front. The conductor takes the breath simultaneously with the performers during this motion. The baton stops momentarily, center front, and then suddenly (unrhythmically) moves

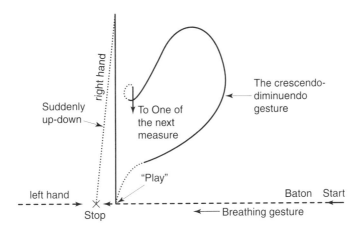

Figure 34. The breathing gesture.

up-down with great vigor, and the attack bursts forth with tremendous brilliance. The attack is followed by a sustained tenuto in the baton. Time-beating as such starts as a rhythmic preparatory beat leading into the following measure.

Example 32 shows this type of beginning. In Example 33, the breathing gesture would be omitted, since only the strings play the sustained C. The first beat of the second measure would be shown by a small dead gesture for the sake of the winds who are "counting measures."

Example 32. Beethoven, *Egmont*, Op. 84. Overture (measures 1–2).

Example 33. Beethoven, *Coriolanus Overture*, Op. 62 (measures 1–3).

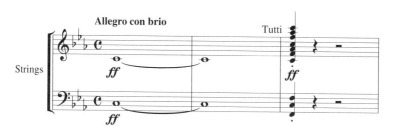

When the instruments have to execute a grace note at the beginning of a piece, the conductor can arrange with the musicians beforehand that they are to play the small note exactly on the principal beat. A case in point is the entrance of the four trumpets plus marimba in the third measure after letter D in *Music for Prague* [BAND] by Karel Husa,* a Pulitzer Prize–winning composer. On beat Three:

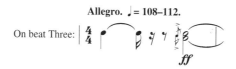

In the opening measures of the overture to Mozart's *Magic Flute,* the preparatory beat sets the tempo but no time-beating follows (Figure 35). The half notes are sustained (tenuto) and cut off. Each sixteenth note is articulated, indicated by a downbeat, followed immediately by a second downbeat for the half

*1968. Associated Music Publishers. International Copyright Secured. Used by Permission.

note, providing sufficient spacing between the two. The GoS is not applicable here until measure 3.

Figure 35.

There is one facet of the preparatory beat that must not be overlooked. **When the first beat of the piece comprises three or more notes of equal value (♩♪♪♪ | ♪♪♪♪), the preparatory beat must take the form of a legato line, connected directly to the playing beat.** Regardless of the dynamic, there must be no stop between the prep-beat and the playing beat. The length of preparatory motion states precisely the rhythmic length of the coming beat.

Is there ever a staccato preparatory beat? Yes. The stop is imperative when the first entrance is after the beat. The downbeat will be a gesture of syncopation (for example, the opening of the Fifth Symphony by Beethoven: $\frac{2}{4}$ ♪ ♪ ♪ ♪ | ♩). Also, the staccato prep-beat is useful when the first measure comprises even quarter notes, staccato marcato. The prep must be absolutely rhythmic.

One last word on the preparatory gesture: It is possible to clarify the beginning of the preparatory motion by a tiny incentive in the hand. It shows the instant of an ictus just as the hand starts to move upward. Care must be taken that there is no motion before it. This gesture is recommended by some very fine professional conductors and is useful with the 100-member professional symphony orchestra.

Exercises for Practice: Developing Expression in the Gestures

1. Practice applying the legato, staccato, tenuto, and dead gestures and the gesture of syncopation to the beat patterns of Chapters 2 and 4. Watch the tip of the stick in the mirror as you practice until each beat shows the distinctive style being worked on at the moment.

2. Practice the following exercises, repeating each several times without stopping. Be careful not to change the speed of the takt when the style changes to staccato. *Keep the takt steady.*

a. Six measures in ONE staccato and six measures in ONE legato.

b. Four measures in ONE staccato, *forte,* and four measures of dead gesture (silence). Use very small beats for the dead gesture here; center them in the wrist only.

c. Three measures in ONE tenuto and one measure as a gesture of syncopation with the group playing *after* the beat:

d. Two measures in TWO staccato and one measure in TWO tenuto:

e. Two measures in THREE tenuto and one measure in TWO silent (dead gesture).

3. Four measures in $\frac{2}{4}$: the first two measures in TWO staccato; the last two measures in ONE sustained-tenuto. ♩ = ♩ throughout.

4. Two measures in FOUR tenuto and one measure in THREE silent.

5. One measure in TWELVE staccato and one measure in divided-FIVE (3 + 2 pattern, divided). Repeat without stopping. ♪ = ♪ throughout.

6. One measure in TWELVE staccato, followed by one measure in FIVE silent (dead gesture).

7. Obtain any full score and look for places where the GoS might be used effectively (for example, entrances on part of a beat and notes tied to sixteenths).

Recommended Videotapes

It is strongly recommended that these tapes be seen, especially the Kleiber tape.

Carlos Kleiber, dir. *Beethoven Symphonies Nos. 4 and 7*. The Concertgebouw Orchestra, Amsterdam.

Phillips Video Classics, 070-200-3 NTSC VHS. Every gesture bespeaks the music itself. Notice the excitement and the timing when the musical character is about to change.

Dvořák in Prague: A Celebration. Seiji Ozawa and the Boston Symphony, with soloists: Firkusny, Piano; Yoyo Ma, Cello; Itzhak Perlman, Violin; Frederica von Stade, Vocalist. "As featured on the PBS Broadcast." Sony: Classical Films and Videos, NTSC VHS Hi-fi Stereo. Dolby/ SHV 53488. Some interesting staccatos in this one.

Music for Performance

Example 34. Mozart, *La Clemenza di Tito* (K.621). Overture (measures 1–12).

Time-beating in FOUR. Measure 1: Rhythmic prep-beat; show beats One and Two, and cut ON beat Three. The cutoff states the beat. A sudden GoS ON beat Four is all that is needed to continue. Measure 4: Observe the fermata. Keep hands in the ready position; then use the GoS for the entrance.

Example 35. Liszt, *Les Preludes* (measures 1–12). B-flat clarinet, cued.

No preparatory motion to start. Just show One straight down, Two in rhythm, small dead gestures. As soon as Two is indicated, start a large, preparatory gesture into Three-stop; Four, One, Two, dead, and prepare Three again.

*For the best sound in the pizzicato, there should be a point of resistance for the plucking finger to pull against, and the plucking finger should "twist" or "roll" the string as it plucks. For the tone to continue to sound throughout the beat, the finger holding down the pitch should remain firmly pressed to the fingerboard. Conductor: Carry through the third beat and make a cut-off on Four.

Recommended Reference Readings

CHRISTIANI, ADOLPH F., *Principles of Expression in Pianoforte Playing.* In applying Christiani's writings to massed performance groups, substitute the word *emphasis* for *accent.* This is one of the great works on expression in music.

LEINSDORF, ERICH, *The Composer's Advocate.* Chapter 3, "Knowing What Composers Wanted." Read sections on pages 51–63: "The Risks of Interpretation" and "The Limits of Interpretation of Music."

MALKO, NICOLAI, *The Conductor and His Baton.* Chapter 5, pp. 123–220. This is probably the greatest chapter in print on the conductor's gestures.

MCELHERAN, BROCK, *Conducting Technique.* Chapter 16, pp. 83–84: "Moulding the Music"; Chapter 18, pp. 91–92: "Ears."

SALZMAN, ERIC, *Twentieth-Century Music: An Introduction.* A well-written introduction to contemporary thought.

Recommended Videotape

For readers who are interested in the history of the conductor's technique, the following videotape is recommended. It is highly revealing.

The Art of Conducting: Great Conductors of the Past. Teldec Video. VHS Hi-fi 4509-95038-3. NTSC Dolby System.

6 Phrasing, Tempo Changes, Endings

Can you imagine how startled (and perhaps furious) you would be if you opened a new book and saw line after line of closely spaced words with no paragraphs, no capital letters, no periods to show where a thought ended, and no commas to explain the progress of the thought—just line after weary line trudging on, and on, and on . . .

Bear that thought in mind as we explore musical phrasing.

A well-written score is filled with "punctuation"—slurs, rests, staccato dots, dynamic markings, and so on. The composer has used phrase after phrase to lead the listeners onward, just as in literature the writer carries us forward from comma to comma until we encounter a period.

As conductors, we must understand our musical phrasing most potently, because we have to "interpret" it for our audiences, many of whom do not speak our musical language. To the listeners, "our" music that needs conducting is just a blur until we clarify it for them. This we do by what they hear and what they see.

All audiences have at least one ear on the music and one eye on the conductor. When our performance is "good enough," we can entice that other ear to listen and perhaps the other eye to observe the quality of the music as shown by the conductor's gestures.

The point that should be made here is that too often the hands are showing things that have no reference to what is sounding at the moment. We owe it to our players and our audiences to listen intently to what we are producing and to notice what our hands are saying.

Phrasal Analysis and Phrasal Conducting

Both analysis and conducting deal with three aspects of the phrase: the beginning, the contour, and the ending.

The Beginning   Does the phrase start ON the beat (gló-ri-a)? Or does it start on an afterbeat—a "pickup" note or notes (a-wáy down south in Dixie)?

The note on which the phrase begins must establish itself clearly. Too often we become conscious of a phrase after it has already passed several of its important notes. We must not permit accompanying instruments to blot out a section as it introduces a melody line or a principal performer beginning an important solo.

The Contour   Which note is the most important after the first note? Is it the highest note or the longest note? Or is it the last note in the phrase, its termination? Does the phrase lead toward a climax that is followed by a decline to its last note, or does it end on a climax note?

To conduct **contour,** we depend largely upon our ability to **vary our speed of motion between beats.** Here are four beats in $\frac{4}{4}$: 1- - - -2- - - -3- - - -4- - - -. Whereas the beat-points occur rhythmically, our speed of motion between beats changes to enlarge or diminish the contour. See Figure 26, page 46, for various contours. The contouring of Example 36 is now spelled out.

Example 36.

In conducting Example 36, and beating in TWELVE, there are several changes in speed of motion of the baton. The first beat moves toward its ictus in tempo. For the divisions of the beat (1,2,3), the hand moves slower, covering less space, but moving slightly faster as it leads into small beat 4.

As the crescendo takes over, the contour is enlarged and the speed of motion increases (beats 7,8), becoming rapid as 9 covers more distance while swinging into 10. Beat One of measure 2 signifies that the climax has been completed and the speed of motion gradually slows down, covering less distance, as the diminuendo takes over for the termination of the phrase. All of this takes place without disturbing the takt—the rhythmic drive of the tempo itself. See Last Training Exercise, pages 158–159.

Example 37 is a second version of the phrase, leading to a more brutal ending. How would you conduct this one?

The eventual size of the contour-arc tells the player just how much stress is needed on the important notes (see also "Contouring the Phrase," page 93). You

Example 37.

can think of all of this in terms of the size if you prefer, but you cannot change size without changing speed of motion unless you want to disturb the majesty of the takt (the rhythm). **The size of the gesture is a by-product of the speed at which you are moving.** And adjustment of speed of motion relies upon mental and physical flexibility in the conducting process. Rigidity just won't work.

Ending the Phrase   Does the phrase end on a full beat? Or does it end on part of a beat? Is there a whole beat of rest following? Is it a split beat? Does the next phrase start immediately, or is there time to breathe?

This is where much of the trouble starts for inexperienced conductors: Just when does the phrase end? The following should clarify your thinking.

1. For a phrase ending on a full beat, followed by one or more full beats of rest, cut on the ictus of the first rest. Since an ictus starts the sound (or the silence), cutting on the ictus of the notated rest brings silence with it.

2. For a phrase ending on part of a beat, cut on the beat itself. The line leading into the beat becomes a cutoff as the ictus occurs.

3. For a phrase followed closely by a new phrase, simply approach the last note of the present phrase using slow speed of motion and stop the motion exactly on the ictus. No cutoff. Continue immediately after the stop by giving a good preparatory gesture into the new phrase that starts on a full beat. (See also item 5.)

4. In fast tempos (no written rest involved), stop the baton exactly on the ictus of the last beat of the phrase and continue instantly.

5. For a phrase ending on a full-beat note that is followed immediately by an afterbeat entrance in the new phrase, stop on the ictus of the ending note; use a gesture of syncopation for the rest in the afterbeat entrance and continue.

6. *In all of the above, guard against shooting the phrase down in midflight. Don't "chop it off."* **Coming to a phrase ending is like a train approaching a stop. Its motion slows down.** But to retard the end of every phrase would be musically ridiculous. Therefore, we substitute a slight diminuendo and we **slow the motion of the baton between beats without interrupting the forward drive of rhythm.**

Example 38 will provide experience in most of the items enumerated above. Sincere appreciation is expressed to composer Robert Jager for this very clever training exercise (used by permission).

PROBLEMS

1. Practice the music as written, applying the material given above to solve its problems. (See 1 and 5 under "Ending the Phrase.")

Note: Conduct all silent beats by using **dead** gestures. Prepare the entrances immediately after the ictus of the last beat of rest.

Example 38.

2. Practice the music omitting all the rests except the one in measure 9. Link the music into a continuous sequence as if it were one longer phrase, but show the sub-phrases within. (See 3, 4, and 5 under "Ending the Phrase.")

3. Try both 1 and 2 at various metronome settings. Retard the last three notes if you wish.

Marking Phrases

Marking phrases into the score proceeds differently from conducting them. *Conducting deals with the musical aspect; marking deals with the structural aspect.* The basic principle in marking is this: **Disregard any phrasal introductory notes** written before a barline and begin your measure-count with beat One of the first full measure occupied by the phrase.

To mark, extend the barline down into the bottom margin, and write next to it the number of measures in the coming phrase. Thus you will know where the phrase is heading. To conduct, you must start with the "pickup" notes that come before the barline. The most important note in the phrase is its first note. See Example 39.

MUSIC FOR PERFORMANCE

Example 39. Schubert, String Quartet in A minor, Op. 29. Beginning (measures 1–22).
Apply the material on phrasing. No ritards at phrase ends, but slow your motion for smaller gestures. A slight diminuendo can replace the ritard. Let your ear tell you.

Tempo Changes

From Slow to Fast Tempo

Important: When the music changes from a slow to a fast tempo at a double bar, place the last ictus of the slow tempo **low** in space. Bring the baton to the center front near where the ictus of One took place. The baton will stop momentarily to permit the slow tempo to complete itself, then will make a sudden rhythmic preparatory beat upward to set the new tempo. Figure 36 diagrams this technique.

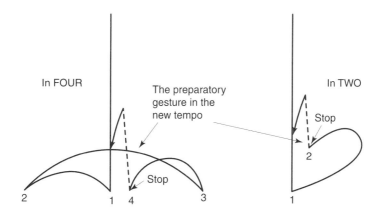

Figure 36. Change of tempo—the return to center.

Example 40 presents a pertinent passage. Here the baton has to prepare the coming Presto by a fast legato gesture after the ictus of Four in the slow tempo. Note the reiterated notes on the first fast beat in the violins. Since these players enter after an eighth rest, the conductor will do well to look sharply to the ictus of his or her first Presto beat.

Example 40. Mozart, *Cosí fan tutte.* Overture (measures 14–15).

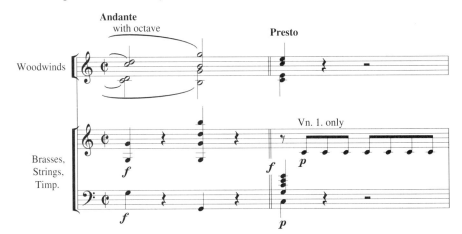

Drill: Practice the following exercises showing a *change to a faster tempo* when the meter changes. Make the change exactly on One of the new measure, and use a precise preparatory beat *in the new tempo.* Start with several measures in the first tempo. Remember to **control the rebound of the last beat of the slow tempo, returning the baton to center front** near the ictus of beat One, and making a gesture of preparation thereafter in the new fast tempo.

a. $\frac{4}{4}$ to $\frac{3}{4}$

b. $\frac{2}{4}$ to $\frac{3}{4}$

c. $\frac{3}{4}$ to $\frac{6}{8}$ in SIX

d. $\frac{2}{4}$ to $\frac{5}{4}$ in FIVE

e. $\frac{3}{4}$ to $\frac{4}{4}$

f. Divided $\frac{3}{4}$ to $\frac{4}{4}$

g. $\frac{4}{4}$ to $\frac{2}{4}$

h. $\frac{5}{4}$ in a 3 + 2 pattern to $\frac{6}{8}$ in TWO

i. $\frac{6}{8}$ in SIX to $\frac{4}{4}$

j. $\frac{4}{4}$ to $\frac{5}{4}$ in TWO, 3 + 2 division

k. $\frac{4}{8}$ in TWO to $\frac{3}{16}$ in ONE

l. $\frac{6}{8}$ in SIX to $\frac{3}{4}$ in THREE

From here on, the student should be conscious of both *score* and *interpretative technical means.*

Subtle Tempo Variations

If the student will set a metronome going while playing a fine recording of a major work by a major symphony orchestra, he or she will perhaps be surprised that the two will not continue to coincide in the takt. Music is a living thing, and as such it cannot become entirely mechanistic. But in the hands of a skilled conductor, it can give the illusion of perfectly timed beats without sacrificing the right to breathe freely.

Tempo variations, when they exist and are not indicated by written directives, must be very subtle. It is easier to fool the human ear than it is the metronome. When these variations occur, they must be so skillfully performed that they do not call attention to their existence as such. The adding of a bit of **tenuto** to a certain note in a legato passage may lend color to the whole passage—but, inconspicuously, it has stretched the beat, which stretching is often compensated for by an equally inconspicuous deletion in the next following beat. When the composer requests such performance, and wishes it to be of a slightly more obvious nature, this is indicated through the use of the word *rubato*. It is a delightful word that permits emotion to reign with an authority superior to the inherent majesty of the takt. The French interpretation of the word is one that recognizes irregularities *within* the measure but keeps the length of the measure itself intact.

When it is necessary for the conductor to hold back the tempo, the addition of more tenuto in the gesture can accomplish it. When the conductor wishes to urge ahead, the use of staccato gestures will help. Also, a factor in urging ahead is the cheating, slightly, of the longer notes. Gestures become smaller, not larger.

In very slow movements (especially in Adagio tempos), the entrance of the second theme is usually the signal to relax the intensity and to urge the tempo ahead slightly—enough to negate any monotony that might otherwise prevail.

In Example 41, the tempo is sometimes subtly broadened after the fermata with a *very gradual* accelerando all the way to the end of the piece. This makes for a thrillingly brilliant ending.*

Example 41. Weber, *Der Freischütz.* Overture (measures 287–292).

Accelerandos and ritardandos marked by the composer are not quite so subtle. The important thing with these devices is that the change of motion in either case be gradual, not sudden, and that both may be brought under control again when the music demands the resumption of its original tempo. For immediate changes from slow to fast tempos, see page 76.

---

*There are two accepted interpretations for the passage given here. The second is as follows: The tempo is slightly slower following the fermata, tutti rest; it then resumes its original brilliance at (a).

The Closing Measures

A few words now about the almost imperceptible tempo deviations that lead to the final note of a composition.

Some pieces end with a tremendous rush of time-beating right to the last note, which is performed as a brilliant cutoff. Accelerando is well nigh unavoidable. Other compositions lead to a gorgeous, sustained sound crowned with a fermata. When the **fermata** exists, pay attention to it. Usually it tells you that the composer intended some broadening of the sound (and tempo) with a consequent lengthening of the last note beyond its notated value. Try to achieve the nobility inherent in such an ending.

Note: A fermata over a barline signifies only the termination of a certain section of the piece and does not affect the performance.

For the diminuendo into silence, keep the hands moving downward in a tenuto gesture until the sound disappears. When silence reigns, the conductor stands perfectly still for a moment before releasing the audience from the spell of utter quiet.

Delayed Last Note

Another type of ending must be mentioned. It is the hair's-breadth delay of the very last note where no ritard has occurred. It is pertinent to pieces of a light, airy, and often humorous character that bounce along right up to the end with no ritard. The performance of the last note, just later than the audience expects it, brings with it a bit of a chuckle and a storm of applause. It has a charm that is difficult to match in any other way. Example 42 shows a place where the delayed last note can be used.

Example 42. Lalo, *Symphonie espagnole,* Op. 21, for Violin and Orchestra. Second movement (last four measures).

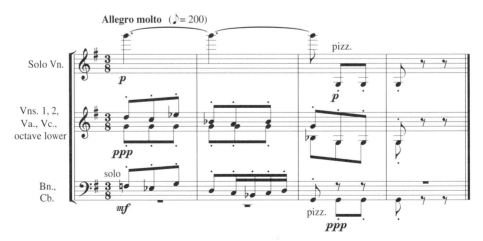

A second example of the delayed last note occurs in the Minuet forms. On occasion the bass instruments have an ending note on the second beat of the measure. This is usually in the form of an octave skip. In cases where there has been no ritard, this last note is generally played a fraction of an instant late. The effect is that of putting a definite period on the end of the sentence.

The necessity often arises, in theatrical performances, to stop the music in the midst of its onrush, as it were. When the "act" finishes, the applause must start regardless. The old circus bands customarily resorted to their C major chord, playing it instantly when the act terminated and holding it *forte* until the applause was well established. In the theater, often the tonic chord of the selection being played is used for the ending chord, and it is inserted whenever the applause is due. The theater orchestra understands that one of its biggest jobs is to crescendo the endings so that the audience reaction will be enthusiastic, spontaneous, and sustained.

Finally, let us mention the old "showmanship" ending. This is used when the theater orchestra is performing on the stage and is itself the main attraction. The conductor wishes to force the applause to start before the orchestra has finished playing its last note. (This presupposes a loud ending.) He or she can warn the musicians, during the rehearsal, to "keep pouring it on" until the applause starts. The conductor then forces the applause by turning suddenly to the audience while still holding out the last note and, if necessary, jerking the baton upward a little, very quickly. It is almost foolproof in its results if the conductor has confidence in himself or herself as the gesture is performed. The cutoff for the orchestra is performed after the applause has started and while the conductor is still facing the audience. Remember, this is pure showmanship—not formal concert etiquette. When your *band* soars to a great climax—*fff* plus fermata on the last note—don't shoot it down in midflight. Take time to enjoy the view while you are up there! Let your band show you how long they can sustain without changing pitch. You may be surprised.

The Up-Ictus

Caution: One will, upon occasion, see a type of time-beating in which the ictus, the playing point, comes at the top of the rebound. The hand, instead of "bouncing the ball" on each beat, acquires the feeling of tossing the ball. *The moment of impact shows at the top of the rebound instead of at the bottom of the beat.* This is something to be avoided as a basic habit. It makes life difficult for the performers, since the beat-point is no longer at the lowest moment of the gesture. Rhythmic precision suffers and rehearsal time is lost. In choral music, the *rare* conductor who uses this beat feels that it gives "lightness" to the tone and helps to keep the pitch from sagging.

There is, nevertheless, one place where the up-ictus is useful, and that is in the One-to-the bar waltzes. Once the rhythm has been established, the conductor can subtly slip over to the up-ictus. It can add a charming lilt to the performance.

We have mentioned the up-ictus at this time because one should be able to recognize it when it is seen. But we caution against its use as a general facet of time-beating.

As a final word for this entire chapter: Teach your performers to see and recognize the first beat of each measure—and then be dead sure your own downbeat is clearly recognizable as such.

MUSIC FOR PERFORMANCE

Example 43. Mozart, *Così fan tutte*. Overture (measures 1–22).

Time-beating in FOUR. Set tempo in your mind. Then prepare and show One; cut on Two using a GoS. Continue in rhythm on Three, Four. Measure 4: GoS on Four. Three measures before the double bar: Show each chord, but use the rests only to prepare the next chord.

*Keep beat Four low in space: no high rebound. **Caution:** When the prep-beat for the fast tempo is made at the top of One, it is too high for the players to see it. See Figure 36, page 76.

Note: Measures 1 and 5 are the problem measures in Example 43. They illustrate the difference between "time-beating" and "conducting." Set your tempo by humming measures 2 and 3. Measure 1: Legato prep-beat in tempo, solid ictus on One. Cut off the quarter note ON beat Two. The STOP of the cutoff IS the beat-point of beat Two, and it is followed by an upward GoS flick, on the "and," in the baton before it swings into Three, which is cut off ON Four. The GoS is the printed dot.

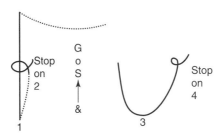

Example 44. Mendelssohn, Symphony No. 4 in A major, Op. 90 *(Italian)* (measures 1–10).
Time-beating in FOUR. Legato and tenuto. Apply the GoS if you need it for the afterbeats.
Performance suggestion. Feel as if you are lifting the orchestra over the sixteenth note, and use a
gentle GoS for the third beat in the first two measures. See that cellos and basses are clearly
heard on their entrance. Balance the dynamics.

*Take time to end the phrase. Stop the baton for one instant on the third beat. You still have a half-beat coming to allow you to prepare the fourth beat. Don't jump away from the phrase ending. The bass line will keep you on the beat.

Recommended Reference Readings

BRAITHWAITE, WARWICK, *The Conductor's Art.* Chapter 4, pp. 22–35: "Sudden Changes of Time."

EARHART, WILL, *The Eloquent Baton.* Chapters 6, 7, 8, pp. 36–67: "Phrasing"; "Phrasing Beats"; "Other Properties of the Beat."

KAHN, EMIL, *Conducting.* Chapter 20, pp. 146–154: "Phrasing."

MALKO, NICOLAI, *The Conductor and His Baton.* Chapter 5, pp. 123–220: "The Conductor's Gestures." This is still the greatest chapter in print on the gestures.

7 Developing the Left Hand

The technically developed left hand plays an important part in the overall musical result. Although this hand should be able to beat time efficiently, it should not constantly mimic the rhythmic motions of the right hand. The left hand has its own eloquent language to speak, and it should eventually be trained for **independent** action.

To introduce this facet of the technique, it is helpful if the reader has some understanding of the structure of the brain. The human brain is made up of two "mirrored" halves, each complete in itself. Medical science has shown that the left half of the brain controls the right side of the body; the right half controls the left side of the body. The two halves can set up independent controls, aided by habit formation, so that each hand can do a different kind of work simultaneously with and independently of the other.* Witness the violinist!

By use of the Positron Emission Tomography (PET) scan, the intuitive, spatial recognition, and music centers have been located in the right half of the brain; the emotions occupy the frontal portion. When trained musicians judge musical pitches, both halves of the brain show activity. This should tell us something about how important it is to have both halves of the brain developed, especially in our field of physical-mental-emotional-creative conducting.

---

*"Each hemisphere contains the control centers for several activities that can occur simultaneously." Excerpts from *The Brain: The Last Frontier* by Richard M. Restak, M.D. Copyright © 1979 by Richard M. Restak. Reprinted by permission of Doubleday & Company, Inc., a division of Bantam, Doubleday, Dell Publishing Group, Inc.

The two hemispheres are interconnected by an intricate network of fibers, called the *corpus callosum,* that acts to correlate the functions of the two halves when, for example, simultaneous or similar actions of the two hands are desired.* If you have read the footnote, you will realize that as a young conductor you can have confidence that you are "built to function!"—but it takes practice. For an update, see under *Calvin, William H.,* in the Bibliography, page 279.

Building Independent Action in the Hands

During the activating of the left hand, the right hand will be functioning largely by habit—the habits you have established in your conducting thus far. Two goals now emerge: first, to be able to activate and deactivate the left hand without upsetting the time-beating in the right hand; and second, to be able to perform long, smooth, slow motions with the left hand without showing either pulses or momentary stops in its motion while the right hand continues its time-beating.

Training Exercise 5

Let the left arm hang loosely from the shoulder, completely relaxed. Begin time-beating in FOUR with the right hand. Bring the left hand up in a fist gesture on a third beat and then drop it back immediately to its full-length relaxation. Do this every second measure while the right hand continues to beat time. See that the rhythm of the right hand is not upset by the left-hand motion. When this exercise is easy, bring the left hand up on the first beat of each measure. This is more difficult because the right hand will be coming down while the left hand is coming up. Continue with 4, 3, 2, 1 (in consecutive measures), then 1, 2, 3, 4. The left hand returns to *complete relaxation* each time.

Repeat this same study with your left hand resting near your diaphragm and returning to this position after each gesture. This is the more normal position for the left hand when you are standing on the podium.

Cuing

First a word about the position of the fingers of the left hand. If allowed to spread widely apart, they show great tension and assume a grotesque appearance. Keep the three middle fingers together. With relaxation, they will curve naturally. The thumb and little finger can "float."

---

*Restak, p. 172. "Events in one hemisphere can be immediately telegraphed over this 200-million-fiber network [corpus callosum] to the opposite hemisphere. If we suppose that each fiber has an average firing frequency of twenty impulses a second, the *corpus callosum* is carrying something like four billion impulses a second right now as you are reading this sentence."

To Cue: Use a small, definite motion toward the recipient(s); palm toward the floor, middle fingers together. If you prefer to "invite" them to play, turn the palm slightly upward and indicate the entry beat. Make eye contact if possible.

To Practice Cuing: Direct your cues to specific musicians and visualize where they would sit in the ensemble. Choose a time-beating pattern for the right hand. Left hand, palm upward, rests near your diaphragm and returns to this position between cues.

First, cue ON the beat in each measure: measure 1 on One; m. 2 on Two; m. 3 on Three; m. 4 on Four. Then cue on beats 4, 3, 2, 1; on beats 2 and 4; and so on. Repeat.

Second, bring the left hand into play one beat before the cue-beat and make a rhythmic preparatory beat leading to the cue. Both of these are good for improving your "timing." Vary your time-beating patterns as you wish. You are drilling your left hand to respond instantly to the directions sent out by your mind. Meanwhile your right hand is working through habit. To give effective cues, you must know where the various singers or instrumentalists are positioned in the organization you are about to conduct. If you are in doubt, it is permissible to ask at the beginning of the rehearsal. It is best if you can be provided with a seating chart beforehand. Several types of seatings are to be found in Appendix A.

When Are Cues Given?

Cues are customarily given under the following circumstances:

1. When an instrument or a group of instruments enters the music for the first time after the piece has already begun
2. When an instrument or a group of instruments enters after a long rest
3. When a single instrument begins an important solo or melodic line
4. When an entire section takes over the main theme
5. When melodic interest or rhythmic figures (motifs) are tossed from one instrument to another
6. Whenever entrances are tricky and difficult
7. When the conductor wishes to control exactly the moment of the sound
8. When instruments enter on *double forte* attacks
9. When there is a cymbal crash or an entrance of the cymbals for a prolonged passage
10. When there are isolated pizzicato notes or chords

How Are Cues Given?

Cues are given in the following ways:

1. By the baton in the manner of a time-beating gesture directed specifically toward a player or a group of players customarily seated on the conductor's right or in the center of the orchestra.

2. By the left hand in a special motion (not a time-beating gesture), sometimes with a preparation gesture preceding the cue and sometimes with just an indication on the beat-point. The left-hand cues are used for players sitting left of center.

3. By the eyes, a lift of the eyebrows, or a nod of the head. This last is used in very quiet passages where anything other than the most subtle of motions would disrupt the mood. These gestures are also used when both hands are already fully occupied with other necessary conductorial gestures.

Caution: The two hands should not cross over each other in giving cues. *Do not lean over toward the performers when giving a cue.*

Training Exercise 6

Beat eight measures in TWO with the right hand. The left hand is going to make a four-measure crescendo motion upward followed by four measures of diminuendo as it returns downward to its starting position. Let the palm of the hand face upward on the crescendo gesture, as if actually carrying the sound up. At the peak of the upward motion (forehead level), the hand is turned to face the performers. Bring it back down to the starting point at the side, indicating diminuendo. You will find that at first the left hand will not perform smoothly. Watch it with your eyes. Its motion will tend to pause here and there and to be somewhat jerky, influenced by the rhythmic motion of the right hand. Smoothness comes rather quickly, however. Later, the right hand can vary the size of its time-beating gestures to match the crescendo-diminuendo dynamic of the left hand. When this exercise becomes smooth and easy, you can be assured that the two hands have established their fundamental independence. The brain has gone through its period of initial development.

Contouring the Phrase

Let the right hand beat a two-measure group in $\frac{4}{4}$. Let the left hand carry the phrase upward in about a twelve-inch arc, its peak coinciding with the beginning of the second measure; then turn the palm toward the floor and bring the phrase back down again. Practice this on Example 45, which presents two passages where phrasal contour gestures may be used effectively. In (a), two four-measure phrases are shown with the peak at the beginning of the second measure; in (b), a series of two-measure phrases of increasing intensity is given. Use the gesture of syncopation in measures 1, 5, 9, 11, 13, 15.

Example 45. Dvořák, *Slavonic Dance*, Op. 72, No. 2, in E minor. (a) Measures 1–8; (b) measures 17–24. First violin only quoted.

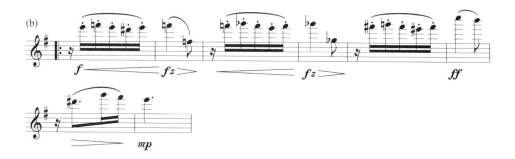

Other Facets of Left-Hand Technique

In addition to its duties in cuing and phrasing, the left hand gives valuable assistance in controlling dynamics and adding to the emotional drive. When the palm faces the players, it is usually read as a caution to soften; when it faces the conductor, the musicians read it as a command for more power. *Keep the three middle fingers together in using the left hand.* For the *piano subito,* bring the left hand up suddenly, palm toward the performers and fingers pointing *straight up.* The more sudden the motion, the softer the response.

A left hand, working without panic, can often prevent mistakes from happening. It can say "Not Yet" so beautifully.

Exercises for Practice: Cuing and Left-Hand Independence

Repeat each of the following exercises many times without stopping. Repeat until easy.

1. Beating time in FOUR, cue with the left hand on One of the first measure and on Three of the second measure; on One of the third measure and Three of the fourth measure; and so on.

2. Beating time in THREE, cue on One of the first measure and on Three of the second measure and repeat. Direct the cues toward the two different players in an imaginary ensemble.

3. Beating time in ONE, cue on the first beat of the third, fifth, and ninth measures.

4. Beating time in FOUR, cue on Three to the left and in the next measure cue on Four to the right (baton cue).

5. Beating time in FOUR, cue on the first beat of the first measure, the second beat of the second measure, the third beat of the third measure, and the fourth beat of the fourth measure, repeating instantly from the beginning.

6. Beating time in THREE, cue on Three; in the third measure, cue on Two with the baton.

7. Beating time in SIX, give no cues in the first measure; in the second measure, cue on Four to the left and on Six to the right with the baton.

8. Beating time in TWO, let the left hand show four measures of steady crescendo (upward rise) and four measures of steady diminuendo (downward gesture, palm toward players).

9. Beating time in TWO, let the left hand show a two-measure crescendo, a three-measure diminuendo, a three-measure crescendo, and a four-measure diminuendo, and repeat.

10. Beating time in FOUR for four measures, the left hand is to show a phrase contour, rising and falling in an arc from left to center front, ending the phrase on the second beat of every second measure.

11. Practice cuing on all the full-score excerpts in Chapters 10, 11, and 12. Direct the cues to the proper place in the imaginary band, chorus, or orchestra. (Seating charts may be found in Appendix A.)

Recommended Reference Readings

BRAITHWAITE, WARWICK, *The Conductor's Art*. Chapter 7, pp. 46–50: "Use of Left Hand and Arm."

EARHART, WILL, *The Eloquent Baton*. Chapter 11, pp. 88–93: "The Left Hand and Signaling."

GROSBAYNE, BENJAMIN, *Techniques of Modern Orchestral Conducting*. Chapter 12, pp. 75–80: "Left Hand."

KAHN, EMIL, *Conducting*, pp. 74–75: "Cuing."

MALKO, NICOLAI, *The Conductor and His Baton*. Chapter 6, pp. 251–266: "The Left Hand."

RESTAK, RICHARD M., *The Brain: The Last Frontier*. Chapter 10, pp. 164–206: "The Jekyll and Hyde Solution."

For the left hand, see the videotape recommended on page 241.

CHAPTER

8

The Fermata

Every fermata ($\frown$) is a law unto itself. Only one thing do they all have in common, and that is a nonrhythmic execution. The fermata is held out as a sustained tone with no rhythmic pulsation and, except in chorales, is lengthened beyond the written value of the note.*

The fermata is used in two ways:

1. In early church music (chorales), the fermata indicates the ending of the phrase. Sometimes this ending is elongated, but that is not an invariable custom.

2. In other types of vocal composition and in instrumental music, the fermata is written to lengthen a particular note when the drama of the situation demands it or when the expressive qualities of the music require such highlighting.

When the young conductor begins working with the fermata, he or she must clarify three points:

1. What the emotional quality of the particular fermata is and, therefore, **how long it should be held.**

2. **Whether it cuts off completely at its termination or leads directly into the next note** with no moment of silence between.

---

*It is of serious concern today that the length of the fermata is being so greatly disregarded. One hears performance after performance of the less-than-professional choruses, bands, and orchestras in which the fermata is being given exactly the length the note would have had if the composer had failed to write the fermata above. The ability to *stop* the rhythmic feeling inside oneself seems to be a lost art. In response to the question "What is the most difficult thing for the students to acquire?" many teachers of conducting, both here and in Europe, have answered, invariably, "The handling of the fermata."

3. In the event the fermata is to cut off completely, **what direction this cutoff should take so that the baton may be in position to move easily into the following gesture,** whatever it may be. (Check back on the cutoff diagrams on page 14.)

Every fermata should be "solved" in the light of the foregoing three points before an attempt is made to execute it with the musicians.

Definition of the Fermata

The fermata is a cessation of rhythm. In Italian, the word *fermata* means "stop." One does not beat time during a fermata. The hands simply perform a sustained tenuto gesture during the length of the sound.

In general, it is preferred to keep the baton moving slowly while sustaining, but there are occasions that warrant the striking of a dramatic pose with the stick and "freezing." When this is done, intensity must show in the baton grip. The tension in the hand keeps the players sounding their tone until a cutoff occurs or the music continues. Sometimes this intensity is shown by a small but purposeful shaking of the stick. When the baton stands still, there is always the danger that a diminuendo will occur. The sustaining motion may be transferred to the left hand if preferred, the stick remaining static.

Fermatas Classified by Length

There are two basic types of fermata by length:

1. **The fermata that is determinate in length.** The duration is a certain definite span in relation to the speed of the takt, such as twice as long as the composer's written notation of the fermata note. This type of fermata appears in certain places in Haydn and Mozart, especially in fast movements of solo accompaniments. It is, however, the exception to the rule.

2. **The fermata that is indeterminate in length.** The duration of such a fermata is left entirely up to the conductor, but it should be *longer* than the written value of the note or rest over which it is placed. This is the more common type of fermata.

In the handling of either type, *no time is beaten*. One's inner feeling of continuous rhythm must halt. The fermata must not be curtailed. One is reminded of Wagner's "as if Beethoven cried, 'HOLD my fermatas!'"

The cutting off of the fermata should leave the baton (hand) in position to move easily into the next gesture. When the cutoff feels clumsy, check the direction of the cutoff loop—clockwise or counterclockwise? Choice of the correct loop will leave the hand in good position to continue. See Figure 51, page 140. In many cases the left hand can be most serviceable in showing the termination of the fermata. This hand is also valuable in helping to control the general fermata dynamic, in reinforcing the sustained tone, and in adding a hypnotic quality to a very long diminuendo-fermata.

Important: After any fermata there must be a rhythmic preparatory gesture if the following note comes directly ON a beat. But if the entrance comes after a beat (on part of a beat), the use of the gesture of syncopation ON the beat will be sufficient to ensure accuracy of execution. (Afterbeat entrances can be seen in Example 46; Example 47, last measure; and Example 49.)

The Fermata That Continues the Music without a Stop (Caesura)

Note: The caesura lines (//) indicate a complete cutoff, a complete stop but of momentary duration.

Certain fermatas lead directly into a continuation of the music without a complete cutoff. The musical thought carries on through the rhythmic interruption contributed by the fermata. The next six examples deal with fermatas of this type.

Example 46 shows the fermata slurred to what follows. Here the baton sustains the fermata while moving slowly (tenuto) to the right and slightly upward. To terminate the fermata, the baton shows Two (after the manner of a gesture of syncopation). This gesture actually states the dot on the fermata note, and the music continues in the given rhythmic tempo. No preparation is necessary. The showing of Two terminates the fermata at the same time that it resumes the tempo of the music.

Example 46. Beethoven, Symphony No. 3 in E-flat major, Op. 55 *(Eroica).* Finale (measures 95–96).

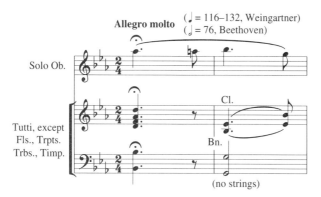

Example 47 shows a tutti fermata with no caesura indicated. At the termination of the first hold, the baton loops directly into One of the next measure. The cutoff of the second fermata is Two of that measure, again stated suddenly as a gesture of syncopation (no preparatory loop), thus resuming the rhythm. The downbeat of each fermata measure should be shown by a very small down-up in the stick as it sustains the tie from the preceding measure. The left hand becomes valuable here also in preserving the sustained sound. The reason for not cutting off the first fermata completely is given by Felix Weingartner (an authority on Beethoven): The passage is "a closed harmonic and melodic complex," thus not allowing a break in its sequence.

Example 47. Beethoven, Symphony No. 1 in C major, Op. 21. Finale (measures 234–236).

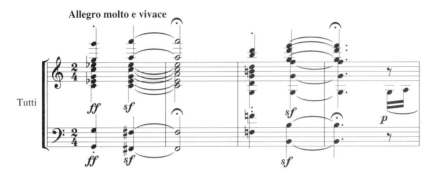

Example 48 presents another type of direct continuation of the music. The fermata is held on One, the baton moving to the right and slightly upward. This motion changes to an outward, rhythmic preparatory loop, and Two is stated with good impulse of will. This cuts off the fermata at the same time that it commands the strings to continue the music *on* Two.

Example 48. Beethoven, Symphony No. 7 in A major, Op. 92. First movement (measure 88).

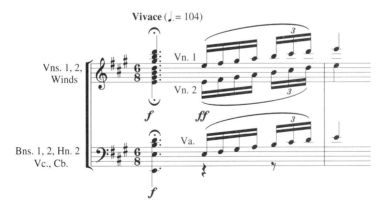

In Example 49 we see Beethoven's very careful notation of just exactly what he means. The pizzicato A-flat in the strings is to continue immediately on the heels of the fermata. Notice Beethoven's notation of the fermata *between the rests* in the string parts. This signifies that the gesture of cutting off the fermata becomes a rhythmic Two.

Example 49. Beethoven, Symphony No. 3 in E-flat major, Op. 55 *(Eroica)*. Finale (measure 31).

Not infrequently a fermata appears just before a double bar. This is seen in medleys and overtures. If the pause is on a dominant seventh chord, a complete cutoff is out of place. It leaves the resolution chord, to the right of the double bar, stranded. Sometimes an arranger marks the cutoff. Be wary in such places.

When the **fermata before the double bar** precedes a change of tempo, the fermata is held, after which the baton makes a **rhythmic preparatory gesture in the new tempo** leading into One. (Check page 77, "From Slow to Fast Tempo.")

In Example 50, the first beat of the new tempo entails the playing of six notes on that first beat, violins and violas. The Allegro preparatory gesture should be legato and connected directly to the downbeat. Refer to page 63.

Example 50. Beethoven, *Nameday Overture*, Op. 115 (last measure of the slow introduction and first measure of the Allegro).

Finally, in Example 51, we find a leading-through on the fermatas with an interesting articulation in the timpani (stems down in the bass-clef line). In measure 1, the timpanist is shown the ending note by a gesture of the left hand as the right hand begins its rhythmic preparatory loop into the first beat of the second measure. In measure 2, after the timpanist has performed the roll, the conductor gives the left-hand cutoff gesture. But now Beethoven has written a fermata on a rest, *after* the timpani cutoff, showing that the fermata is still in effect and is to be sustained after the timpani stops.

Example 51. Beethoven, *Consecration of the House Overture*, Op. 124 (measures 200–202).

The Fermata Followed by a Complete Cutoff (a Rest or Caesura)

In the performance of **fermatas on rests,** the duration of the silence is influenced by the dynamic preceding it. Extreme *piano*s or massive *double forte*s usually lead to a longer silence. In Example 52, the note preceding the rest is a phrase ending. The cutoff can be handled effectively by the left hand. The baton stops on Two and stands still during the fermata-rest; then it makes a rhythmic preparatory beat into One.

Example 52. Beethoven, *The Ruins of Athens Overture*, Op. 113 (measures 23–24).

When the fermata cutoff is followed by a single full beat of rest, the silent beat is used only to make a rhythmic preparation for the next entrance. If there are several beats of tutti rest, the left hand can control the silence while the baton makes very small dead gestures showing the passing of the beats; or the baton can move directly into position for the next beat and wait until it is time to make the preparation. If time is beaten, the small gestures should be in the direction normally taken by the pertinent time-beating pattern.

When the composer has not specified rhythmically how long a silence should last, then it depends upon the conductor's own innate musical taste. In general, the longer the fermata, the more the silence can be stretched in that magic moment following the cutoff.

The Fermata with Caesura Lines (//) Continuing Immediately

The caesura lines indicate a complete break between the fermata and what follows—just enough of a break to show that the fermata is not connected to what *immediately* follows.

The Fermata on One

In $\frac{4}{4}$, the line of sustaining for a **fermata on One** would move to the right; the cutoff gesture would circle upward, counterclockwise, and cut to the right, leaving the hand in position to move leftward into Two (Figure 37). In $\frac{3}{4}$ meter, the line of sustaining would move left, the loop would be clockwise cutting left, and the hand would be in position to make the customary Two to the right. In every case, a slight lift of the stick after the stop would act as a preparatory motion into the next beat—as if you were saying "and Two," "and Three," as the case may be.

Figure 37.

From the foregoing, it will be seen that (except in time-beating in One) when the fermata occurs on One, the line of sustaining will move in a direction *opposite* to that of beat Two when that second beat follows immediately.

Note: When conducting a fermata, if the cutoff and reentrance feel clumsy, check on the direction of the circle used for the cutoff. Reversing the direction will often solve the problem.

The Fermata on Two

Figure 38 shows the **fermata on Two** in $\frac{4}{4}$. In (a), the line of sustaining continues leftward and slightly upward after the ictus of Two. A clockwise loop cutting left is made, and the baton arches into Three. In $\frac{3}{4}$, the fermata sustains to the right, uses an upward counterclockwise gesture, cuts to the right, and proceeds into Three.

Important: Look now at Figure 38b. After showing the ictus of Two, the hand would now sustain to the *right* so that the cutoff could be made on the customary ictus-point of Three (the tie of the fermata note), and would then be in position to loop directly into Four. This is an example of what is meant by "baton in position for the next beat after the cutoff." Be sure the baton stops cleanly after a cutoff.

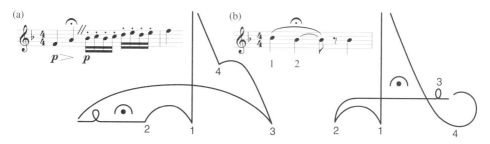

Figure 38.

The Fermata on Three

When the **fermata is on Three** (in $\frac{4}{4}$), the line of sustaining moves to the right, the cutoff loops counterclockwise and cuts to the right (Figure 39).

Figure 39.

The Fermata on the Last Beat of Any Measure

With the **fermata occurring on the last beat of any measure,** it is necessary to **keep the rebound of the preceding beat low. The ictus of the last beat will then be also in a low position.** The line of sustaining has two choices. It can move normally upward, very slowly so as not to go too high; the cutoff can circle right or left, leaving the hand ready for a short preparatory motion into One (Figure 40). Or, if the fermata is to be extremely long, the baton can take a horizontal sustaining line, to the right and back or to the left and back, before starting its climb upward. If there is a rest on One, the baton can simply cut the fermata on One, beaten rhythmically, and then prepare Two.

Note: The slow-moving horizontal line is the preferred line, in general, for sustaining. The wrist can lead the hand (exercise 1, page 10) with the thumb facing the ceiling; the hand is then always in position to take the next beat. *Perpendicular* lines are usually time-beating in character.

Figure 40.

Some More-Difficult Types of Fermata

As you have seen, every fermata requires intelligent study. Of all composers, Beethoven stands out in precision of notation and in a variety that is all-encompassing. Every rest, every dot, every caesura says exactly what he means. We shall close this chapter by dealing with some specialized types of fermata.

The Rebeaten Fermata

In Figure 41, we have a series of fermatas that playfully interrupt the melody's rhythm but not its sequence. Imagine that this same melody has occurred earlier in the piece without the fermatas. To perform this music, breaking the rhythm but not the melodic sequence, the conductor has to show *two* second beats in each measure, one to start the hold and another to signify the ending of the fermata and the resumption of the rhythm. The first of the two second beats will show its ictus and move into a slow, tenuto gesture of sustaining. This sustaining gesture will go to the right. This will be followed by a sudden gesture of syncopation also to the right stating Two again and proceeding rhythmically into Three.

Figure 41.

Example 53 shows a **different type of rebeaten fermata.** Here we have a triple meter, beaten in One-to-the-bar. The measure preceding the fermata is often taken in THREE to gain precision in the ensemble for the slight ritard marked by the composer. If THREE is used, the first two beats of the measure are in tempo, the ritard being reserved for the third beat. The fermata rises upward from the ictus of One. The cutoff is made upward and becomes, rhythmically, the first beat of the fermata measure, rebeaten in tempo, the musicians playing on the last one-third of the beat. The gesture of syncopation is practical for this rebeaten One.

Example 53. Beethoven, Symphony No. 5 in C minor, Op. 67. Third movement (measures 7–9).

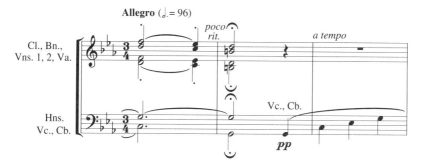

Specialized Problems

In Example 54, we have a gentle **rhythmic interruption in a continuous melodic line.** Compare Example 54 with Example 53. In Example 54, there is no break: The fermata is held out on a sustained Two, the hand then looping without a stop into One. Beat One cuts the fermata as the new instrument enters. On the last measure of the example, a small One is shown in the baton, the sustaining motion moves to the right and upward, preparing the stick for the sudden down-up, *double forte* ictus of Two.

Example 54. Beethoven, Symphony No. 4 in B-flat major, Op. 60. Finale (nine to six measures from the end).

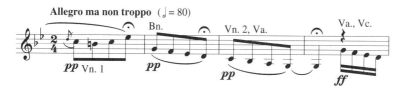

In Example 55, the caesura lines are missing. The usual solution for handling this famous place is to consider the downbeat One of the third measure as the cutoff of the fermata. However, the author has seen at least one of the great conductors use a very quick cutoff gesture upward with an instantaneous One. In that instance the auditorium was a large one, and he may have resorted to this device to clarify the written eighth rest for the audience.

Example 55. Beethoven, Symphony No. 5 in C minor, Op. 67. First movement (measures 1–6).

One other comment on Example 55: Your attention is called to the fact that the fermata in the fifth measure comes on the *second* downbeat of that note. Both downbeats must be shown, the second One very small so as not to interrupt the tenuto motion of the tie.

In Example 56, the cutoff is performed whenever the conductor wishes to end the sound. The following rest is used only for the purpose of making a preparatory gesture into One of the next bar. The rest is a tutti rest.*

Example 56. Berlioz, *The Damnation of Faust*, Op. 24 (last measure of Scene XVI and first measure of Scene XVII, recitative).

Example 57 presents a **fermata written against a moving voice.** This type of fermata is rather common. Although the fermata appears to begin on the first beat of the measure for those instruments playing the whole note, actually it does not start as a *fermata* until the last beat of the measure. The position of

---

*This type of fermata is very rare. There are hundreds of examples to be found with notes followed by fermata-rests, but very few with fermatas followed by *rhythmic* rests for the balance of the measure.

the fermata in the *moving voice* (in this case the first violins and the cellos) states the onset of the hold as such. In conducting this type of fermata, *continue the time-beating until the last beat of the moving voice.* When that beat begins to sustain, the real fermata starts.

Example 57. Beethoven, *Fidelio Overture,* Op. 72b (measures 247–248).

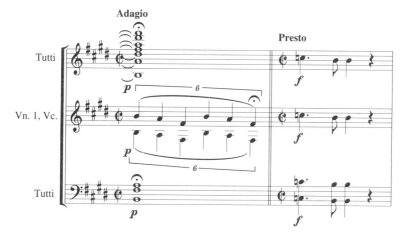

The Adagio marking with the cut time signifies two major accents in the measure but a time-beating pattern in Four. Beethoven, in writing six notes in this fermata measure, has stretched his phrase with a subtle type of written ritard. Beats One and Three would be emphasized in the preceding measure. They would become rhythmically One-Four of this last Adagio measure, beaten in a SIX pattern.

In Example 58, the **fermata is placed over the rest,** indicating two things: (1) The last note before the rest must be given exactly its written value and not lengthened unless qualified by the word *ritard.* (2) There is a long moment of silence following the note before the next entrance is made.

Example 58. Rossini, *L'Italiana in Algeri.* Overture (measures 31–32).

In the quoted example, the first beat (One) would be cut on Two. In measure 2, after the cutoff, the baton stands still as long as the conductor wants the silence to last. Then he or she makes a tiny flick with the fingers of the left hand, which is not seen by the audience. This flick tells the players, "Here is Two *in the Allegro tempo.*" The baton then beats Three as a sharp gesture of syncopation, and everything follows in due course. The flick of the left hand shows the ending of the fermata-rest and simultaneously states Two in the Allegro tempo. Three is the gesture of syncopation, after which the musicians play. Careful timing is necessary here to see that Two-Three are exactly in tempo.

When there is no change of tempo after the fermata and the silence is of rather short duration, the left-hand flick is not needed. The tempo of the piece has already been well established in the minds of the players during the rendition of the measures preceding the fermata. The baton beat alone is sufficient to reestablish the tempo.

Some pieces start with a **fermata on the very first note.** This is a dramatic call to attention and is usually a *double forte.* It means *no rhythm* on the first note. See page 61, Figure 34, "The breathing gesture."

In Example 59, we have a fermata followed by two beats of tutti rest. When this type of notation is used, it signifies the immediate resumption of the rhythm when the fermata is cut off. The baton shows One and sustains to the right. The gesture of cutting off becomes Three (to the right), and Four (moving upward) prepares for One, the pizzicato chord.

Example 59. Rossini, *Semiramide.* Overture (measures 173–174).

Note: When a single pizzicato note, surrounded by rests, is to be played ON a beat, use a legato preparation that leads directly into the pizzicato without stopping. If a stop occurs between the preparation and the command to play, the result will probably be ragged. The stop "reads" as a gesture of syncopation with the note coming after the beat.

Finally, let us mention a specialized type of fermata. It is that which **occurs on a sustained tone** or a rest for certain members of the ensemble while one or more instruments perform cadenza-like passages. Here a bimanual handling is usually best; one hand devotes itself to controlling the nonsolo instruments (the fermata) while the other hand beats as necessary, if necessary, to give the needed direction for the cadenza performance. The beat following the cadenza must be made in the correct direction of the time-beating. A good reference score is *Sheherazade.*

Although the foregoing examples provide some methods for studying fermatas, and some solutions for handling them technically, it is important to caution again that every fermata is a law unto itself. Its proper handling is determined by the context in which it occurs. Intelligent thought should be brought to bear upon the problem each presents, and the gestures ought to be practiced to ensure effective performance of the fermata and efficient resumption of the rhythm thereafter. The fermata is inserted for the chief purpose of making the note *longer* than its written value. HOLD the fermatas!

Application to Your Repertoire: A Reference Index

Analyze what type of fermata you are dealing with. Locate it on the following list.

  I. **Fermata cuts off completely**
     A. Music starts thereafter ON a beat. Refer to Examples 52, p. 101, and 59, p. 108. Fermata cuts off: on **One,** Figure 37, p. 102; on **Two,** Figure 38, p. 103; on **Three,** Figure 39, p. 103; on **Four,** Figure 40, p. 104.
     B. Music continues on an **afterbeat:** Example 49, p. 100; moment of silence, Example 58, p. 107.
 II. **Fermata continues without a cutoff**
     A. Music continues ON a beat. Refer to Examples 48, p. 99; 50, p. 100; 51, p. 101; 54, p. 105; 55, p. 106; 57, p. 107.
     B. Music continues on an **afterbeat:** Examples 46, p. 98; 47, m. 2, p. 99; 49, p. 100; 53, p. 105; 55, p. 106.
III. **Fermata interrupts a continuous melody line, no cutoff**
     A. Continuing ON a beat: Example 54, p. 105.
     B. Continuing on an **afterbeat—the rebeaten fermata:** Figure 41, p. 104; Example 53, p. 105.

Exercises for Practice: Handling the Fermata

  1. Practice all the examples given in the chapter.
  2. Apply your knowledge to the following problems.

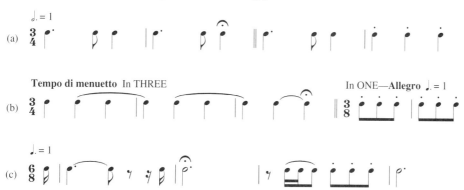

9 Fast FIVES, SEVENS— Twentieth-Century Innovations

Rhythm is universally defined as heavier emphasis followed by lighter emphasis, repeated—a succession of heavy–light recurrent accentuations.

In basic time-beating, you encountered the "divided" beat where all beats were of the same length (duration) and the number of pulses between beats was constant throughout.

In the twentieth century, composers have chosen to upset the duration of primary beats, so that some beats may be extended by an extra half-beat, others curtailed by an equal amount. (See Example 60, second measure.)

Example 60. Stravinsky, *L'Histoire du soldat*. Introduction: Marche du soldat (measures 78–80). © 1924 by J. & W. Chester, Ltd. By permission of the copyright owners, J & W Chester/ Edition Wilhelm Hansen London, Ltd.

If the second measure is beaten in ONE, it must account for an extra "and" beat; if it is beaten in TWO, the second beat must be shortened by a half-beat. All of this has resulted in what we have termed **lopsided time-beating.** All beats will not be rhythmically even.

Lopsided Time-Beating

In addition, the composers have chosen to *regroup* the smaller pulses within the measure. What was formerly a nicely balanced nine-beat measure (3 + 3 + 3) may now become an uneven grouping of 4 + 5, or 5 + 4. Such groupings occur most often in faster tempos where the smaller pulses are not shown as such, but their existence is accounted for by lengthening (or shortening) the duration of the primary beat (Example 61).

Example 61. Stravinsky, *The Rite of Spring.* (a) Sacrificial Dance: The Chosen One (measures 15–19; rhythm only); (b) The Play of Abduction (measures 19–21; rhythm only). Copyright 1921 by Edition Russe de Musique. Renewed 1958. Copyright and Renewal assigned to Boosey & Hawkes, Inc. Revised Edition Copyright 1948 by Boosey & Hawkes, Inc. Reprinted by permission.

* The broken lines are in the score.

When conducting these complicated rhythmic variations, the conductor must think in the value of the shorter notes (in (a), the sixteenths; in (b), the eighths) and then adjust the duration of his or her primary beats to accommodate the added (or deleted) pulse where it occurs. In (b), the composer himself has indicated his groupings by the addition of parenthetical signatures and dotted lines of demarcation.

Fast FIVES

There is a helpful adjustment in the time-beating pattern to accommodate measures beaten in TWO where lopsided beats are called for (Figure 42).

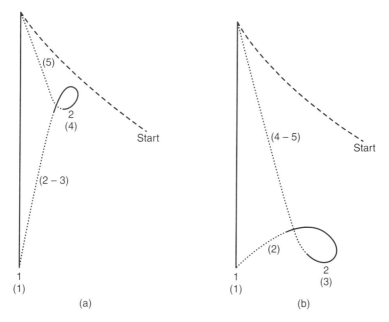

Figure 42. Fast FIVES beaten in TWO (lopsided pattern). In fast SEVENS, (a) = 4 + 3; (b) = 3 + 4. Malko *originated* these accommodations.

In Figure 42a, the **high rebound of One accounts for the added duration** (the 3), leaving only a shorter line for the curtailed half of the measure (the 2). In 42b, the **rebound of One is kept low, leaving the long upward line for the lengthier second beat** (2 + 3). The speed of motion of the gestures will vary appreciably, faster on the short gestures, slower on the longer.

Example 62 shows a 3 + 2 followed by a 2 + 3 in the second measure. (Figure 42a followed by 42b is an excellent example for reiterated practice.)

Example 62. Stravinsky, *L'Histoire du soldat.* Music from the first scene: Little Tunes Beside the Brook (measures 64–65). © 1924 by J. & W. Chester, Ltd. By permission of the copyright owners, J & W Chester/Edition Wilhelm Hansen London, Ltd.

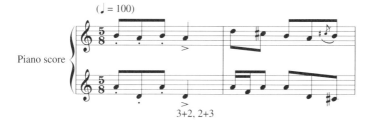

The patterns of Figure 42 can also be adapted to the fast SEVENS, 4 + 3 and 3 + 4, beaten in TWO. Reemphasizing, **the conductor must keep the pulse-notes clicking through his or her mind in** *even succession,* **showing their group-ings with unbalanced gestures.**

Strange Combinations of Pulses in Slow Tempos

Figure 43 presents diagrams for showing odd combinations of phrasings within the measure.

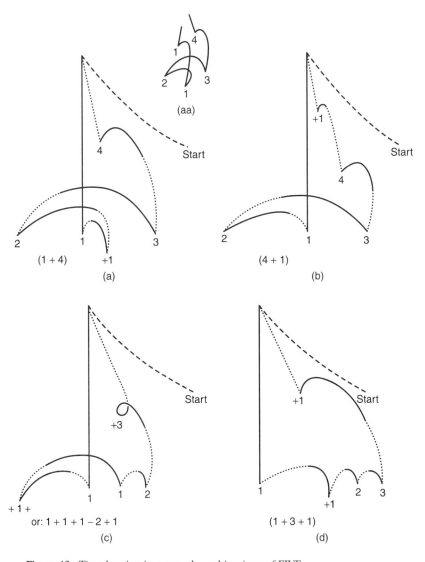

Figure 43. Time-beating in unusual combinations of FIVE.

Figure 43a (1 + 4), a heavy downbeat followed by an attached FOUR pattern, tells us that the composer has written a *forte* One and a subsequent four-beat phrase. Figure 43aa, with a small first One, would be applicable to the excerpts given in Example 63a and b. Added Ones are small gestures.

Example 63. Stravinsky, *The Rite of Spring.* (a) The Sacrifice (measure 55); (b) Games of the Rival Tribes (measure 27). Copyright 1921 by Edition Russe de Musique. Renewed 1958. Copyright and Renewal assigned to Boosey & Hawkes, Inc. Revised Edition Copyright 1948 by Boosey & Hawkes, Inc. Reprinted by permission.

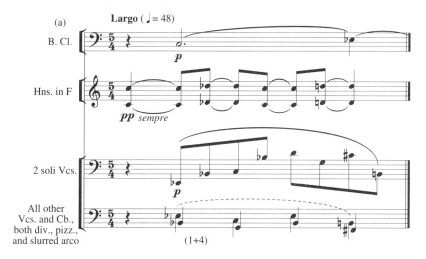

Figure 43b shows the 4 + 1 pattern—a normal FOUR plus an extra small beat at the top for the fifth beat.

FIVES may also be found in combinations of 1 + 1 + 3 (Figure 43c), 1 + 3 + 1 (43d), and 3 + 1 + 1. In (d), there are three groupings within the measure, and a basic THREE pattern is feasible adding the small pulses as demanded by the music. Example 64 shows 1 + 3 + 1. (See next page.)

The Principle for Creating Gestures

To create gestures for things not yet written: Choose the primary beat pattern by the number of groupings within the measure and add the subdivisions as notated. The long lines of the primary beats lead to the beginning of the following pulse-grouping.

Example 64. Stravinsky, *The Rite of Spring.* Games of the Rival Tribes (measure 22). Copyright 1921 by Edition Russe de Musique. Renewed 1958. Copyright and Renewal assigned to Boosey & Hawkes, Inc. Revised Edition Copyright 1948 by Boosey & Hawkes, Inc. Reprinted by permission.

Such patterns define precisely the structure within the measure and are visually clear for the musicians performing the notes.

SEVENS

Seven beats to the bar may be broken up into the following groupings: 3 + 4, 4 + 3, 2 + 3 + 2, 3 + 2 + 2, 2 + 2 + 3, and combinations of a 1 and several 2s. If there are two or four groupings in the measure, start with a four-beat pattern. (Figure 44a). If there are three groupings, use three primary beats—a three-beat pattern (Figure 44b).

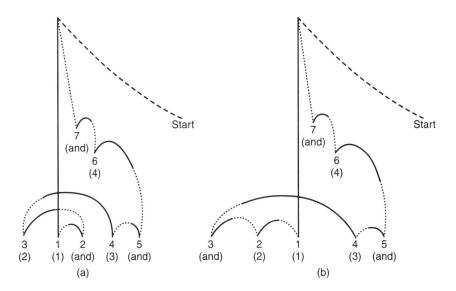

Figure 44. Time-beating in SEVEN: 3 + 4.

Figure 44a shows the deleted divided-FOUR; 44b shows the augmented divided-THREE. Figure 44b could serve either a 3 + 4 phrasing beaten in THREE or a 3 + 2 + 2 grouping. The choice would depend upon subtleties found in the score.

In Example 65, the composer's dotted lines state a 3 + 2 + 2 pattern (Figure 44b). The left hand would be useful in cuing the horns (top score) and the violins at the end of the last measure if necessary.

Example 65. Copland, *Concerto for Piano and Orchestra*. First movement (measure 4). © Copyright 1929 by Aaron Copland; Renewed 1958 by Aaron Copland. Reprinted by permission of Aaron Copland, Copyright Owner and Boosey & Hawkes, Inc. Sole Publishers and Licencees.

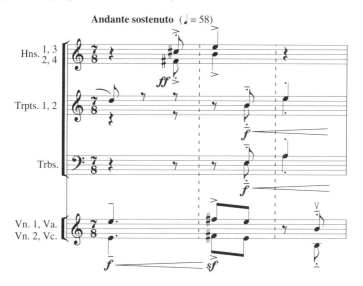

Example 66 might be conducted using either (a) or (b) of Figure 44.

Example 66. Barber, *Medea's Meditation and Dance of Vengeance,* Op. 23A (measure 110). Copyright © 1956 (Renewed) by G. Schirmer, Inc. International Copyright Secured. Used by Permission.

Figure 45 deletes the divided-FOUR pattern: in (a), 2 + 2 + 1 + 2, and in (b), 2 + 2 + 2 + 1.

Thus it shows the 4 + 3 patterns springing from a divided-FOUR. In (a), the "and" of Three has been deleted, and in (b), the "and" of Four has been eliminated.

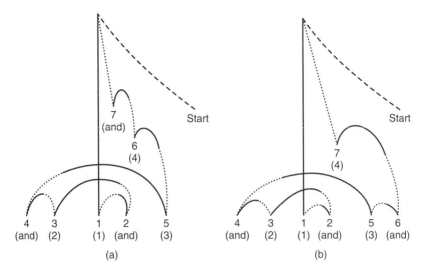

Figure 45. Time-beating in SEVEN: 4 + 3.

Figure 46 enlarges the THREE-beat pattern.

Note: In **fast tempos,** conduct in primary beats but **think** in values (groupings) of the shorter notes, extending or deleting the primary beat as necessary.

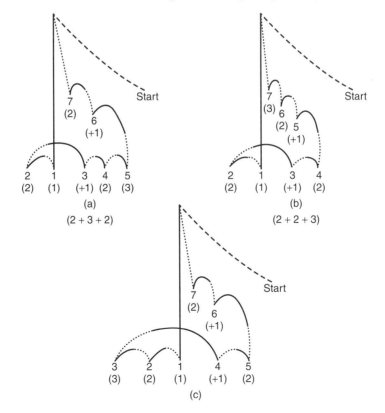

Figure 46. Time-beating in SEVEN springing from a THREE pattern.

Example 67 combines SEVENS and FIVES: 2 + 2 + 3 and 3 + 2.

Example 67. Stravinsky, *L'Histoire du soldat*. Music from the second scene (measures 35–37). © 1924 by J. & W. Chester, Ltd. By permission of the copyright owners, J & W Chester/ Edition Wilhelm Hansen London Ltd.

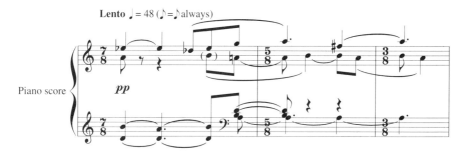

Example 68 moves from 3 + 2 + 2 (Figure 45c) to 2 + 2 + 3 (Figure 45b), a "mirrored" image, rhythmically.

Example 68. Stravinsky, *The Firebird* Suite (measures 41–42, melody line only.) © 1920 by J. & W. Chester, Ltd. By permission of the copyright owners, J & W Chester/Edition Wilhelm Hansen London Ltd.

* The broken lines are in the score.

PROBLEMS, Series 5

1. Choose the FIVE pattern you believe would be best for each of the following and give your reasons for your choice. Beat in FIVE.

2. Choose a SEVEN pattern for each of the following. Beat in SEVEN.

3. Time-beating in TWO for the FIVES and SIXES that are eighth notes. All other notes are quarter notes. Keep the eighths running through the mind throughout. Use both 3 + 2 and 2 + 3. Each number represents one measure.

Sequence: in 2 3 2 5 6 4 3 1 1 2 5 3 4 6 5 1 1 5 4 2 1 beats per measure.

4. In the SEVENS, use 3 eighths plus 4 eighths beaten in TWO. Each number is one measure.

Sequence: in 4 2 5 3 2 7 4 3 5 7 2 2 6 3 5 2 7 1 1 beats per measure.

The Misunderstood Example

Attention is now called to Examples 69 and 70: the first, written in FIVE and beaten in TWO; the second, written in SEVEN but beaten in THREE.

Example 69. Stravinsky, *The Rite of Spring*. Glorification of the Chosen One (measures 1 and 18). Copyright 1921 by Edition Russe de Musique. Renewed 1958. Copyright and Renewal assigned to Boosey & Hawkes, Inc. Revised Edition Copyright 1948 by Boosey & Hawkes, Inc. Reprinted by permission.

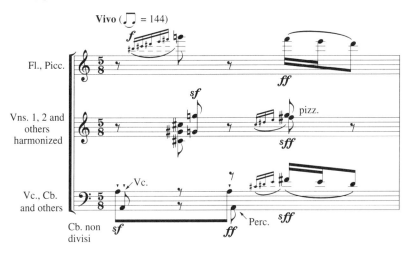

Example 70. Ibid., measure 19.

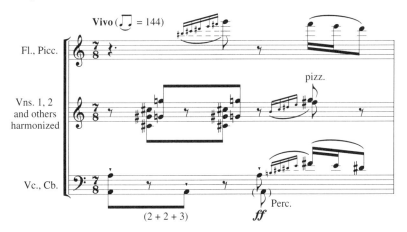

The tremendous *ff* and *sff* (strings) on the last notes of measure 1 immediately attract attention. The tendency is to accept a 3 + 2 and to apply it again as a 3 + 2 + 2 analysis of the $\frac{7}{8}$ measure (Example 70), the conductor preparing and showing the last beat with great vigor. But this does not work in performance. What must be conducted here is the *ff* timpani line, using a sudden vigorous gesture (similar to a gesture of syncopation) on the final beat of each excerpt. The pattern is a 2 + 3 and a 2 + 2 + 3. The sudden percussion "whack" precipitates the grace notes, which are the real problem in producing good ensemble. Trust the other players who enter on those last three notes; they will be fine if they hear that percussion beat emphasized.

Example 71 is simpler. Again the bass line is the clue to solving the conducting.

Example 71. Stravinsky, *L'Histoire du soldat*. Music from the first scene: Little Tunes Beside the Brook (measure 67). © by J. & W. Chester, Ltd. By permission of the copyright owners, J & W Chester/Edition Wilhelm Hansen London Ltd.

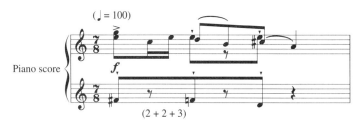

Caution: In twentieth-century music, a distinction is to be made between the length of measure and the length of note. If the note length is a constant, then the measure length will vary; if the measure is to be uniform throughout, then the extra notes squeezed in will have to adjust. Try the following drill.

Drill: Time-beating; *the duration of each measure is identical.* The number of beats per measure changes.

Counting as follows, complete the count within the duration of the measure. Start in slow tempo on the first line.

PROBLEM 1	PROBLEM 2
3 beats per measure 1 2 3	Increasing speed of beats.
4 beats per measure 1 2 3 4	Set metronome on 40.
5 beats per measure 1 2 3 4 5	Count the numbers aloud,
6 beats per measure 1 2 3 4 5 6	arriving on 1 as metronome clicks.
7 beats per measure 1 2 3 4 5 6 7	
8 beats per measure 1 2 3 4 5 6 7 8	
9 beats per measure 1 2 3 4 5 6 7 8 9	

Note: An interesting example is to be found in Respighi's Sonata in B minor for Piano and Violin, second movement. The piano has a $\frac{10}{8}$ signature against a $\frac{4}{4}$ in the violin, further complicated, here and there, by measures containing two triplet figures in quarter-note values in the violin part.

Strange Combinations of NINES, TWELVES, ELEVENS

Refer again to the basic principle as stated on page 115. See also Example 61b on page 112. With the discussion already completed in this chapter, the reader should be able to adjust the time-beating patterns to accommodate the demands of any combinations of NINES or TWELVES. In cases where ELEVENS and other odd and rare meters are called for, the basic principle still is to use the long gestures when leading into the rhythmic accents (groupings) and to intersperse them with the short "and" gestures as needed. When the ELEVEN comprises eleven equally accented beats, a simple counting of eleven identical downbeats can be used (Example 72). When the conductor uses this solution, he or she should warn the players of those intentions verbally, then make the rebound of the eleventh beat move to a totally new position in space. This tells the performers that the next beat will be One of the next measure.

Example 72. Stravinsky, *The Rite of Spring*. Mysterious Circle of the Adolescents (last measure). Copyright 1921 by Edition Russe de Musique. Renewed 1958. Copyright and Renewal assigned to Boosey & Hawkes, Inc. Revised Edition Copyright 1948 by Boosey & Hawkes, Inc. Reprinted by permission.

Training Exercise 7

First, refer to Training Exercises 1 and 2 (pages 5–6). Speed up the motion, ending in a staccato stop at each end of the line. See that the hands have not changed their position before the stop. Turn hands on demand and proceed.

You now come to the most challenging of all the Training Exercises. Be patient! It will gradually come under control.

Using the horizontal (Training Exercise 1) gestures, make the left arm staccato (fast) and the right arm legato-tenuto (slow). The left arm stands perfectly still while the right arm completes its motion. Watch the staccato arm while you train it in this motion. You will improve faster. Try to start both arms at the same instant. It will finally come. Change arms, staccato in the right arm, legato in the left.

Training Exercise 8

Refer to Training Exercise 2, page 6.

Apply the new technique of Training Exercise 7 to the perpendicular lines of Training Exercise 2. Both arms staccato. Then left arm staccato, right arm legato, moving in the same direction. When that is good, use the opposite direction. One arm goes down staccato while the other moves up legato. Switch arms, right arm staccato, left arm legato. Drill both arms in all facets of this exercise. **Note:** The legato arm is working through habit. You can usually disregard it. Concentrate on the staccato arm.

Conducting Accents and Cross Accents

The conductor's gesture must show that the accent is to occur on the coming beat. The rebound of the preceding beat usually rises somewhat higher, and sometimes the baton stops for an instant just before it swings into the accented beat. Stopping the motion momentarily after the ictus of the accent or suddenly retracting the hands helps to prevent a crescendo following the accent.

In nonprofessional ensembles, there is always the tendency to make the accent loud and then to retain that dynamic. This is especially true in *sforzato*s on sustained tones. Such a rendition denies the accent completely. An accent is an accent only if the dynamic falls away instantly, following the accented sound. As to the amount of tone on the *sforzato* itself, the professional rule is "one degree louder than the passage in which it occurs." Lack of understanding of this dictum explains why so many amateur groups "crush" the *sforzato* in *piano* passages.

For accents occurring just *after* the beat, use the gesture of syncopation *on* the beat.

Cross accents are regularly recurring accents sounding in one meter but written in another. Example 73 is an excellent illustration. The clarinet is accenting in $\frac{5}{4}$, the singer in $\frac{2}{4}$, and the violas in $\frac{3}{4}$, but all parts are notated in the $\frac{2}{2}$ measure.

Example 73. Dallapiccola, *Divertimento* for Soprano voice, Flute (Piccolo), Oboe, Clarinet, Viola, and Cello. III: Bourrée (measures 134–136). Reprinted with authorization of Carisch S. p. A. Milan (Italy), owner of the author rights all over the world. © 1956 by Carisch S. p. A.

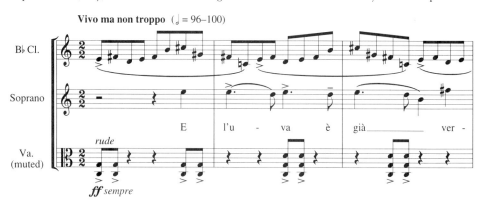

Let us say we have a series of measures in $\frac{4}{4}$ with accents occurring every three beats. $4 \times 3 = 12$. Write down the numbers 1 through 12, well spaced. Above numbers 1, 4, 7, 10, write an R (right hand). Below numbers 1, 5, 9, write an L (left hand).

```
    R        R         R          R
    1   2   3   4   5   6   7   8   9   10   11   12
    L            L             L
```

Count aloud, rhythmically, and tap with the correct hand as marked. With a little practice, you will feel a definite rhythm emerging thus:

```
Both
hands         R   L        R        L   R
 ↓            ↓   ↓        ↓        ↓   ↓
    1   2   3   4   5   6   7   8   9   10   11   12
```

Beat 7 is the beginning of the second half of the measure. Your rhythm is: Both, rest rest, right-left, rest, right, rest, left-right, rest rest.

For FOUR against FIVE, start with the number 20.

The most common form of cross accentuation is found in three-beat measures with the accent coming every two beats. Example 74 is a well-known case in point. To preserve the three-beat pattern and still show the accents, proceed as follows: Say to yourself One-Two, One-Two, One-Two, instead of One-Two-Three, One-Two-Three, while continuing the time-beating pattern in THREE.

Example 74. Schubert, Symphony No. 8 in B minor, Op. posth. *(Unfinished)*. First movement (measures 134–142). Score condensed.

Then make a large, vigorous gesture each time you say One and a very small gesture when you say Two. The pattern that will emerge will look like Figure 47. The dangerous beats are the small Two of the first measure and the small One of the second measure. Control will be needed to keep them small.

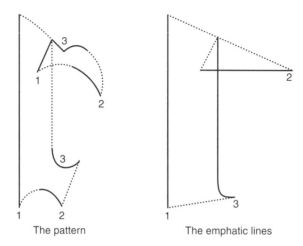

Figure 47. Cross accentuation.

Note: The aleatoric ("allowing for chance") score is discussed on page 206.

Accompanying

Almost every instrumental organization will have to do a job of accompanying sometime in its career. It may be that a chorus has been added to the production or a special soloist is to perform with the group. Or the accompanying activity may be just a simple background for a solo melody line within the composition itself. In any case, accompanying is an art in its own right and merits a few words here.

First and foremost: **The soloist must be heard.** This may mean cutting down on the size of the accompanying group, or just an underplaying of the marked dynamics. Second, the conductor, in general, follows the soloist and tries to give the soloist confidence and a feeling of musical ease in the performance of the number. (After all, the success of the program at the moment depends upon that soloist.) The conductor should know the soloist's part about as well as the soloist knows it. The conductor must also know how every note of the accompanying part fits against that solo line. He or she must be alert to quick adaptation to the soloist, and the musicians must watch with all attention to catch instantly any new subtlety that may be added to their previous rehearsing of the score. The timing of the conductor's preparatory gestures is of vital importance so that the beat itself will coincide with the soloist's rendition.

When the accompanying group has an interlude, this interlude should enhance the general character of the drama of the music itself. It should also act as a momentary release—a breath for the audience—from the concentrated intensity of the solo. The interlude should take over in its own right, furnishing the contrast of the full beauty of the instrumental ensemble to the continuing line of the music. In light opera, the orchestral interlude often heightens the characterization on the stage, sometimes humorously, as happens in many Gilbert and Sullivan operettas. A bit of overplaying, even in a single measure of interlude, can add a humorous touch to the comedy going on beyond the footlights. In all interludes, the accompanying instruments carry the burden of the performance. When a group is accompanying the soloist, total control of the softer dynamics is imperative.

In instrumental works that have a lengthy unaccompanied passage for the soloist, the conductor can show the first beat of each measure by a dead gesture One, and nothing more. Go straight down and *immediately* up. Wait at the top of the beat for the next One. When the solo passage happens to be a long cadenza, the conductor does not beat time. He or she simply tells the musicians, "I shall begin to beat again ____ measures before our entrance."

Note: The accompanying of the recitative is discussed on pages 223–225.

The Metronome

This little beast must not be entirely ignored in a book on conducting. Many are the sins that may be laid at its door; nevertheless, it is good for the young conductor to test every so often against the metronome. In doing this, the conductor subjects himself or herself to a severe but conscientious taskmaster, and a little disciplining now and then is good for almost anybody.

The metronome came into existence during Beethoven's lifetime. He himself placed metronome markings in his scores, but because of his deafness, conductors do not always accept them as accurate. When the conductor sees metronome markings on scores predating Beethoven, he or she knows that they are suggestions of the editor of the music, not of the composer. When the metronome marking is authentic, it should be given intelligent attention.

A metronome marking at the beginning of the piece and at double bars with change of tempo signifies that the given note, or its equivalent, occurs the stated number of times per minute. For example, *metronome: quarter note at 126* means that the quarter-note value comes 126 times per minute.

It is important to work out the mathematical relationships at double bars where tempo changes occur.

PROBLEM

Andante, $\frac{4}{4}$, quarter note equals 80; followed by Allegro vivace, alla breve, half note at 120. (Tchaikovsky, Fifth Symphony, finale.) Dividing 80 and 120 by 4, we have 20 against 30 or 2 against 3. The lowest common denominator for 2 and 3 is 6. On the last beats of the Andante, think triplets. Use two of the triplets to set the new tempo.

Andante $\frac{4}{4}$ at 80:	Beat One		Beat Two			Beat Three		Beat Four		
Think:	1	2	3	4	5	6	1	2	3	4	5	6

Allegro vivace in TWO:	1	2	1	2	1	2	1	2	1	2	1	2
half note at 120:	One		Two		One		Two		One		Two	

Memorizing the Metronome

At the time the author was studying with Dr. Malko, the following advice was given:

> Sing a common tune—one that is so common it almost ceases to be music. Take the tempo which is your own most natural way of rendering it and then find this tempo on the metronome. Remember that such-and-such a tune correlates with such-and-such a marking on the metronome. When you have built up a good collection of these tunes together with their metronome markings, you will be able to arrive quite accurately at the marking requested by the composer, even when the metronome is not present.

It is, as all his advice notably was, very good advice.

Exercises for Practice: Cross Accents, Irregular Time-Beating

1. Time-beating in THREE, accenting every second beat. Continue the THREE pattern but say One-Two to yourself throughout. Accent on "One."

2. Time-beating in TWO, accenting every third beat. Beat in TWO but say to yourself One-Two-Three throughout, and give the large beat on One each time you speak it.

3. Time-beating in FOUR, accenting every third beat. Beat in FOUR but say to yourself One-Two-Three and accent on the Ones.

4. Choose five common melodies and gear them to the metronome at your own tempo. Check several days in succession to see that your own tempo is consistent.

Think in eighths throughout. ♪ = ♪

5. $\frac{12}{8}$ | $\frac{5}{8}$ | ⁒ | $\frac{12}{8}$ | $\frac{5}{8}$ | ⁒ | $\frac{12}{8}$ | $\frac{3}{8}$ | ⁒ | $\frac{4}{4}$ ♩ ♩ ♩ ♩ | ♩ ♩ ♩ ‖

In Four 3+2   2+3

6. $\frac{6}{8}$ | $\frac{5}{8}$ | $\frac{2}{4}$ | $\frac{5}{8}$ | ⁒ | $\frac{4}{4}$

In Two

$\frac{4}{4}$ ♩ ♩ ♩ ♩ | $\frac{3}{4}$ ♩ ♩ ♩ | ♩ ♩ ‖
        > >

Notice the difference in time-beating between 7a and 7b.

Irregular time-beating.

7a.

7b. Regular time-beating.

8.

In FIVE

Think in sixteenths.

9.

Example 75. Stravinsky, *L'Histoire du soldat*. Music to Scene II (measure 30 to the end). ©
1924 (Renewed) by J. & W. Chester, Ltd. International Copyright Secured. Used by Permission.

Two ways to practice this one: (a) Time-beating in eighth notes throughout, using divided
beats in the $\frac{3}{4}$ measures, etc. (b) Time-beating in eighth notes, but in quarters for measures 3–7.
Use lopsided beats in measures 6, 7, 8, and so on. Be sure the time-value of the eighth note remains constant throughout.

MUSIC FOR PERFORMANCE

Example 76. Schubert, Symphony No. 8 in B minor *(Unfinished)*. First movement (measures 122–176).

Time-beating in THREE. Use left hand to control dynamic and swell-dim. in the violins. For the cross accents, (a) beat time and leave it to the players; if they cannot manage, then (b) use large gestures on the accents and small gestures on the unaccented beats. See Figure 47.

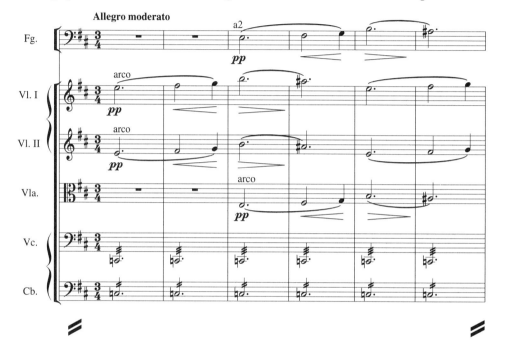

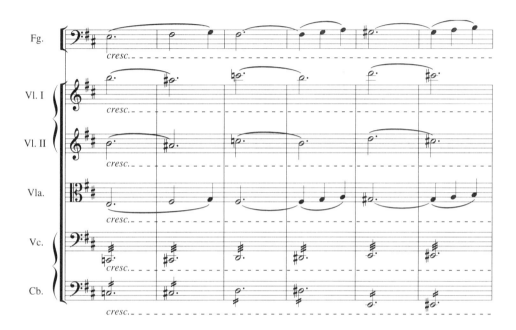

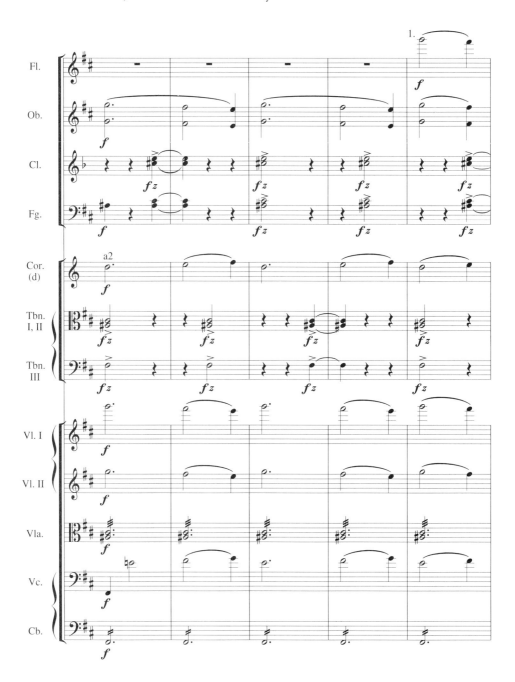

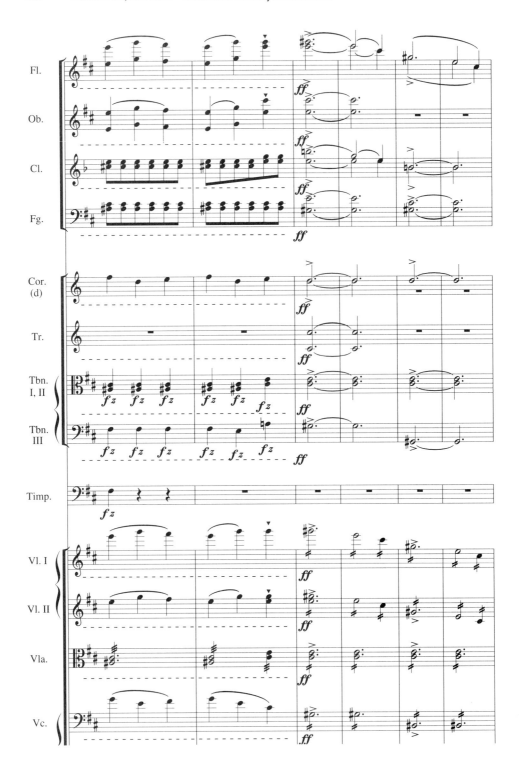

Recommended Reference Readings

BOULT, ADRIAN C., *A Handbook on the Technique of Conducting*. Section 10, p. 26, "Accompanying."

BRAITHWAITE, WARWICK, *The Conductor's Art*. Chapters 2, 3, pp. 13–21: Exercises in Fives and Sevens at the ends of these chapters. Chapter 6, pp. 40–45: "Indefinite Problems"; Chapter 12, pp. 80–82: "On the Conducting of Concertos."

CHRISTIANI, ADOLF F., *Principles of Expression in Pianoforte Playing*. Chapter 17, pp. 296–303: "Sudden Changes of Tempo."

COOPER, G. W., and L. B. MEYER, *The Rhythmic Structure of Music*. Very erudite. Everything that deals with rhythm.

Recommended Videotape

HISTORICAL OVERVIEW, CONDUCTORS IN ACTION

The Art of Conducting: Great Conductors of the Past. VHS Hi-Fi Stereo #4509-95038-3. An IMG Artists/BBC Production in association with TELDEC Classics International and Sender Freies Berlin. © 1994 TELDEC Classics International GmbH Hamburg. A Time-Warner Company. There is much to learn and much to avoid in studying this tape. Do not criticize, but instead *learn* from it. It reveals the manual adequacy and inadequacy of those who have gone before us.

10 Melding and Psychological Conducting

Time-beating is a monotonous process, but it is not necessary to show every beat of every measure. Tutti long notes are often indicated by a prolonged tenuto gesture. This technique is termed *melding*.

Melding

Melding means "merging, blending." It is the combining of two or more time-beating gestures into one long, sustained gesture that has a duration equal to that of the combined beats. The term was introduced in the first edition of *The Modern Conductor* and has become part of the conducting vocabulary.

To execute the meld, show the ictus of the first of the gestures to be combined. Move the baton through the contours of the melded beats without showing any time-beating icti, arriving ultimately at the ictus of the beat following the meld. The last of the melded beats becomes a prep-beat for what follows.

Figures 48, 49, 50, and 51 are self-explanatory.

To show the presence of a tutti whole note, the ictus of One is shown and then all the remaining beats of the measures are melded into one long gesture. The pattern might look like any of those given in Figure 51.

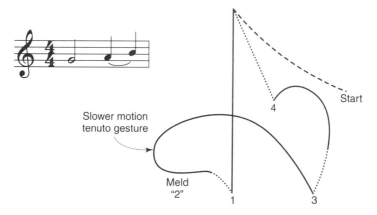

Figure 48. Melding the first two beats.

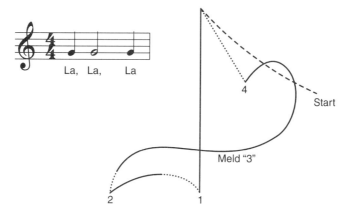

Figure 49. Melding "Two-Three" in $\frac{4}{4}$.

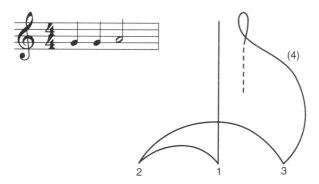

Figure 50. Melding "Three-Four" in $\frac{4}{4}$.

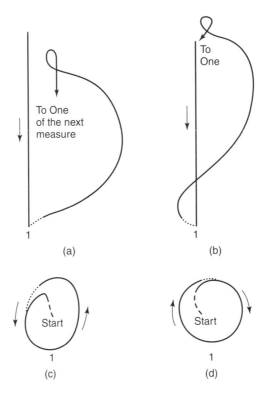

Figure 51. Melding the whole measure.

As shown in Figure 51c, the meld of the full measure is sometimes performed as a circular motion. The ictus of One is the lowest point of the circle. The second measure of Example 77 might be conducted as shown in Figure 51a.

Example 77. Mozart, *Don Giovanni.* Overture (measures 17–19).

The melded gesture is the very soul of **phrasal conducting.** When changing to phrasal conducting, the conductor must be sure that the rhythmic drive of the music is such that the musicians can carry on perfectly without his or her time-beating gestures at that point. Melds are much used in choral conducting.

Let us examine two more examples from the orchestral repertoire where phrasal or melded gestures may be successfully used.

In Example 78, the first two beats of measures 2 and 4 may be melded, the baton showing One, then moving toward the right, where the third beat is performed as a cutoff gesture. The baton would stand still during this tutti fermata-rest. A sudden, sharp, upward gesture of syncopation would then state Four, precipitating the triplet entrance at the end of the measure.

Example 78. Mozart, *La Clemenza di Tito.* Overture (measures 3–6).

The familiar passage in Example 79 lends itself well to the use of phrasal conducting and the melded gestures. The first measure is beaten out fully, thus setting the tempo securely. Measure 2 melds the first and second beats but shows the ictus for Three. Measure 3 shows One and then melds the remainder of the measure. The fourth measure is beaten out in full, indicating each of the quarter notes. Measure 5 is like measure 2. In measure 6, the first beat is shown. This is followed by a gesture of great sustaining power, *double piano*–tenuto. This last gesture sustains for three measures, showing only the slightest dip for the first beat of measures 7 and 8. The entrance of the sixteenth notes in the ninth measure is prepared by a rhythmic, legato gesture on Three of the eighth measure. This gesture would be similar to the preparatory beat at the very beginning of a piece. Once the violins enter in measure 9, normal time-beating takes over. (See also Example 80.)

Example 79. Schubert, Symphony No. 8 in B minor, Op. posth. *(Unfinished).* First movement (measures 1–8).

Before initiating the psychological conducting, it would be practical for you to begin practicing Training Exercises 9 and 10. These complete your long route to competent control of your hands and the several sections of your arms. You will not conquer them in a day, but they are well worth the effort you will expend until you "arrive."

Example 80. Schubert, String Quartet in D minor, Op. posth. *(Death and the Maiden).* Second movement, beginning and ending.
    Time-beating in FOUR. Meld One-Two. Pattern: Down, up-up, as in time-beating in divided-TWO.

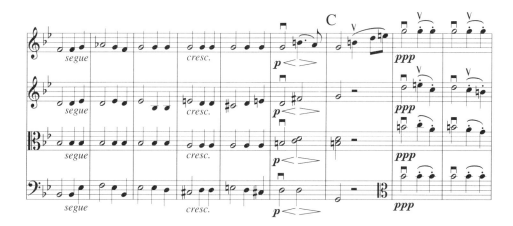

Training Exercise 9

Rest your upper arms, shoulder to elbow, securely on your sides, immobilizing the upper arm.

Swing your lower arms from the elbows, freely forward, upward, and back down. Using only the lower arms, perform the perpendicular gestures of Training Exercise 2, page 6.

Bring the hands up to the shoulder and return. Hands hang down on the way up and are up on the way down. Do not allow upper arms to move.

Use parallel motion, legato, staccato; opposite directions with legato, staccato; and finally legato against staccato, parallel motion and opposite motion. In short, the whole series.

Training Exercise 10

With upper arms immobilized, raise lower arms to form a right angle at the elbows, palms facing floor.

Curve the fingers into a gentle fist.

Apply the whole series of Training Exercise 9 to the hands only, moving in the wrist joint: up, down, legato, staccato, parallel, opposite, and legato against staccato also parallel and opposite. The application to the hands alone is more difficult because the command from the mind has farther to go and must deny other motion in the arms.

Psychological Conducting

As your baton technique clarifies, you will find it possible to produce from an ensemble, *on a static pitch, musical excerpts for which the performers have no music and which they have not seen or heard before.* This is termed *psychological conducting.* Examples follow.

Example 81. Robert Jager, Class example (seventeen measures). Used by permission.

Example 82. David Bates, Class example (thirteen measures). Used by permission.

When a true independence of the hands is gained, it is not impossible to perform a dual rhythm such as that given in Example 83. In this case, the ensemble is divided into two groups, one of which follows the directions given by the conductor's right hand while the other responds to the signals of the left hand.

Example 83. Don Wilcox, Class example (nine measures). Used by permission.

(It might be a good idea to mention that the examples used here were taken from student performances on final examinations. The examples were written by the students themselves and successfully performed—without classroom rehearsal—as one phase of the final test. Only two copies existed—one for conductor, one for instructor. Singers had no music to read.)

In the quoted examples, the staccato dot signified the use of the staccato gesture, the long line over a note showed the tenuto gesture in action, unmarked notes were simply performed legato, notes of more than one beat's duration were "melded" (see pages 138–144), and notes coming after the beat were handled by use of the gesture of syncopation. Rests were indicated by dead gestures. Notes followed by rests were conducted as cutoff gestures on the beat on which the note was written. The cutoff replaced the time-beating gesture. (This is necessary when the performers do not know beforehand that a rest is about to occur. Otherwise they will sing ON that rest.) After a rest, a preparatory motion is made if the next following note is ON a beat. If it comes just after the beat, the gesture of syncopation will handle the problem. In psychological conducting, any GoS must immediately precipitate the following preparatory beat to control an entrance on that beat.

Technical Proficiency

Psychological conducting is the technical phase of the virtuoso technique. It tests the readability of the conductor's gestures, impulse of will, and mental alertness.

Psychological conducting we now define as the process of getting a group of singers or players to respond, *on a single pitch throughout,* to the messages it receives from the conductor's hands and baton alone. The group has no music to read, and the conductor announces, "Perform one note on each beat and do whatever you think the baton says."

Psychological conducting implies a transfer of ideas from the conductor's mind to the performer's mind through the medium of precise conductorial technique without the use of verbal directions. After all, isn't that what conducting is? The impulse of will must be strong.

Caution: Psychological conducting cannot handle everything that can be written in music. For example, it cannot show more than one note per beat unless the time-beating is so very slow that a divided beat can be inserted here and there. The things that are possible are listed on pages 147–148.

Let us now become specific. Figure 52 deals with the performance of the cutoff gesture, mentioned a moment ago, synchronized with the beat itself.

Figure 52.

In the second measure of Figure 52, the second beat is a quarter note. This is followed by a rest on the third beat. The tempo is Allegro moderato. The second beat of this second measure will, therefore, be conducted with a cutoff gesture instead of a time-beating gesture. This cutoff occurs on the ictus of the time-beating gesture. If the regular time-beating gesture is made, followed by a cutoff, the latter comes too late and the group sings a note on the rest. This again emphasizes that **every conductorial gesture has to be made in sufficient time for the group to respond properly to it.** Continuing with the example, beat Three may be conducted either as a dead gesture or simply as a preparatory motion leading into the fourth beat. Beat Four must show good impulse of will. Beat One of the next measure will again have to be an active gesture of cutting-off. In all of this, the underlying rhythmic pulse should be steady and exact.

Note: The cutoff, performed simultaneously with the beat, is *not* necessary when the group is reading music, but it becomes a valuable piece of technique, repertoirewise, in very fast tempos. In slower performance tempos, it is perfectly safe to show the beat with the cutoff following on the rest—but not in psychological conducting.

For psychological control of all entrances *after* the beat (the eighth rest followed by the eighth note in all the foregoing examples), the gesture of syncopation is used. Remember, the stick must stand perfectly still momentarily before this gesture, and the sudden, sharp motion of the gesture must coincide exactly with the moment of the takt after which the note is to be sounded. This gesture gives no warning that it is about to happen. It is seen too late for the group to respond ON the beat, and they therefore respond *after* the beat.

Writing Examples

In all musical examples used **for psychological conducting, the notation must be limited to notes requiring one or more beats for their performance, or to single-note entrances after the beat.** This is true throughout unless the beat is so slow that it can be adequately subdivided to show the "and" and, therefore, the presence of two eighths for that beat. (Example 81 shows this.)

The student should now write his or her own exercises for psychological conducting. Two copies should be made. One is used on the conductor's stand, and the other is given to the instructor so that the latter may see whether the young conductor is producing from the group what he or she intended. There is no better way to develop the "impulse of will" than practice in "psychological conducting."

The following list of possibilities will serve as a guide in the writing and conducting of the original examples.

1. Write one note per beat, or notes requiring more than one beat per note.
2. Notes requiring more than one beat per note may be performed by use of the melded gestures.
3. Any number of beats of rest may be written and conducted by use of the dead gestures. All tutti rests are to be so shown during these drill studies.
4. The last note before a rest must be beaten as a cutoff gesture in Moderato and faster tempos. The cutoff replaces the time-beating ictus.
5. The eighth note followed by the eighth rest is usable if a *very short* staccato gesture is made to indicate it, or if each beat so written is performed as a very demanding and very short cutoff gesture.
6. The eighth rest followed by the eighth note is usable and may be produced by the gesture of syncopation on the rest.
7. The dotted quarter with eighth is usable, since the conductor can control the eighth by making a gesture of syncopation on the second beat of the quarter note. When this is done, however, the conductor will have to "drive" for the next beat following the eighth note. Unless this following beat has great impulse of will, and is made precipitously, the singers will not sing a new note on it.
8. Fermatas are always usable and good.
9. All dynamics may be used and should be carefully marked in the written example.
10. All the expressive gestures may be used and should be indicated in the manuscript as follows: A dot over or under a note indicates the staccato gesture; a long line signifies tenuto; no marking for notes of the simple legato character.
11. Accelerandos and ritards are usable and good.
12. Crescendos and diminuendos are usable and good.

13. Changes of meter are excellent.
14. The left hand may bring in or cut out some of the singers independently of the right hand.
15. Accents of individual notes may be shown by enlarging the preparatory gesture leading into the accent.

Young conductors who can produce what they want in the foregoing categories from the musicians—who have no music and to whom no verbal instructions have been given—need have no worries about their control of the situation when they are working with a future orchestra, band, or chorus. Their technique is a true technique of the stick. They are no longer cheerleading. Their hands have been trained to speak a recognizable language of the baton.

On the job, a little psychological conducting in front of your band, orchestra, or chorus once a week or so will soon tell you whether you are slipping. It is a good drill for the players, too. They watch, understand, and become flexible when these drills are used often. Conductor and conducted benefit mutually. Don't be afraid to use them!

Exercises for Practice: Classroom Performance

Produce the following studies by conducting someone who has no music to read from. (The conducted person can be a singing or playing musician, or a nonmusician who hums a monotone in response to the gestures.) One note per beat. Meld all half notes.

Staccato = •
Tenuto = –
Legato, no marking

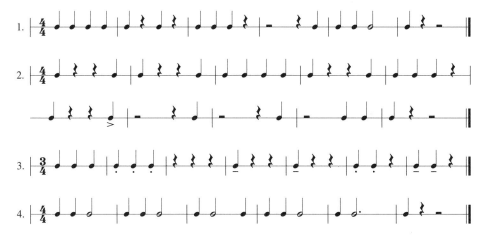

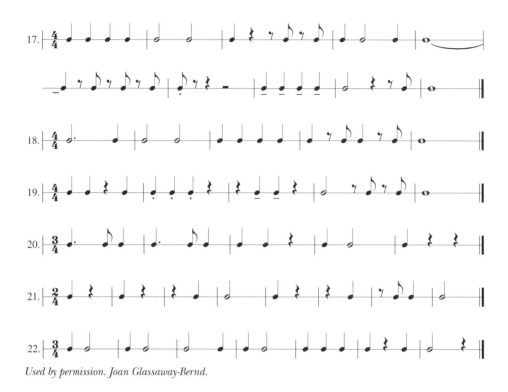

Used by permission. Joan Glassaway-Bernd.

11 The Virtuoso Technique

Ivan Galamian in his *Principles of Violin Playing and Teaching** contrasts "interpretative" (controlled) technique with "virtuoso technique." What you have been building thus far is the **interpretative technique.** It is the technique that you labor over in studying any art. It is the technique that comes instantly to your assistance when the virtuoso technique accidentally slips. An interpretative (controlled) technique is the "know-how" technique, the developed skill to show the music with your hands—your tool of interpretation.

Virtuoso technique is the free-wheeling, uncontrolled, let-it-ride technique that takes over when all of your attention is centered on the sound of the music and the performance itself. Every public performer has used it. It is not always reliable.

A truly fine virtuoso technique rests upon a strong foundation of personal know-how and mental-physical labor. The conductor's hands-arms have come, honestly, to the point where they respond automatically and perfectly to the musical thoughts in the mind. The conductor is free to let his or her imagination soar. Too often, performances that fail do so because the performer has never acquired a controlled technique. How recurrently we see it on the podium!

If you have continued to practice the technical exercises for ten minutes a day, you should find good things happening when you are on the podium, concentrating upon the musical sound from your ensemble.

*© 1962, 1985 by Prentice-Hall, Inc., a division of Simon & Schuster. Used by permission

The Shift from Technique to Music Making

Music is not a static art. It plows through time, measure by measure, in an ever-changing panorama. As their skills mature, young conductors find that the active concentration on technique is gradually being replaced by their own personal response to the music itself, influencing the gestures and lending an individual quality to the work. This quality differs from one conductor to another. No two mature conductors conduct exactly alike.

Musical consciousness eventually achieves supremacy, and with it comes the paramount need for flexibility and variety in the technique. Nothing is more monotonous than the changeless repetition of the time-beating gestures.

Suppressing the Time-Beating

Time-beating may be negated as follows when all parts are momentarily safe without it.

1. In melody lines: Show smoothly only the contour and the dynamic.

2. In rapid, consecutive motifs: Indicate only the beginning of each repetition, as in the overture to Mozart's *Impresario,* measures 47–50. GoS on One:

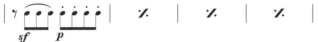

As we strive for variety in our gestures, we approach the virtuoso technique that can unlock our musical ideas for the performers and the audiences.

Creative Conducting: Variety—Seven Types

Freedom of expression is not a stereotyped thing, but in conducting, it has one controlling factor—namely, that we do not become so "original" that our gestures are meaningless to the performers. It is not necessary to sacrifice clarity to be flexible.

Flexibility and the avoidance of monotony may be attained in several ways:

1. By variety in shape of beats
2. By variety in size of gestures
3. By variety in style of gestures (legato, staccato, etc.)
4. By variety in speed of gesture-motion
5. By variety of position in space
6. By variety of melding (combining time-beating gestures)
7. By variety in texture and emphasis

All of these have their "imaginative" qualities, linked to the sound of music. When the ear takes over our existence, musically, for a space of time, the imagination quickens and unpredictable things can happen. An unimaginative performance is a dead performance—a thing of skin, bones, cold notes, and ossified rhythms.

In the following exploration of possible variations from the norm, let us still retain, subconsciously, our commitment to clarity of communication with our players.

1a. Variation in Time-Beating Patterns: In TWO.

The greatest possible variety in adjusting the time-beating rests with the TWO patterns. Enumerating, we have, in Figure 53, (a) the straight down-up One-Two, termed the rigid takt; (b) the clockwise turn into Two; (c) the counterclockwise circle so helpful in phrase endings; and (d) the "common garden variety," which was introduced on page 28, shown here with (e) its divided pattern.

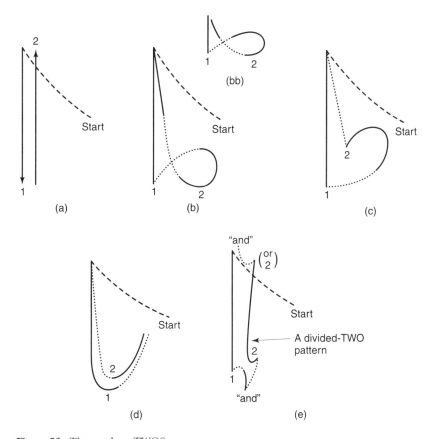

Figure 53. The modern TWOS.

(a) The Rigid Takt   One is straight down. Two is straight up. Nothing more is shown. The ictus of One is at the bottom, and that of Two is at the top.

This type of time-beating is used when there are many rhythms going on simultaneously in the music and all that the musicians desire from the conductor is to be shown the most exact definition possible of the takt—and then to be left alone. A passage such as that quoted in Example 84 might very well lend itself to this kind of treatment.

Example 84. Barber, *Medea's Meditation and Dance of Vengeance,* Op. 21A (measure 221, rhythm only, quoted) © 1956 (Renewed) by G. Schirmer, Inc. International Copyright Secured. Used by Permission.

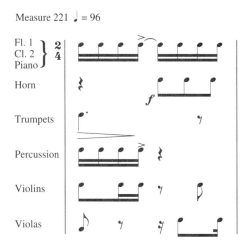

The rigid takt, in TWO, is also much used in the conducting of marches for the band where the musical content is somewhat subordinated to the rhythmic drive. In such cases it assumes a rather staccato character, changing to the traditional TWO for the more melodic trios of the march form.

(b) The Clockwise Loop   The baton rises sharply upward after One and makes a loop outward to the right, coming downward into the ictus of Two. Attention must be paid to the rebound after One so that it does not rise too high for good clarity.

This clockwise turn into Two is most valuable when the conductor wishes to carry a phrase into and through the second beat. It is endowed with tremendous sustaining power because of its possible extension of the horizontal line as shown in Figure 53bb. Example 85 is a case in point.

(c) The Counterclockwise Loop   Here the baton spreads its rebound after One outward to the right rather than moving instantly upward. Contrast diagram c with the much sharper reflex of diagram b in Figure 53. After the outward swing to the right, the baton curves back toward the downbeat line as it comes into the ictus of Two. When this counterclockwise gesture is used, the ictus for the second beat is somewhat higher up in space than was the ictus of

One. This counterclockwise loop serves very well when the phrase ends on Two. To close off the phrase, the hand slows its speed of motion (not the speed of the rhythm) as it approaches Two and stops still for an instant on Two.

The counterclockwise loop may also be adapted to the closing of a phrase on the last beat of any measure regardless of the meter. For a complete phrase ending, the beat is brought to a gentle stop on the ictus-point. Great delicacy and charm are possible.

Example 85. Schoenberg, *Gurrelieder.* Part II (measure 420 of the Berg piano reduction, page 152 of the piano score). © 1912, renewed 1940 by Universal Edition A.G., Vienna. Used by permission of Belmont Music Publishers, Los Angeles, California, 90049.

Example 86 shows an excellent contrast of clockwise and counterclockwise loops. In the third and fourth measures quoted, the clockwise loop is practical because the composer so obviously leads the phrase through One into Two. In the last two measures, the counterclockwise gesture matches the reverse phrasing, the emphasis on One with the close on Two.

Example 86. Schubert, *Rosamunde.* Overture (measures 340–347).

(d) The Traditional TWO   The traditional TWO depicts well a flowing motion, swinging along with great ease, showing two accents in each measure.

Erik Tuxen, before his death the conductor of the Copenhagen (Denmark) State Radio Orchestra, used all four of the TWO patterns very closely juxtaposed in the conducting of a certain Scherzo movement. The music was a $\frac{6}{8}$ meter. A staccato section in the rigid takt was followed by the counterclockwise looping for several measures. This gave way to the clockwise gesture, which, in turn, was followed by the traditional TWO. Then came a passage similar to that quoted in Figure 54, in which the conductor dealt most imaginatively with the rebound after One, gradually changing its height to match the contour of the melody and changing its speed of motion on the rebound of One.

Figure 54.

Example 87. Rimski-Korsakov, *Russian Easter Overture*, Op. 36 (measures 9–11 from the beginning).

(e) **The Divided-TWO Pattern**   This little-known pattern (down-down, up-up) is effective when, instead of resorting to a four-beat solution, it is preferred to retain the more visually obvious down-up of the principal TWO-beat design. An ideal excerpt for this type of divided-TWO is given in Example 87.

1b. Variation in Time-Beating Patterns: THREE and FOUR Varied

The patterns for THREE and FOUR are, in general, static. Their variations come largely under the heading of "6. Variation by Melding the Gesture." One thing, however, can be said here: The second beat of the THREE pattern is sometimes reversed in direction, moving left instead of right. Used upon occasion in the opera pit for ease of visibility by the stage performers, it can also show an antiphonal character between the violins (left on Two) and the cellos (right on Two). See Figure 55.

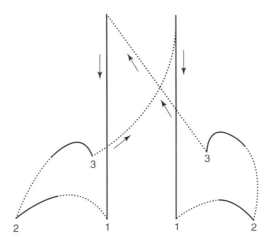

Figure 55. Reversal of direction in time-beating in THREE.

In FOUR, the size of any beat may be varied to show subtle changes in the phrasal dynamic within the measure. See Example 36 and details on page 72.

2. Variation in Size of Gesture

This has been previously mentioned, linked to the dynamic—large gestures for the *forte*s, small for the *piano*s. However, Nicolai Malko trained his students also to reverse the size of the dynamic gestures, showing a large, very gentle, floating motion that still reads *piano;* and, contrariwise, commanding a brilliant *double forte* by a sudden, small preparatory beat of tremendous vigor with momentarily added muscular tension. This latter gesture was valuable when a large preparatory beat was undesirable, the intention being to take the audience by surprise.

3. Variation in Style

See all of Chapter 5.

4. Variation in Speed of Gesture-Motion

Here we have a facet of conducting technique too often ignored. Although the rhythmic reiteration of the takt remains a constant, the speed of motion of the conductor's gestures will vary. This topic covers all the unmarked subtleties: the illusion of stretching the beats, of dwelling momentarily on a particular note, of making imperceptible accelerandos and ritards, and of closing off a phrase among other phrases. All these musical attributes of the great performance rely upon skill in the variation of speed of motion, the takt remaining recognizable.

Inserted among faster gestures, a suddenly slower motion gives the impression of "stretching the beat."

The need for this momentary dwelling on a note is apparent to all fine musicians. Our innate musical feeling takes over. We delight in a beautifully written bit of music, and we cannot shoot down a fermata in midflight.

The great performer listens.

Conductors who are naturally gifted will feel these things happening in their hands. But a conductor still needs the technical "control" to make them clearly and vitally understandable to the players and to enable him or her to show just enough to get effects without the undue exaggeration that results in cheap sentimentality.

When control of the speed of motion has become automatic (habitual), the players will see that the conductor expects them (allows them) to utilize their own fine musicianship in producing the sounds they contribute to the performance.

We approach now the last and the most musically effective of the Malko training exercises. Its mastery releases the conductor to step across the threshold into the realm of virtuoso conducting.

Note: More than one on-the-job conductor has exclaimed, "Since practicing this exercise, I find I am hearing my band (orchestra) better."

So here it is: the summation of all of the training leading to it. Introducing it too soon builds tension. The infinite control demanded leans heavily upon the previously acquired, free-flowing, habitual gestures that have finally acquired their automatically relaxed response.

The Last Training Exercise

Set the metronome at 92 for an effective first tempo. Practice with baton in hand (right hand only).

Time-beating in FOUR, using the "balanced" patterns: Beats Two and Three are *equidistant* to the left and right of the ictus of one. See Figure 2, page 11.

Start with a quarter-inch square. The four beats (at the tip of the stick) are confined within that tiny square thus: Beat One drops down ¼ inch. Beat Two moves ¼ inch left; beat Three ½ inch right (¼ inch beyond One). Repeat several times for control, then continue.

Without stopping, move to a half-inch square. Guard the balanced design throughout, and keep the height of One within the given square. Repeat and proceed as follows.

Use 1-inch, 2-inch, 3-, 4-, 5-, 6-, 7-, 8-, 9-, 10-inch squares. Move to 12 inches and add three inches each time from here on: 15, 18, 21, 24.

Reverse the sequence (24, 21, etc.) and proceed back to the quarter-inch square. The change in square-size occurs on the last beat of any unit, thus preparing the change.

Note: The lower arm can remain static until about 5 inches, when it will have to come into play.

Variations: Try different metronome settings, faster, slower. Also use one setting but change from 2 to 10; from 15 to 3; from 24 to 2; from one to another number. Once mastered, the time-space factor should flow freely and unconsciously to match what the music is saying.

Timing   There is another facet of speed of motion that should be mentioned here. **Not every gesture the conductor makes will be rhythmic.** There are times when a sudden unrhythmic gesture is necessary to produce an exact rhythmic response from the players. That introduces the topic of "timing" the gestures—the most advanced skill of all and the one that grows only with experience in front of the ensemble.

We have what we call "**precipitating the beat**"—often addressed to players sitting far from the conductor (Trombones, String Basses, etc.) to ensure that their entrance is synchronized exactly with that of the players up front. Very often those in the rear will hear the sound too late. To control the situation, the baton, raised above the line of vision of the front rows of players, will indicate the beat infinitesimally ahead of its rhythmic takt.

Note: The sound waves of the lowest-pitched bass instruments are of such length that the pitches are not instantly heard.

Cautionary gestures to prevent accidents also require sudden, unexpected, and nonrhythmic motions.

5. Variation of Position in Space

One facet of this was mentioned in time-beating in ELEVEN, page 123. A second aspect is found in time-beating in ONE at fast tempos where a heavier stressed measure is followed by a second measure of lighter accentuation in a sequential series. Beating in ONE throughout, the ictus-point for the lighter measure is placed higher up in space and slightly to the right, thus accounting for the two-measure phrasal grouping. (See Example 88 and Figure 56.)

Example 88. Beethoven, Symphony No. 6 in F major, Op. 68 *(Pastorale)*. Third movement (measures 1–2).

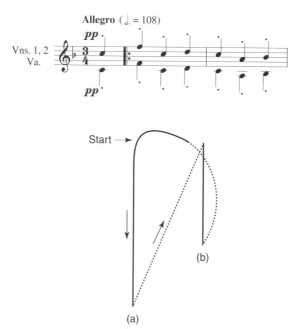

Figure 56. Change in the position of the ictus in time-beating in ONE. No preparatory beat shown here.

6. Variation by Melding the Gestures

For a review of melding techniques, see pages 138–144.

7. Variation in Texture and Emphasis

The quality of the line between beats bespeaks the texture of the sound: gentle sound, gentle curves; in fast tempo, vigorous beat-points with more angular connections for the big *fortes*; and so on. There is the Toscanini story in which he tossed his open handkerchief into the air, letting it float down to show the texture he was trying to produce in the sound.

Conclusion

Summing up the virtuoso technique, let us refer to Beethoven's Third Symphony *(Eroica)*, first movement. This movement is a veritable symposium on time-beating in THREE. Much of the movement is done in ONE—the first two measures, for example. In THREE, measures 83–90. In THREE staccato, measures 65, 70, 186–193. Baton shows the slower-moving Two—the dwelling on Two starting in measure 44. One, Two-accented, with Three unbeaten, being used only to prepare the next One, starting in measure 236. Showing One, using Two, dead gesture, then preparing Three, measures 152–165 (second ending). Many passages show accents every two beats (cross accentuation): measures 25–26; 28–34; see Figure 47, page 126.

When the technique has become habitual, such interpretative conducting takes place without conscious effort, even in sight reading. Make a distinction in your mind between monotonous time-beating and interpretative conducting. **Let your imagination take over.** Couple that with intense listening and you have a source of infinite inspiration. The freedom you allow yourself becomes your individuality as a conductor.

MUSIC FOR PERFORMANCE

Example 89. Haydn, Symphony 104 in D major *(London)*. First movement, Introduction (measure 7 to end of Intro). Ten measures.

Time-beating in divided-FOUR. To control the thirty-second notes, use GoS on the second dot, upward, immediately after the "and" of Two, which falls on the first dot, and continue the time-beating or sustain the half note in rhythm.

Example 90. Beethoven, *Coriolanus Overture,* Op. 62 (measure 276 to the end). Thirty-nine measures.

In FOUR. Note tempo cue at bottom of second page. Meld the whole notes, but show beat One of each measure (see Figure 51). Use a legato pre-beat on Four for the coming chords on One. Small dead gestures for the rests. Measures 11–15 beat all quarter notes. Dead rests. Prepare each entrance after a rest. Follow indications above last 18 measures.

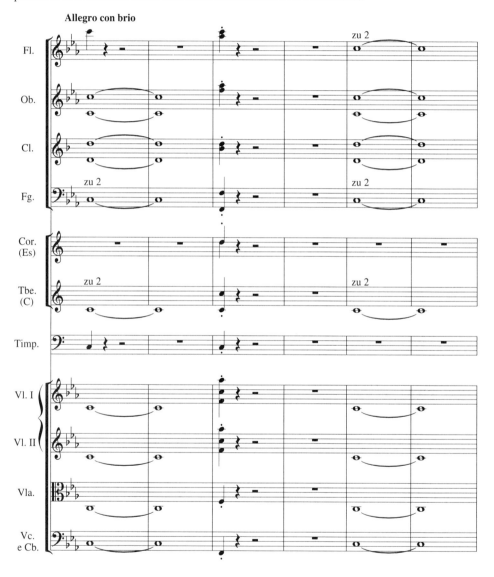

(tempo cue)

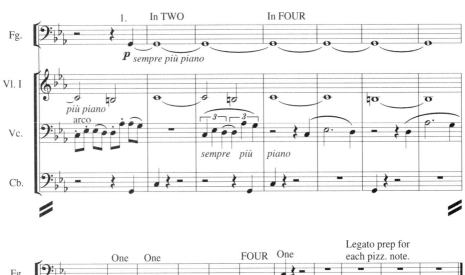

Recommended Reference Readings

BARRA, DONALD, *The Dynamic Performance.* Ideas on musical expression and interpretation. Worth reading.

BOWLES, MICHAEL, *The Art of Conducting.* Good chapters on interpretation.

VAN ESS, DONALD H., *The Heritage of Musical Styles.* A great book, profusely illustrated with beautiful reproductions of art.

Recommended Videotape

FOR VIRTUOSO TECHNIQUE

Carlos Kleiber, dir., *Beethoven Symphonies Nos. 4 and 7.* The Concertgebouw Orchestra, Amsterdam. Phillips Video Classics, 070-200-3 © 1987. (UNITEL, 1983). Every student should have the opportunity to see this video. Every gesture *shows* exactly what the music is expressing or is about to express.

P A R T   2

Score Study

It is necessary to read a score in **two directions: horizontally,** part by part, to understand the performers' problems; and **vertically** for interrelationships of rhythms, dynamics, cues, and harmonic analysis. Regarding the last named, look first at the **bass line,** the foundation of the chord; then **read upward through the parts,** applying correct transpositions as you encounter them. (See Chapter 12.) Make sure in your mind that you are distinguishing "written pitch" from "sounding pitch."

The Steps of Score Study

1. Look first at the instrumentation. Memorize it!

2. Read through the entire score, casually noting tempos, climaxes, changes of style, type of ending.

3. Have you now understood the general aspect of the music? Is it decisive? lyrical? tragic? majestic? meditative? What is its reason for existence?

4. Do you like what you have discovered? Can you make an interesting performance? Does this score challenge your imagination?

5. Will it work with your ensemble? with solo instruments? Is the melodic line clear of obstructions, or is the music too heavily scored against it? How will you produce good balance?

6. Now make a complete phrasal analysis. Count the number of measures in each phrase. Mark that number in the **bottom margin under the beginning of the**

phrase, thus: 4/; 6/; 2 × **4,** showing repetition of two measures, four times. Count measures beginning with the *first full measure of the phrase.* Pay no attention at this time to notes that introduce the phrase before the barline.

7. **Check for dangerous places where *you* must be in absolute control:** difficult rhythms; **cues after many measures of rests. Mark the name of the instrument** (abbreviated) **in the TOP MARGIN of the score directly above the entrance beat** where you **can see it instantly. This makes for a cleaner score.**

8. Compare "parallel passages," a section near the beginning that comes in again **later on** in the music. Be sure that you have located the very first note in the second passage that is **different** from the first passage. This note is the "switch in the track" that sends the music forward instead of committing it to circular repetition.

9. Check on the cymbal crashes, especially the first one of a series. Mark them in red. Put a cue in your score a measure or two ahead.

10. When speaking to any player of a transposing instrument, state whether you are referring to the **written pitch** or the **sounding pitch.**

Recommended Reference Readings

For more detail on score study, you may wish to peruse Green and Malko, *The Conductor's Score,* Chapter 3 (Malko), "Studying the Score," pp. 12–27, and Chapter 4 (Malko), "Marking the Score," pp. 30–76. Also, Benjamin Grosbayne, *Techniques of Modern Orchestral Conducting,* Chapters 21–24, pp. 192–226. Fine material on Score Analysis, Editing the Score, and Preparing the Rehearsal. See the Bibliography.

BATTISTI, FRANK, and ROBERT GAROFALO, *Guide to Score Study for Wind Band Conductors.*

MORRIS, R. O., and HOWARD FERGUSON, *Preparatory Exercises in Score Reading.* For use at the piano.

12 Clefs and Transpositions

Before students begin a perusal of the various types of conductor's scores, their attention should be called to two facts: (1) They will have to deal with the C clefs in addition to the G (treble) and F (bass) clefs; and (2) in the instrumental scores, they will come into vital contact with the problem of the transposing instruments. We shall take these up in order.

The C Clefs

The C clefs are not difficult to understand. The small pointer of the printed clef sign points to the line or space of the staff that is to be read as *middle C,* as shown in Figure 57.

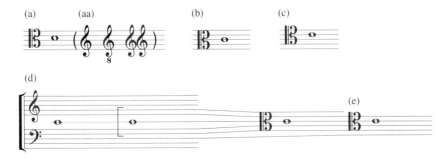

Figure 57.

There is a possible C clef for every line and every space of the staff. Those given in Figure 57 are the most used in present-day printing, although the reader will come across others as his or her experience with music scores enlarges. Figure 57a is the C clef that is called the *vocal tenor clef*. It designates the third space of the staff as middle C. Since this third space is also C in treble clef, the lines and spaces of these two clefs have the same letter names. When this C clef is used for the tenor parts in choral music, it recognizes that the male voice is *an octave below the corresponding female voice*. Nevertheless, it is not used consistently. The other designations for the tenor voice are given in parentheses in Figure 57aa.

Figure 57b shows the pointer of the clef sign designating the middle line of the staff as middle C. This clef is called the *alto clef*. The viola parts in the orchestra are written in this clef, with occasional lapses into the treble clef to eliminate leger lines for the highest notes. For that reason the clef is sometimes referred to as the "viola clef." But the violas do not exercise exclusive ownership, since the first trombone parts, in the European editions of orchestral works, are often found in this clef. When it is used, the part is often called "Alto Trombone."

The third C clef, Figure 57c, is the fourth-line C clef, called the *instrumental tenor clef*. This clef is used for the higher notes of the cello and bassoon parts and, in certain European editions, for the second trombone parts, which are therefore designated "Tenor Trombone." Upon rare occasions the string basses may encounter this clef in their parts. Today the bass clef is customarily used for all trombone parts (especially in American publications), occasionally resorting to the use of the tenor clef for the higher notes of the first and second trombones. The third trombone part is invariably in the bass clef.

The instrumental C clefs are formed as shown in (d) and (e) of Figure 57. Starting with the grand staff, we know that between the treble and bass clefs there is one line missing: the middle-C line. If this line is extended, it becomes the C line in the C clefs. Thus, for the alto clef, we borrow two lines from the treble clef above it and two from the bass clef below it, and our new five-line clef is formed. When the lowest line of the treble clef is used above the C line and the three top lines of the bass clef are marked below it, we have the tenor C clef, instrumental. Bearing this in mind helps with the initial steps in reading these two clefs, but they should, certainly, be learned subsequently as individual clefs by practicing them at the piano.

An interesting vocal use of the C clefs is found in Schoenberg's *Drei Satiren*. The first song, entitled "Am Scheideweg" ("Concerning the Departure"), opens with the words "Tonal or atonal" (Example 91). Such writing is seldom seen in our day, but, as the example shows, it does exist.

Example 91. Schoenberg, *Drei Satiren für Gemischten Chor,* Op. 28. No. 1: "Am Scheideweg" ("Concerning the Departure") (measure 7). © 1926, renewed 1953 by Universal Edition A.G., Vienna. Used by permission of Belmont Music Publishers, Los Angeles, California 90049.

The Transposing Instruments

The wind instruments are classified either as "transposing" instruments or as "nontransposing" instruments. Simply defined, the **transposing instruments** are those that sound pitches different from the notes actually written in the score. The **nontransposing instruments sound as notated.** They match the corresponding notes on the piano and are designated as C instruments. A written C sounds C.

The transposing instruments are identified by title: clarinet in B-flat, clarinet in A, French horn in F, and so on. When a transposing instrument plays a written C, it actually sounds the pitch for which the instrument is named. Clarinets in B-flat playing C will *sound* the B-flat.

The relationship between C and the name-pitch of the instrument is called the **interval of transposition.** Each written note will sound below (or, in a few cases, above) its printed pitch as determined by this interval of transposition.

Caution: A note that drops a whole tone in performance must be written, by the composer, one whole tone higher than the desired sounding pitch.

The resonance of a wind instrument depends upon the length of its air column. This length must be determined, for the particular type of instrument, by three things: (1) the range of the notes it is to play, (2) the resulting efficiency and tone quality produced by the chosen length, and (3) its adaptability to the size of the human hand. The shape of the instrument, the manner in which the air is set into vibration, and, according to some authorities, the material of which it is made all add their bit to the resulting tone.

Through years of experimentation and improvement, certain standard instruments (as to length of air column) have emerged as functioning most efficiently for the player. This means that such instruments cover their entire usable range with good quality and fairly easy execution, and this accounts for the existence of the transposing instruments. See "Table of Transposition Intervals" on pages 179–180.

The **C instruments,** sounding as notated, are flute, oboe, bassoon, trumpets in C, trombones, baritones and euphoniums in bass clef, and tubas. (For exceptions, see the next section.) The strings are all "C" instruments, matching the piano in pitch, with the exception of the string basses, which sound an octave lower than notated. Customarily, the string bass part duplicates, in the lower octave, the cello part.

Now a word about the **brasses** in particular. When Haydn, Mozart, Beethoven, and their contemporaries were writing, the horns and the trumpets were not provided with valves as they are today. (By use of the valve mechanism, our present-day instruments have control over the complete chromatic range.) Instead, "crooks" were used. These were of varying lengths, and each crook placed the instrument in a certain key. The crooks were removable, and when the music modulated, the player had to have time to make the exchange. The use of the crook permitted the following notes to be played in the given key: root (not playable on some instruments), octave (not used on the trumpets and the cornets), fifth above, double octave, third, fifth, out-of-tune seventh above the double octave, plus scalewise progression thereafter, including the raised fourth—in other words, the succession of notes playable on the trumpet as open tones today. If the D crook was in the horn, the D major series would sound, and so on.

On the French horn, the player could also make other pitches by inserting his hand into the bell of the horn, but the tone quality changed on those notes, and composers tended to avoid them.

Since these early horns and trumpets would necessarily play in the key of the crook, it is easy to see that accidentals had little or no place in the writing of such parts in those days. The composer stated the crook to be used, and that took care of the situation. The accidentals of that key functioned automatically.

With our modern valve horns, all accidentals are playable. The contemporary notation of the horn parts is generally without signature and with all accidentals marked in as they occur. In classifying a score as to the period in which it was composed, much can be inferred from the presence or absence of accidentals in the horn and trumpet parts.

The conductor will feel insecure with the early horn parts unless he or she is acquainted with the transpositions of various crooks in use during the eighteenth century. These will be explained under "Rules for Transposition."

Some Additions and Exceptions

The following comments will give the reader some idea of the variations found in notational customs. This is not an exhaustive listing.

Certain C instruments sound at an interval of an octave above the notated pitches: piccolo in C, xylophone, chimes, and celesta. The glockenspiel sounds two octaves higher than written. Richard Wagner preferred to write for it in its sounding octave!

When the **bass clef** is used for the bass clarinet, the written notes sound one whole tone lower. But this instrument may also find bass-clef parts written in concert pitch and even designated "clarinet in A." Notated in treble clef the sound drops a major ninth.

The contrabassoon sounds an octave below its notation. However, parts are to be found written at sounding pitch: *Iberia* by Debussy; *Parsifal* by Wagner.

The bass clef is used for the trombones and the baritone (euphonium). They sound as written. When treble-clef parts exist, they are B-flat transpositions. Customarily only one part is scored for these instruments; however, some English editions, as well as early American scores, include a specialized part for the baritone, written in treble clef.

The tubas sound as notated in the bass clef. A famous exception is the sustained tone starting in measure 485 of Tchaikovsky's *Romeo and Juliet*. Traditionally it is played an octave lower than written. In certain French scores for band, tuba parts are found in BB-flat, E-flat, and C scorings. Professional orchestra players will change to the smaller E-flat and F tubas for performing lengthy parts written in the upper registers. They sound as written.

In certain earlier English scores for military band, parts designated "E-flat piccolo and flute" are to be found. There does exist an E-flat soprano flute (in addition to the E-flat alto flute, rarely seen today), so that the conductor must, in such cases, determine whether piccolo or flute is intended.

The Two Basic Rules for Transposition

The young conductor can quickly master the two basic rules for transposition. The first rule tells the conductor exactly what pitch should *sound* for each note written in the score—the *concert pitch*. The second rule tells the player what to do when the composer calls for an instrument other than the one the player has in his hands.

The First Rule for Transposition

Most prevalent are the transpositions that *sound* a pitch somewhat *lower* than the written note. To determine the downward interval of transposition, proceed as follows:

Write on the staff the note C. (In treble clef the third space is best; in bass clef use middle C.) *Below this note write the pitch of the instrument designated by the composer* (clarinet in B-flat, trumpet in A, French horn in F or D, or whatever is called for). **The *drop* in pitch from the C to the name of the instrument will tell you the interval of transposition.** Each written note will sound as much lower as the interval of transposition states. Refer now to Figure 58. This will state the most common of the transposition intervals.

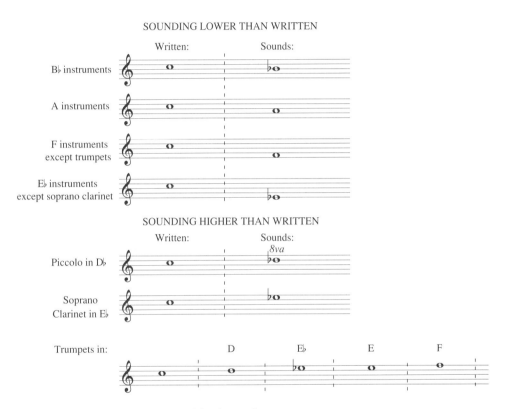

Figure 58. Common transposition intervals.

With the exception of the four trumpets mentioned in Figure 58, the early instruments with crooks all transposed downward. These were trumpets in B (natural), B-flat, and A; French horns in B-flat alto (one whole tone lower), A, A-flat, G, F, E, E-flat, D, C basso (an octave lower), and B-flat basso (a major ninth lower). The designation "horn in C" generally refers to the "C basso." For further specific information, see "Table of Transposition Intervals" on page 000.

When horn parts are notated in the bass clef, the transposition interval is the inversion of the interval in the treble clef. This is because the direction of the notation is reversed in bass-clef writing for the horns, each written note rising to the concert pitch above instead of dropping to the concert pitch below. This form of writing is not strictly adhered to in modern works. When the composer chooses to lay aside this custom, he or she will call attention to the fact by a brief sentence in the score and parts.

A very few instruments **transpose upward.** These are piccolo in D-flat (a minor ninth higher); soprano clarinet and trumpet in E-flat (a minor third higher); trumpet in D (a major second higher), in E-natural (a major third higher), and in F (a perfect fourth higher). You will have to memorize this short list of upward transpositions. Applying the first rule of transposition in these cases, the C will be written on the staff, and the keynotes of these instruments will be written *above* the C. Each written note in the part will then sound at the resultant interval above. (The composer will have to write it that much under pitch.)

The Second Rule for Transposition

This rule tells the player what to do when his or her instrument is not built in the key specified by the composer. Here again the rule is simple: The player writes on the staff **the key of the instrument in his or her hands** ("horn in F," for example). The relationship between that instrument and the instrument called for will state the interval of transposition. The student will have to read each note of the written part transposed by that interval. In the case of a horn in F going to a written horn in D, each written note will be read downward a minor third. If horn in A were called for, the A would be written above the F, since in the table of horn transposition, that is the A designated by "horn in A." Figure 59 will help to clarify this point.

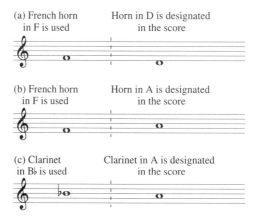

Figure 59.

Some students may need to think "the long way around." Write C for horn in F = 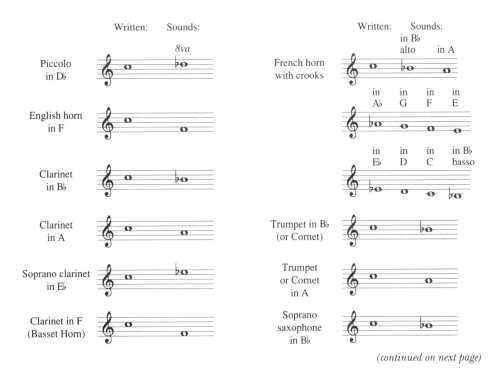 . Write C for horn in D = . For horn in F to sound the required pitch of horn in D, the F horn would have to transpose a minor third downward = . It is difficult to think in minor thirds downward. There is a shortcut. Notice that the part for horn in D shows no written signature. The performer is therefore playing in *his or her* key of C (no sharps, no flats to read). Take *this* key and carry it through the interval of transposition (a minor third downward), and you arrive at the key of A, which has a signature of three sharps. To play the D part on the F horn, the player proceeds as follows: Any note on a line is dropped to the next line below. Any note on a space is dropped to the next space below. And the player uses a three-sharp (key of A) signature.

Note: The written part for horns with crooks will show a C signature. Carry the C signature through the interval of transposition to obtain the key for the transposed part. *Again: When going from instrument to instrument, start with the instrument in the players' hands and go from there to the instrument called for in the score* (for example, horn in F to horn in whatever).

When the conductor names notes, he or she specifies "written pitch" or "concert pitch" (sounding pitch).

TABLE OF TRANSPOSITION INTERVALS

(continued on next page)

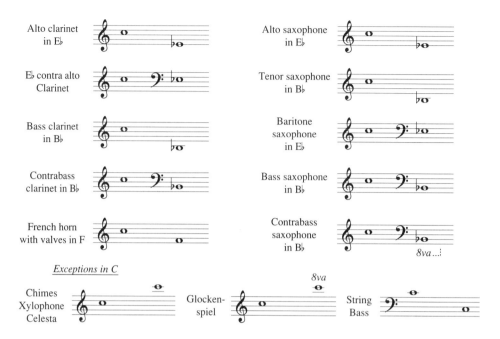

Timpani sound as written in all modern notations.

Exercises for Practice: Skill in Clefs and Transpositions

1. Play the following examples on the piano, or on your major instrument.

2. Refer to the orchestra scores given in Chapter 13 and play through all the C-clef parts.

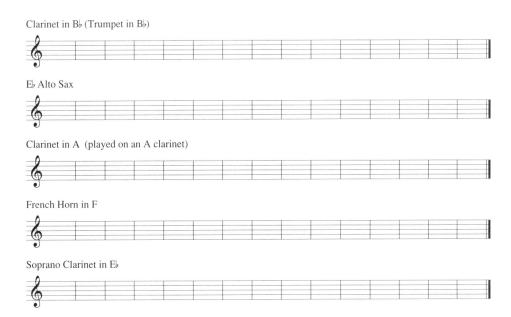

Clarinet in B♭ (Trumpet in B♭)

E♭ Alto Sax

Clarinet in A (played on an A clarinet)

French Horn in F

Soprano Clarinet in E♭

3. Notate the pitches actually sounded by the designated instruments.

4. If the given notes of exercise 2 were designated Horn in D, notate the notes played on the Horn in F to arrive at the correct sound. In other words, transpose the D part for Horn in F (page 178). If designated Horn in A, then what?

5. Use the scores in Chapter 13 and work at the piano. Reading from the bottom upward, play each *sound* called for on the first beat of each measure. Make the correct transposition for each instrument as you come to its part. Remember, the string basses sound an octave lower than the cellos when they are playing the identical written notes.

6. Sing exercise 5 without help from the piano. Sing the *sound* for the transposing instruments, not the written note. Place the pitches within your own voice range.

Recommended Reference Readings

BOWLES, MICHAEL, *The Art of Conducting*, pp. 99–140. Specific information on each of the standard orchestral instruments, winds and strings.

GOLDMAN, RICHARD FRANKO, *The Concert Band*. Chapters 2–5, pp. 18–146. Very complete information on band instrumentation and the functions of the instruments.

KENNAN, KENT, and DONALD GRANTHAM, *The Technique of Orchestration*. Complete information on the instruments of the symphony orchestra.

LANG, PHILIP, *Scoring for the Band.*

PIETZSCH, HERMANN, *Die Trompete* ("The Trumpet"). The American edition is filled with excellent information of a detailed nature on this instrument, its history, transpositions, and uses in the literature.

RIMSKI-KORSAKOV, NICOLAI, *Principles of Orchestration*, Vol. 1. Chapter 1, pp. 6–35. The manner of presenting the instruments in this book is unique. It is highly recommended. It states comparable resonances for various groupings of instruments, pp. 33–35.

13 Instrumental Conducting: Orchestra and Band Scores

There is no good reason today why a fine conductor, equipped with an adequate manual technique, must confine his or her expertise exclusively to either the band or the orchestra. With knowledge of the pertinent repertoire and an understanding of the "typical sound" or the "musical goals" of each organization, the thorough musician can be successful on either podium. It is being proven constantly in concert halls today.

Specialization can follow classroom training, but the basic training should open both doors for the student. Who knows what opportunities may come?

The international competitions for young conductors deal with the symphony orchestra repertoire. They present a challenge, during classroom days, to prepare to go as far as one's talent will permit.

Band and Orchestra: Comparisons and Contrasts

There are many principles of musicianship that apply equally to both organizations. There are also fundamental differences between the band and the orchestra of which the conductor should be cognizant.

Contrast of Basic Sound

The most basic difference between the symphony orchestra and the symphonic band has to do with the volume of sound. The wind instrument deals with an immediate force—wind is blown into the mouthpiece and sound waves as such emerge directly into the air, unhampered by the transference to and through the wood of the stringed instrument. In the latter, the vibrations initiated by the bow on the strings pass through the bridge (wood) to the top of the instrument (wood) and finally to the air inside, where the sound wave then forms. A certain loss of energy occurs in the process. Thus it is easy to see that a 100-piece symphonic band will have a greater volume than a 100-member symphony orchestra, where some sixty percent of the players are functioning on stringed instruments.

The orchestra relies greatly on its string tone for its basic sound. Each wind instrument now becomes a unique tone color in its own right. In general, a solo wind will stand out more individually, as a color, against a string background than it will when accompanied by other wind instruments. **The orchestra sound, then, deals with the contrast of color between strings and winds**—an effect that might be regarded as a type of transparency.

The wind player sitting in the orchestra will find himself or herself using the finest solo tone with its obvious projection much of the time, whereas in the band, he or she will also be more conscious of blending with the section in order not to protrude unduly. (This is similar to the customary choral practices of blend of tone.) **Balance and blend of sound** among players in a single section and among instruments of different tone color are fundamental problems in the band. Orchestrally, dynamic balance is also affected by color balance.*

The orchestra conductor standing in front of the band for the first time is likely to feel a bit overwhelmed by the sheer mass of the sound. Contrariwise, the band conductor in front of the orchestra may feel that the overall sound is a bit "thin." The conductor is working in a different medium with a different type of resonance. The exciting auditory volume of the band is replaced in the orchestra by the visual excitement of the fast-moving bows, functioning in unison and showing the same emotional drive.

Scoring

An important and recognizable change has been taking place in the scoring for symphonic band. One of the pivotal compositions was Persichetti's *Symphony for Band,* published in 1958.† Here Persichetti began to experiment with emphasis on tonal colors rather than relying on the massive sectional sound. Witness, for example, the vastly empty pages: In the first movement, measures 27–32, three clarinets and first horn only are playing; later, in the last movement, measures 92–97, solo oboe is accompanied only by the saxes (two altos, tenor, and baritone). The instruments are handled in a manner similar to the way the great masters of the past had used them in scoring for the symphony orchestra, thus bringing more transparency into the band sound.

---

*It was the consensus of a panel of Detroit Symphony winds that the orchestral musician has to have under control a wider dynamic range—softer *pianos* in the French horns, louder *fortes* in the flutes and bassoons. Concerning intonation: When playing with strings, infinitesimal pitch adjustments become paramount. As one panel member remarked, "D-sharp is not E-flat!"

†Vincent Persichetti, *Symphony for Band* (Philadelphia: Elkan-Vogel, 1958).

The Melodic Line

In older band compositions, the clarinets assumed much of the melodic function that belonged to the first violins in the orchestra, both often doubled by the flutes. Cornet solos were frequent in band music, but for the orchestra the trumpets were and are preferred. A melody performed by a solo wind still remains more prevalent in the orchestra but not as much so today as in former years.

The Harmony

In the band, the three (or four) tones of the chordal harmony can be completed within one set of identical instruments (first, second, and third clarinets; three or four saxes; three trumpets; a set of trombones or horns). This similarity of tonal quality can help in balancing the tones of the chord. Since wind instruments more often come in pairs in the orchestra, the chordal harmony is likely to be scattered through the instruments of the family (woodwinds, brasses, or strings), thus requiring an adjustment that takes into consideration the tone colors of the several instruments as well as their dynamic balance. The larger the orchestra, the more the harmonic distribution will resemble that of the band. A chord given to two violins, viola, and cello-bass will need attention for resonance.

The Percussion

Over the years, the percussion section has been used somewhat more sparingly in the orchestra than in the band with the exception of the timpani. Twentieth-century writing has brought a change here. A distinction should be made, in either organization, between the percussion as an addition to the general sound and the percussion as a solo section in its own right. In earlier works for band where the percussion becomes a rather constant rhythmic force, it has to be kept subservient to the pitched sounds—like a wonderful heartbeat that permeates the music but is not obviously apparent. Regardless of which organization the percussionist performs with, and regardless of whether the music calls for a murmur, a simple statement, an unrelenting intensification of the emotional content, or a thunderous climax, the performer should be made aware that when pitched instruments are also sounding, the dynamic rendition of the percussion element should be in balance with them. (What a joy musicianly percussion playing is!)

Orchestra Scores

Score Development

Note: Use the scores for practice as you examine them.

Our large modern ensembles began with the developmental change of the early viols to the modern stringed instruments—late sixteenth century in

Italy. As the wind instruments also improved, they joined the ensemble. See Example 92 (Bach, b. 1685).

Example 92. J. S. Bach, *Brandenburg Concerto No. 2 in F.* First movement (measures 1–2).

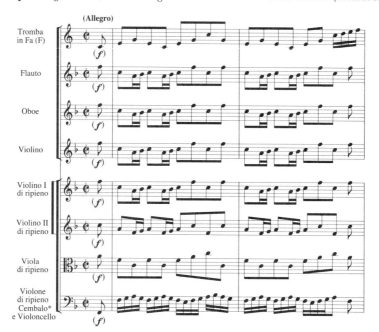

In Example 93 (Mozart, b. 1756), notice that the clarinet is still missing (1787).

---

*Cembalo and Violoncello are on a separate line from the Violone di ripieno in the original score. *Ripieno* is the tutti instruments as distinguished from the solo instruments *(concertino)*, which appear on the four staves at the top of the score.

Example 93. Mozart, Symphony in D major *(Prague)*. First movement, beginning.

Note: Fagotti = Bassoons. Corni = French Horns. Trombe = Trumpets. See Appendix B, pages 252–253.

But in Example 94 (Haydn, b. 1732), the clarinets are functioning. Note the double-dotted eighth notes (Adagio tempo).

Example 94. Haydn, Symphony No. 104 in D major *(London)*. First movement (measures 1–5).

Next, look at Example 95, an opera score (Rossini, b. 1792). The trombones were used in opera and church music before Beethoven (b. 1770) scored them into the Finale of his Fifth Symphony. In the Rossini score, notice the Timpani, H and E. The H signified B-natural. B is B-flat.

Here you have now seen the basic score format: woodwinds at the top, brasses next, percussion, and strings at the bottom. The band score follows the same general outline, lacking the strings, and places the percussion on the bottom line.

Example 95. Rossini, *The Barber of Seville.* Overture (measures 1–9).

On the second page of the Rossini, third and fourth measures, notice the descending chromatics in the cello (bass line). These must be heard.

Note: The Italian terminology is traditional. See Appendix B for terminology in other languages. Customarily, full instrumentation is shown on the first page of the movement. Thereafter the score shows only the instruments playing at the moment. See second page of Example 95. Early scores often show only C and G in the timpani part. The correct tuning notes are stated in the left margin. To show a change in notes (or transpositions), the words *muta in* appear in the part.

Example 96 (Rimski-Korsakov) shows a cadenza played by a solo instrument. Cadenzas often appear in woodwind parts.

One word about the score in C (Example 97): Beethoven requests C instruments throughout. Pitches are as notated.

When the C scoring is used, the composer either specifies French horn in C, trumpet in C, and so on; or writes, "Score in C, parts transposed." When the players read from C parts today, they must transpose to fit the instrument played upon. See Example 97.

Example 96. Rimski-Korsakov, *Russian Easter Overture*, Op. 36. Lento mistico (measures 6–8). The Solo Cadenza.

Example 97. Beethoven, *Leonore Overture No. 3*, Op. 72a (measures 378–389). Score in C.

The story goes that Prokofiev, in his student days, asked his teacher, Glazounov, "Why not write the score always in C and transpose only the parts for the players?" Glazounov is said to have looked the young man up and down rather coldly and then to have replied, "Young man, if it was good enough for Beethoven, it is good enough for you."

Nevertheless, today we find a fair number of Prokofiev's scores in C with the parts transposed for the players only. Recommended for perusal might be the *Lieutenant Kijé* Suite and the Fifth Symphony by this composer.

Band Scores

Example 98 is the total first measure of *Blue Lake,* by John Barnes Chance.

Example 99 is the beginning of a lengthy march for winds and percussion by Beethoven, written in 1809.

Example 100 presents a modern condensed score for band.

Example 101 shows a full page of condensed score. Such a score gives the conductor an instant acquaintance with the sound to be produced. It is playable on the piano, but the conductor has no idea of which instrument plays which note of the harmony.

Since the band uses certain instruments that do not appear in the orchestral score, its symphonic score is lengthier. Also, the band conductor is plagued with infinitely more transpositions, not the keys so much as the octaves in which the notes will sound.

Example 102 (Fauchet) is a well-known work showing full score for band. Note the position of the English horn and the bassoons following the oboe line. This is variable. The E-flat (soprano) clarinet is above the B-flats; and the alto and bass clarinets, below, are followed by the saxes.

A major difference lies in the position of the horns and the cornets. (Remember that "cor." means "cornets," not "horns.") Band scores usually use the English terminology. The position of the baritone-euphonium varies, sometimes above the trombones, sometimes below. The bassoon also jumps around. Compare Example 102 with Example 103. In the Wagner, observe the enharmonic writing: Instruments built in flats are scored-for in flats; instruments in C are scored-for in sharps!

Example 98. John Barnes Chance, *Blue Lake.* Copyright © 1971 Boosey & Hawkes, Inc. International copyright secured. All rights reserved. Reprinted by permission of Boosey & Hawkes.

Example 99. Beethoven, *March for Military Band.* Beethoven placed the bass instruments at the bottom of the score and gave each percussion instrument its own stave.

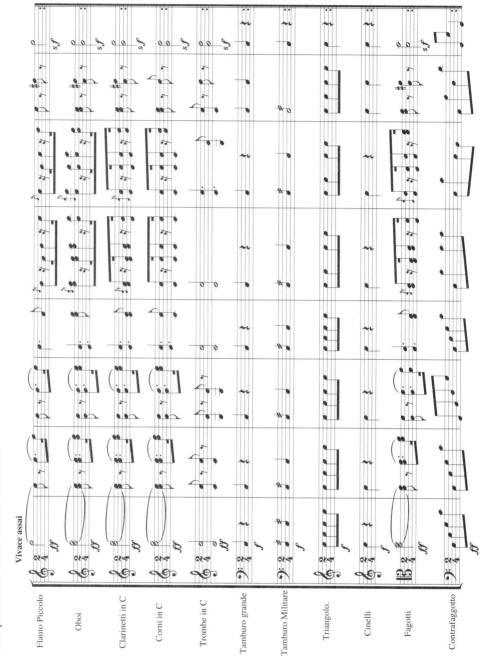

194

Example 100. Moussorgsky, *Boris Godounov.* Coronation Scene, transcribed by Erik Leidzén* (measures 3–4), condensed score. From *Boris Godounov* (Coronation Scene) by Moussorgsky/arr. Leidzén. Copyright © 1936 by Carl Fischer, Inc., New York. International Copyright Secured. All Rights Reserved. Reprinted by permission of the Publisher.

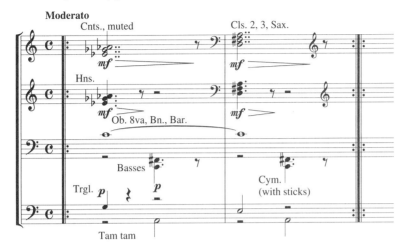

*Respectful tribute should be paid to two great arrangers for band, Erik Leidzén and Lucien Cailliet. Their contribution to the recognition of the musical worth of the fine symphonic band has been of untold value, not only to the bandsmen themselves, but also to the music profession as a whole.

Example 101. Ernest S. Williams, *Symphony in C minor* for band. First movement (measures 1–32). © 1938 by Ernest S. Williams. Copyright assigned by Edwin H. Morris Company to Charles Colin 1958. Reprinted by permission of Charles Colin, 315 West 53rd Street, New York, N.Y. 10019.

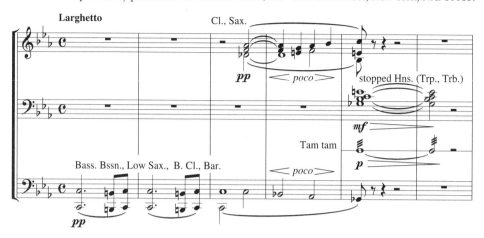

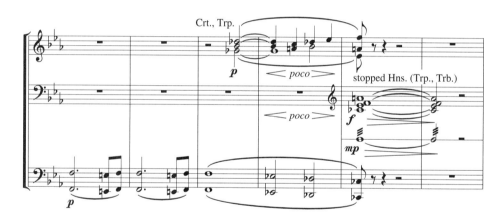

Example 102. Fauchet, *Symphony in B-flat for Band*, arranged by Gillette. First movement (page 17 of the full score). Copyright 1934 by WARNER BROTHERS INC. (Renewed) (Band). Used by Permission.

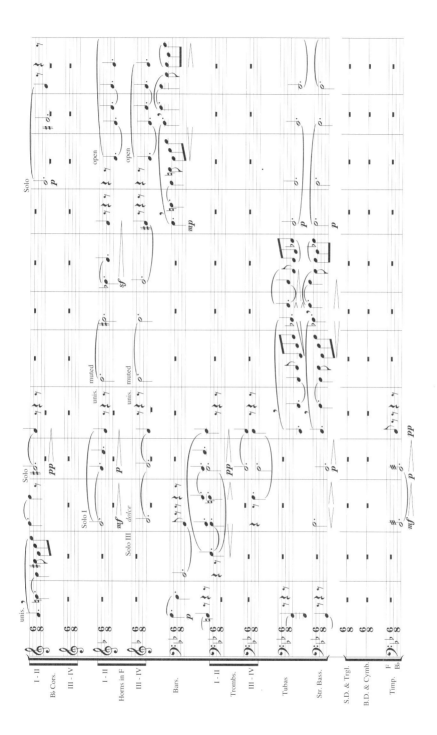

199

Example 103. Wagner, *Lohengrin.* Elsa's Procession to the Cathedral. Arranged for band by Lucien Cailliet. Page 17, full score. © 1938 WARNER BROS. INC. (Renewed) (Band) All Rights Reserved. Used by Permission.

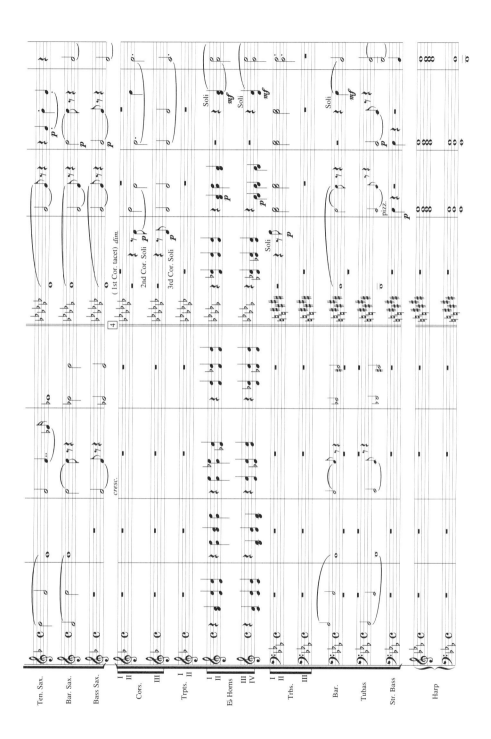

Twentieth-Century Score Innovations

Little has been said regarding the twelve-tone writing. It opened the door for many clashes of dissonance. In rehearsal, when the cacophony becomes unbelievable, it is advisable to take time to sort it out.

1. Start with the lowest written pitch. The players are to sustain throughout the setting of the chord. Tell them to take a new breath (bow) as necessary and reenter the music.

2. Progress **upward** by sequential pitches—not necessarily in score order, but by choosing the next highest sounding pitch. Do not skip octaves. In this way each player hears his or her note as the top note of the chord. When sounding the highest pitch in a discord, it is easier to establish one's relationship to the total sound.

In Example 104 (Milhaud), we see immediately the change in style: more chromatic writing, stranger and more difficult rhythms.

Example 105 (Stravinsky) presents one of the most famous pages in all of twentieth-century writing, taken from Stravinsky's *Rite of Spring*, "The Sacrificial Dance: The Chosen One." Here we see the very essence of modern rhythmic problems. See also Example 114, page 218.

Example 104. Milhaud, *Concertino d'été* for Viola and nine instruments (measures 111–112). © 1952 by Heugel & Cie. Editeurs, Paris. Reprinted by permission.

*The solo instrument in most orchestral scores is placed just above the strings and below the percussion.

Example 105. Stravinsky, *The Rite of Spring*, Sacrificial Dance: The Chosen One (measures 1–10). © Copyright 1921 by Edition Russe de Musique; Copyright Renewed. Copyright and Renewal assigned to Boosey & Hawkes, Inc. Revised Edition © Copyright 1948 by Boosey & Hawkes, Inc. Reprinted by Permission.

Note: The student will find editions in which the second and fifth measures of the passage quoted read $\frac{2}{16}, \frac{5}{16}$ shown here.

Note: *Bouché et cuivré* in the French horn parts mean "muffled (stopped horn) and brassy."

205

The Aleatoric Score

Finally, a sample of an aleatoric score is presented (Example 106). In this particular score, the standard instrumentation is called for. The figures above each measure signify "approximate seconds." Pitches are indicated in certain places, but the performer is left to choose his or her own in other places. The center line in each case represents the "approximate middle range for that instrument." Linear contour shows the direction in which the notes are to progress. Recurrent perpendicular lines state repetitions of the note or figure. *Aleatoric scores explore the minds of the performers.* Such scores are accompanied by a table of signs as the individual composer has used them. Here, crescendos and diminuendos are stated by words. In many scores, the broadening of a line or figure means crescendo; the diminution of size means diminuendo.

In the conducting of the aleatoric score, the technique of time-beating in ONE functions much of the time. Each written barline is clearly indicated by the baton. There is no metrical time-beating in many scores, but the conductor's hands show entrances, cutoffs, and dynamic changes. Players and conductor are "creating" in the process of realizing the score as written.

The Pennington score for band furnishes an introduction to this type of score writing. We follow it with a prestigious work for the symphony orchestra, some measures from Leslie Bassett's *Echoes from an Invisible World*. Here we see measures written in an unmetered notation, inserted into otherwise measured writing, with stated pitches throughout. The performer knows what to play instead of composing on the instant as in completely aleatoric music. Notice the **unmetered time signature** at the beginning of the second page of Example 107—an invention of Mr. Bassett's.

Note: Leslie Bassett won the Prix de Rome, 1961–63, and a Pulitzer Prize in 1966. *Echoes from an Invisible World* was one of the six commission pieces by six composers, underwritten by six major orchestras, for the United States bicentennial celebration. *Echoes* was premiered by the Philadelphia Orchestra (who commissioned it) under Eugene Ormandy on February 26 and 27 and March 2, 1976. It was performed September 26, 27, and 28, 1985, by the Detroit Symphony. There were two performances in 1987 by the Syracuse Symphony Orchestra, and a performance in 1989 by the orchestra of the State University of New York at Potsdam. The recording is CRI No. 429, with the Baltimore Symphony, Sergiu Commissiona conducting. CRI also has issued a compact disc recording, No. 667, which contains *Echoes from an Invisible World* and two other pieces by Bassett.

Example 106. Pennington, *Apollo*, Aleatoric Piece for Band. Page 2 of the full score.

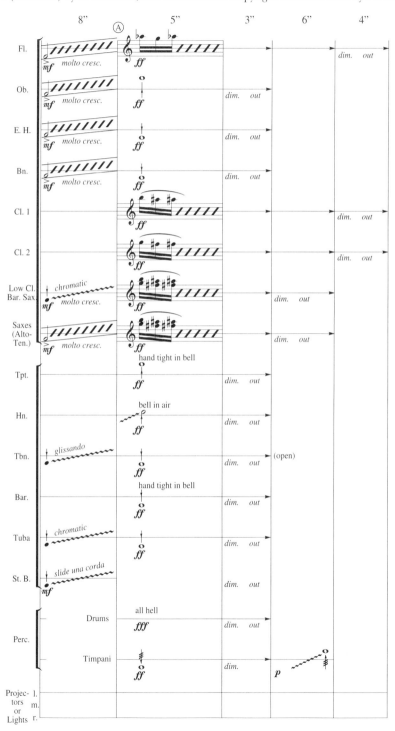

Example 107. Bassett, *Echoes from an Invisible World.* First movement (measure 6 and follow-ing). Copyright © 1976 by C. F. Peters Corporation. International Copyright Secured. All Rights Reserved. Used by Permission of the Copyright Owner.

* Bass Drum inflects pitch by pressure on head.

** Harp harmonics sound **8va.** (Harp here in unison with String entrances)

Exercises for Practice:
Acquaintance with Instrumental Scores

1. Memorize the order of instruments in a standard score such as the *Leonore No. 3 Overture*, Example 81.

2. Familiarize yourself with the order of instruments in the larger form of the score. See Appendix B, Part 1.

3. Study all the full-page excerpts in this chapter, comparing format, transpositions, and so on. Band and orchestra.

4. Analyze each excerpt for the number of parts actually sounding. Notice where the scoring condenses to three or four parts.

5. Go through the score sheets and name each instrument when it enters after a few beats of rest.

6. Take the viola part (middle line is middle C) and play it through on the piano or on your own major instrument.

7. Practice the time-beating gestures for all the excerpts given while either singing or thinking-in-pitches the melody line. Pay attention to the switching of the melodic outline from one instrument to another. If necessary, mark these changes lightly in colored pencil.

8. Refer to Appendix A. Study the seating charts for the standard grouping of instruments in the several types of orchestras given. Then practice the excerpts in this chapter, directing your attention to the place where this or that instrument is situated in the orchestral setup. The orchestral seating is more standardized than is the band seating.

Recommended Reference Readings

BAMBERGER, CARL, *The Conductor's Art.* The section on "Conducting Revisited" by Gunther Schuller. Interesting ideas on contemporary music.

BATTISTI, FRANK, and ROBERT GAROFALO, *Guide to Score Study for Wind Band Conductors.* Excellent!

GREEN, ELIZABETH A. H., and NICOLAI MALKO, *The Conductor's Score* (formerly *The Conductor and His Score*). Many hints on score study, including marking the score.

JACOB, GORDON, *How to Read a Score.* Chapter 6, pp. 39–46: "Aural Imagination." Very fine examples stressing solo passages for the various instruments of the orchestra are to be found herein, as an aid to recognizing these instruments by ear.

READ, GARDNER, *Thesaurus of Orchestral Devices.* A large book containing hundreds of musical examples showing the various uses of the instruments in their many aspects.

14 Choral Conducting

Part One: Score Structure

The three- or four-line choral score is an effective approach to score study in general. All parts are singable and the harmonic outline is clear. Compare Example 112 with Example 111 (pages 216 and 215).

Traditional and Modern Scores

Various types of choral scores are shown in the following pages. As you examine them, follow each part through, then correlate rhythms and harmonization beat by beat upward from bass note to soprano. Pay attention to where the melody lies. It is not always in the soprano. Remember to drop the treble-clef tenor line down one octave as you peruse the scores.

Choral scores range from two to a dozen or more parts for the singers. Example 108 presents an early two-part work. Note the C-clef writing. See page 212.

In some scores, the piano merely doubles the voice parts, lending support thereby but not adding to the musical thought. Example 109 shows such a use of the piano.

In other scores, the piano plays an entirely independent part and in many cases must be conducted as such. Example 110 presents an excerpt in which the accompaniment is given to two pianos, requiring some definite attention from the conductor.

In still other scores, the piano part is entirely lacking; these are called scores for *a cappella* performance, that is, for unaccompanied voices. Example 111 shows an *a cappella* work with a piano part marked "for rehearsal only."

The study of three-part scores (as for three women's voices, Example 112) makes an excellent background for the later study of the orchestral scores of Haydn, Mozart, and even Beethoven where three-part writing is often employed. The auditory recognition of such a structure, harmonically, will come in aptly in many places in scores of larger form.

Scores for large choral ensembles may divide one or another part: first and second soprano, first and second tenor, and so on. Or a work may be written for a double choir composed of two choral groups that are relatively independent of each other. Such writing is often encountered in opera scores, and a case in point is shown in Example 113.

In examining this excerpt, the student will see that it comprises two solo voices; a five-part choir, which, in the staging, is a group of townspeople standing outside the church; and a second choir, which depicts the singing of the people inside the church. Attention should be paid to the brackets in the form of heavy vertical lines outlining these two choirs on the score. These heavy lines are placed at the beginning of the staff, before the clef signs. They will later become a helpful part of the orchestral score study.

Now let us look at the music itself. Notice that in the second measure, only five tones are actually being sung. The solo voices double the notes written on the top two lines of the "External Chorus" parts. (Santuzza is the soprano and Lucia the contralto.) Notice that the second choir is singing the same pitches as the first choir (measure 2) but independence of parts is established by the rhythm and the words. In measure 3, the chord is expanded. The piano part here shows independence from the choral parts. It is a reduction of the orchestral accompaniment.

Note: In musical comedy, instruments are indicated over entrances in the piano-conductor score.

Finally, Example 114 shows eleven measures from Gian Carlo Menotti's *Help! Help! The Globolinks Are Coming.* It is scored for eight soloists, twelve children (a few of them with minor solos), orchestra, and tapes. Here one can see how the tape cues are incorporated into the score and how the stage directions function. This section occurs before the first soloist begins to sing. A companion one-act opera by Menotti is *The Unicorn, the Gorgon, and the Manticore, or The Three Sundays of a Poet.* In this opus a new form emerges. The stage characters perform entirely in pantomime while a chorus replaces the orchestra in the pit, singing the story with charming tongue-in-cheek running comment.

Example 108. J. S. Bach, Cantata No. 212 *(Peasant),* for soprano and bass voices. First duet (measures 1–5).

Example 109. Dvořák, *Stabat Mater.* Blessed Jesu, Fount of Mercy: anthem for mixed voices (words adapted by the Rev. Benjamin Webb) (measures 1–12). Taken from MASTER CHORUSES. Copyright © 1933 by G. Schirmer, Inc. Used by Permission.

Example 110. Copland, *The Tender Land.* Choral Square Dance: Stomp Your Foot, for male voices with piano duet accompaniment (words by Horace Everett) (measures 1–20). © Copyright 1954 by Aaron Copland. Copyright Renewed. Reprinted by permission of Aaron Copland, Copyright Owner and Boosey & Hawkes, Inc., Sole Publishers and Licencee.

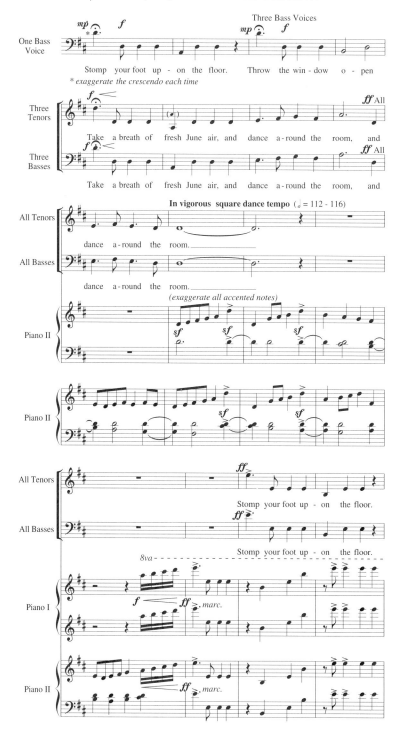

Example 111. Orlando di Lasso, *Good-Day, Sweetheart.* Chanson for mixed voices, *a cappella,* from the A Cappella Chorus Book, edited by Christiansen-Cain (words by Pierre Ronsard; trans. A. C. Curtis) (measures 1–11). 1933 by the Oliver Ditson Co. Reprinted By Permission Of The Publisher, Theodore Presser Company.

Example 112. Palestrina, *Tell Me, What Master Hand.* Canzonet for female voices (ed. and trans. Henry Coates) (measures 1–7). © Novello and Co., Ltd. Used By Permission. Sole Representative, Theodore Presser Company.

Example 113. Mascagni, *Cavalleria Rusticana*. Scene and Prayer (Schirmer's Standard Secular Choruses, No. 2415, page 30). Reprinted by permission of G. Schirmer, Inc.

*Piano reduction of the orchestral score.

Example 114. Menotti, *Help! Help! The Globolinks Are Coming.* Text and music by Gian Carlo Menotti. Piano Score, p. 5, from rehearsal numbers 6 to 7 (eleven measures). © 1969 by G. Schirmer, Inc. International Copyright Secured. Used by Permission.

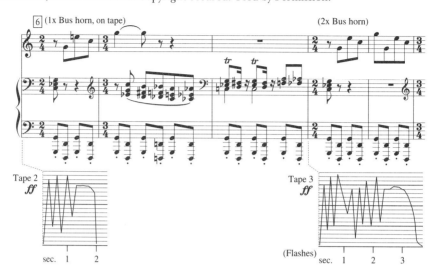

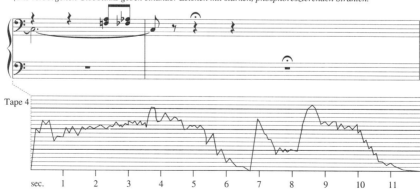

Note: Read also the section on musicianship, pages 231–240. Much of it applies equally to choral conducting. As you read, substitute words as follows: For "play," read "sing"; for "instruments," read "voices"; for "instrumental," read "choral." See also Appendix A for seating charts.

Exercises for Practice: Beginning the Score Reading

1. Take any easy four-part choral composition, preferably with the C-clef tenor printing, and play the voice parts on the piano, reading from the bass note upward on each beat. As soon as one beat is played, sustain it with the pedal and immediately begin to prepare the hands on the notes of the next beat, again *starting with the bass and proceeding upward.* It will be slow work for those who are not expert pianists. If you belong in this category, do not worry about the rhythm at first. Just get the mechanic established of the upward reading and the recognition of the notes in the various clefs. Place the fingers silently, one at a time, on the proper note as you look at each part, and when all notes are correctly under the fingers, play the chord. Sustain it with the pedal while you place, silently, the next chord.

2. Sing each part throughout (same composition as in exercise 1). Jump an octave in the part as necessary to make it fit your voice. Pay attention to the half-step and whole-step intervals as they occur. Concentrate on the pitches this time through, and let the words go. In singing long skips, the unskilled singer will do well to imagine mentally the sound of the missing scale tones between the terminal notes of the skip. In this exercise, start with the soprano line.

3. Sing the notes on each beat vertically upward from the bass note. Place the pitches in your own voice range. Such an exercise is also fine if played on your major instrument, whatever it may be.

4. Conduct the number throughout, handling an imaginary chorus.

5. Now give the words a run-through, beating their articulations instead of the time, just as a practice routine. Sustain with the hand the syllables falling on the long notes of the music.

6. Practice conducting all the longer examples given in this chapter. Imagine the sound of the voices and piano as you do so. Pay attention to the mood as set by the accompanying words of the poem. Try to depict it with your gestures.

Part Two: Score Performance

Choral Style

Choral music has come through a number of stages in its historical development. Early music, largely church-oriented, was sung *a cappella*. There was no recurrent accentuation. The words themselves tied the music together, and stress was laid on a level, continuous dynamic for all long tones. The conductor's hands, instead of beating time, showed the entrances and exits of voices, the length of the sustained tones, the contours of the phrase, and the rise and fall of the several parts.

This style gradually succumbed to the idea that long notes should be made to "come alive." The *bel canto* school of singing took over. This was a style of great lyricism, stressing beauty of tone and the legato line. The sustained vowel sound, when interrupted by the articulation of a consonant, would be interrupted as little as possible. One should feel the legato line as continuous throughout in spite of the consonant interruption. Instrumental accompaniment by stringed instruments became popular. Over the years, the accompaniment emerged from its background position to become an active entity in its own right. Schubert's extraordinary talent for catching the spirit of the poem and transferring it to the music is given credit for this freeing of the accompaniment. Schumann continued this development, and the *Lied* became a duet of sorts between the voice and the piano.

Contrasts: Choral and Instrumental

In choral music, the tangible emotion set by the words is heightened by the music. In instrumental music, the emotional appeal relies upon the intangibility of the music itself. In both categories, however, the historical period in which the music was written shows its influence on our twentieth-century interpretations.

Let us examine for a moment the language aspect of style. A language such as Italian, which has many words ending in vowels, lends itself naturally to *bel canto*. In contrast, a language that bristles with consonants (as does German or Russian) will acquire a somewhat harsher type of articulation and therefore a different stylistic sound in making its musical contribution.

Dynamics in choral composition have an emotional basis. The emotion states the dynamic. (One does not sing a lullaby with either the same dynamic or the same emotional content one would use for an operatic cry of anguish.) In instrumental music, the process is often reversed. The dynamic sounded induces the emotion in the listener. Emotions become tangible in choral music because the words demand it. They exist equally in instrumental music, but they are less tangible.

With all of this in mind, let us now study to conduct.

Preparing for Rehearsal

Here are some practical things to notice as you prepare.

1. *Horizontal motion.* The horizontal or forward motion in each voice in a choral composition should have a certain inevitableness about it. Wide skips between notes in the horizontal line are always difficult and especially so in the inner voices. Notice these as they occur in the score, and solve their problems before the rehearsal begins. Much valuable knowledge is gained through attention to the horizontal line of the choral score.

2. ***Vertical relationship.*** The vertical relationship of the parts is their harmonic relationship. Good ensemble is dependent upon the vertical synchronization of the parts. The best way to study this facet of the score is to sing each beat from the bottom upward, bass to soprano. This clarifies the harmonic outline in the conductor's mind.

3. ***Difficult entrances.*** There are times when the singers have difficulty in accurately locating their entry note following several beats of rest. Often the conductor can clarify such places by calling attention to the sounding of the same pitch a beat or two before by another voice. Example 115 is an excellent illustration of this. The entrance of the new part is made each time on the identical pitch as the *last sung note* in the preceding voice before the new voice enters. In the first measure of the example, the alto sings B on the eighth note just before the soprano enters on that same pitch. Each entrance is similar.

Search diligently during score study to locate possible pitch and rhythm problems. Plan solutions and take them to rehearsal with you.

Example 115. Galbraith, *Out of the Silence* (measures 12–15). 1919 by The Oliver Ditson Co. Reprinted by permission of Theodore Presser Company, Bryn Mawr, Pennsylvania.

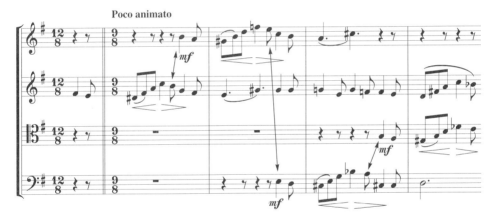

4. ***Breathing in long phrases.*** When long phrases must be sustained, the conductor may suggest "staggered" breathing in which the singers do not breathe simultaneously, but each catches a quick breath as he or she needs it and then reenters the music, thus preserving the sustained tone quality. A breath taken just after a strong beat is less noticeable than one taken before a strong beat. This principle may also be applied to slurred passages. When the breath is insufficient to carry through the slur, take a new breath *after* a note that falls *on* a beat and preferably on a strong beat of the measure.

5. ***Tone quality.*** The conductor of the vocal group is working with what might be termed the most *personal* type of music, namely, the instrument within the self. In everyday life, subjective attitudes are usually apparent in the speaking voice. The choral conductor should face this fact and train the singers to set the mood of the song itself, regardless of their individual and personal feelings at the time.

Any spoken vowel, when sustained long enough, will take on the pitch of a musical sound. Beauty of vowel sound and clarity of consonant articulation are to be stressed. In score study, pay attention to the long vowels. When conducting, see that the singer's mouth is properly opened, without throat tension.

Many beautiful effects may be accomplished by giving the third of the chord spe-cial attention whenever the tone quality is weak or thin. Strengthening this note will add luster to the sound. The third of the chord is also one of the links in fine intona-tion. When a chorus begins to flat, it is frequently because the voices singing the third of the chord have been careless in perfecting the intonation. The seventh of the scale is also dangerous in this respect. Perfect intonation enhances tone quality.

6. Since the choral profession is apparently divided on the next point, we shall briefly state the two views without urging the acceptance of either. The problem con-cerns the vowel that is slurred over several notes. Example 116 is pertinent.

Example 116. Palestrina, *Tell Me, What Master Hand* (quoted in full in Example 78). By permission of Novello and Co., Ltd.

One hears, at times, the articulation of a soft *h* attack in the slurred vowel as the pitch changes. Certain very fine teachers argue against the use of this device for two rea-sons: (1) It tends to interrupt the legato line, which is the main reason for the writing of the slur; and (2) it tends to build breathiness into the tone. Other very fine teachers sanction its use to prevent the glissando that often mars slurred runs in vocal execution. Some opera singers use it, some do not. The young conductor of vocal groups is advised to talk with the finest vocal teachers he or she can contact on this point. The use of this device may depend upon the size of the auditorium and the heft of the accompaniment.

7. ***Final consonants.*** The ending of most tones is given more special attention in choral music than in instrumental performance because many English words end in a final consonant that must be articulated cleanly and together by the singers. This is especially true of *sustained* tones ending in a consonant. The cutoff should be shown in such cases, especially before rests.

Final *s* sounds cause much trouble. They should be spoken softly and placed late in the beat. Final *d*'s and *g*'s, when given clean-cut pronunciation, add immensely to the clarity of the words. There is a tendency for choruses to sustain final *m*'s, *n*'s, and *r*'s instead of the vowel preceding them. These letters, too, should be delayed until the last possible moment.

The clean *articulation* of the consonant makes the speech understandable.* Since the words carry the story of the music, if they cannot be understood, there is no point to singing them. Their ultimate sense depends upon the distinctness of the consonant and the correctness of the vowels.†

---

*There is the story of Chaliapin, the great Russian basso of the past, standing backstage in the opera house during rehearsal and singing over and over the Russian word for God *(Bog)*, fight-ing out an articulation of both consonants that would freeze the blood of the audience when the dramatic moment should arrive.

†The young choral conductor is urged to study diligently the Marshal book on English dic-tion. (See the Reference Readings at the end of this chapter.)

The choral conductor should listen constantly and consciously to the words as the chorus sings them. Too often the conductor's own familiarity with the song gives him or her the illusion of good pronunciation on the part of the singers. Listen to *hear* what your chorus is saying.

A fine exercise for diction is that of having the whole chorus sing together one of the Gilbert and Sullivan "patter songs." It is great fun and an excellent exercise for the tongue.

Conducting the Recitative

The recitative is, fundamentally, an insert in a vocal composition that is to be sung as if spoken. It is often relatively unrhythmic in structure, as speech is unrhythmic. Its purpose is to carry forward the story. It serves to brief the audience on what has transpired before the action continues.

Being of a spoken character, the recitative is usually not fully accompanied throughout. Either it is punctuated by single chords that state the harmonic structure, or it is supported by sustained tones of a static character that change with the harmony as necessary. The conductor's biggest job in the recitative, therefore, is to see that these chords and changes in harmony occur at exactly the right instant, regardless of the unrhythmic character of the general takt. This requires finesse in the timing plus an understanding of the following points:

1. If a chord is to be articulated ON a beat, it should be preceded by a secure and well-timed preparatory gesture that says clearly, "Here it comes."

2. If a chord is to be played *after* a beat, the gesture of syncopation will be used, preceded by a rhythmic staccato preparatory beat.

The first two chords in Example 117 will be conducted as described in point 1. The entrance at the end of the second measure will require the treatment given in point 2, unless, perchance, the soloist keeps a steady takt throughout this measure, in which case simple time-beating may continue with the gesture of syncopation used on beat Three.

3. When the recitative is accompanied by sustained tones, those tones must be played softly and in good balance with each other. They must also be matched against the power of the singer's voice. Since the soloist will take whatever liberties are necessary with the rhythm, the conductor must often resort to a type of irregular time-beating.

Example 118 lends itself to a fairly regular time-beating, but sustained tones have a faculty for sounding a little late with the beat-point. Be doubly alert to anticipate the attacks.

4. The first beat of each measure must be clearly indicated by the baton as the measure passes. This is of utmost importance, since the takt within the measure may vary rhythmically. A simple dead gesture from the wrist (down and immediately up) is all that is necessary. In the case of several measures of tutti rest, the conductor may make a series of several quick downbeats, each beat signifying one measure, and then just wait for the singer to finish those measures.

Example 117. Handel, *Messiah.* No. 5: Recitative, Thus Saith the Lord (last five measures).

*Customarily, such closing chords are played *after* the singer finishes, starting on the last beat and ending on the first beat of an added measure.

Example 118. Mendelssohn, *Elijah,* Op. 70, No. 12: Recitative and chorus (measures 6–10).

5. After the indication of the first beat of the measure, the baton may do one of several things in handling the rest of the measure. It may show nothing except this first beat, which is often done when the entire measure is a tutti rest for the accompanying instruments. Or it may design the beats within the measure according to a rhythmic takt. This is done when the singer, for the moment, is executing a phrase that lends itself to rhythmic speaking on pitch. Or the baton may design quickly all beats of the tutti rests and stop in a position of readiness for the beat that is to be played by the musicians.

6. The conductor must know thoroughly the singer's part, words and music, if he or she is to be successful with the timing in the recitative.

The Operetta

If the show has music, the music must be good. If it is an operetta, everyone should have fun performing it.

In choosing the operetta, the choral conductor should consider carefully the abilities of the voices at his or her disposal. The conductor should also set up committees among the chorus members to take care of much of the non-musical business (ticket sales, publicity, costumes, and so on). The dramatics coach and the customary stage crews should be enlisted to help as well as the orchestra conductor.

Here are some useful hints. (1) Drill the chorus, the soloists, and the orchestra each separately first: the chorus for words and action; the soloists to know their parts thoroughly—the whole show depends on them when they are soloing; the orchestra to read through the music, to mark cuts, to check the parts for wrong notes, to indicate the number of verses and sometimes "cue lines." Stage-exit repeats will have to wait for a stage rehearsal. Anything that can waste time in the full rehearsal should be taken care of beforehand. (2) Have the chorus and the soloists on stage first without the orchestra. Get all stage business working well before bringing in the orchestra. (3) At the first stage rehearsal (without orchestra), make sure that everyone on stage can see the conductor in the pit. Assign certain leaders who must watch the conductor more intently (preferably strong singers). (4) After the speaking parts, it is better to "crash the last line" with the orchestra introduction than to have a wait. The wait kills the show. A good stage show must not be allowed to sag. Call the orchestra to attention before the last speech starts. Train it to *get the music ready for the next number as soon as the end of the previous number is played.* This saves fumbling when it is time to play. (5) Bring the orchestra "into the act." Their introductions and interludes (even one-measure interludes while the singers take a breath) "set the mood" and must be so played. Orchestra dynamics should *project on the interludes;* build them up for those single measures that are important. (6) One fine opera conductor told the author, "Always include *one really slow number* somewhere in the performance. The change of pace sparks the rest of the performance." (7) One solo violin is more apparent dynamically than are two violins playing in unison. (8) Tell the soloists, "In general we shall follow you, so feel free to lead. However, there are certain places where you will have to follow the conductor or the orchestra will not be with you. These places concern entrances on a fraction of an upbeat (usually occurring after fermatas), when the orchestra must play either *with* the singer or on the following beat. In such cases the singer must take the cue for continuing from the conductor." (9) In school performances where the solo voices are weak (especially in junior high school), have the orchestra use the real "musical comedy style," very short notes articulating the beat but with little or no sustaining power. Strings: off-the-string bowings (spiccato), or using a position near the frog of the bow and lifting after all short notes (quarters or less). If the music calls for sustained tones, drop them back to *double piano* immediately after the attack to let the voices through. (10) Do *not* use the piano with the orchestra in performance if it is possible to avoid it. It usually leads out too loudly and the orchestra is blamed for the excessive dynamic. Warn the soloists on stage (and the chorus) that there will not be quite as emphatic an articulation from the orchestra as from the piano. Get them to listen intently to the orchestral sound during the rehearsals.

Who Conducts the Performance?

In the professional theater, opera, and musical comedy, it is always the orchestra conductor who does the performance. In school presentations, however, the choral conductor may take over with, perhaps, the orchestra conductor conducting the overture. Whichever conductor functions, there are facets of conducting that will need special attention.

The **chorus conductor** has been through many rehearsals with the singers and pianist while teaching the operetta. When he or she stands in front of the orchestra, the first tendency will be to show the cutoff for the chorus (at the end of a song) and then to stop conducting—leaving the orchestra stranded. (An orchestra is not like a self-sufficient pianist.) The orchestra measures that continue after the singers have finished must be conducted. They are often written to give time for stage entrances and exits, and their interest has to be kept vital throughout.

Next, the choral conductor should account for the *downbeat in every measure*. The orchestra players depend upon this to "keep the place" when they have a few measures of rest in their individual parts. The readable beat pattern now assumes importance above and beyond what is needed for the chorus. Further, the conductor's hands must not be held so high that the orchestra players cannot see them.

When the **orchestra conductor** does the performance, he or she may tend to forget to make proper cutoffs for the stage performers, thus producing ragged endings. The conductor will have to remember to lift his or her hands when those signals are directed to the singers on stage. Phrasings are important (for breathing), final consonants have to be given attention, and eye contact with the stage is imperative. The left hand can become invaluable in giving a warning gesture a measure or two before a chorus or solo entrance.

Both conductors, working in the pit, will be remote from the singers. The tone of the orchestra may reach the audience a fraction ahead of the singers' sound. The singers may miss the percussiveness of the piano and may therefore lag a bit. Synchronization and balance should be checked from the back of the auditorium during rehearsals.

Dramatic timing becomes important. Variety of tempo spices the show. The conductor should guard against the unconscious habit of permitting his or her own natural pulse-beat to influence the tempo of the music. On stage, the performers have to be trained not to "crash a laugh" but to wait for the audience to "simmer down." The dramatic quality of a fermata and the intensity of a silence that may follow it, or the suddenness of surprise in a *forte* bass drum beat or a cymbal crash, all come under the heading of dramatic timing.

The fine stage performance carries the audience with it by presenting clearly the literary content of the words and the beauty of the music. The excellent rendition of either should not be made the excuse for a poor rendition of the other. The words tell the story. The music heightens the emotional drive. Each must justify the existence of the other.

The Church Organist-Conductor

Finally a word or two for the organist-conductor who directs the choir from a position at the organ. Here the development of the left-hand techniques becomes imperative. Since the ear hears quickest the highest pitches, the audience will not miss omitted notes so obviously if they are in the bass (left-hand) part at the organ. Practice performing the accompaniments using the necessary conducting gestures. If this is not done, the rhythm may be momentarily upset by the functioning of the conducting hand. Sometimes mirrors have to be rigged so that the chorus members can see the organist's hand signals.

Read also Chapters 15, on musicianship, and 16, on memorizing and etiquette.

Exercises for Practice: Difficult Rhythms

Problems 1–3: Think in sixteenth-notes while beating in the stated meters.
Problems 4–5: Think in identical, steady eighth notes throughout. ♪ = ♪.

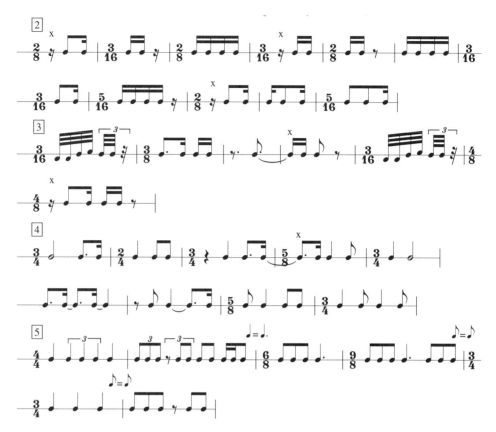

Figure 60. Contemporary Rhythms from Choral Repertoire. Collected by Professor Thomas Hilbish, Choral Conductor. Used by permission.

Exercises for Practice: Choral Interpretation

1. Take the assigned score for class performance and study it following the seven headings given in this chapter on pages 220–222. Thereafter try to synthesize these various aspects into a single, total interpretation of the piece. Set the mood and see the composition in its entirety. The audience is not interested in details. It is interested in the *song*. Failure to synthesize brings with it the same result one gets in plucking the feathers from a bird one by one. In the end, most of the beauty is gone.

2. Prepare to conduct the song without looking at the score. Leave the speaking of the words to the singers who are reading the music, and turn your attention to the mood and the sound of the final result.

Recommended Reference Readings

ADLER, SAMUEL, *Choral Conducting: An Anthology.* A fine selection of music classified according to conducting problems; includes contemporary works.

BALK, WESLEY, *The Complete Singer-Actor.* A method based on the brain research mentioned in Chapter 5 herein, p. 71.

BRAITHWAITE, WARWICK, *The Conductor's Art.* Chapter 13, pp. 83–98: "The Conducting of Choral Works." Part 3, pp. 101–176, devoted to the conducting of opera.

BUSCH, BRIAN R., *The Complete Choral Conductor: Gesture and Method.*

COWARD, HENRY, *Choral Technique and Interpretation.* Pp. 69–87: "Words, Articulation, Diction"; pp. 88–111: "Musical Expression"; pp. 203–248: "Analysis of the *Messiah.*"

DAVISON, ARCHIBALD T., *Choral Conducting.* Chapter 5, pp. 44–73: "Choral Technique." The instrumental conductor is urged to read this chapter.

DECKER, HAROLD A., and JULIUS HERFORD, eds., *Choral Conducting: A Symposium.* Chapter 1, "The Development of a Choral Instrument" by Howard Swan. Don't miss this one! Also Chapter 4 "The Choral Conductor and Twentieth-Century Choral Music" by Daniel Moe.

DECKER, HAROLD A., and COLLEEN J. KIRK, *Choral Conducting: Focus on Communication.*

DEMAREE, ROBERT W., and DON V MOSES, *The Complete Conductor.* Chapters 9–12 on choral conducting. Deals with fundamentals and rehearsing and is very complete in handling choral works from Baroque through contemporary.

HEFFERNAN, CHARLES W., *Choral Music: Technique and Artistry.* The whole book is applicable.

HOWERTON, GEORGE, *Technique and Style in Choral Singing.* Part 2, pp. 79–187, deals with styles of the several historical periods of musical composition and of the various countries and geographical influences as applied to choral singing.

JONES, ARCHIE M., *Techniques of Choral Conducting.* Chapter 3, pp. 37–45: "Diction" (tables on the specific pronunciation of words, vowels, and consonants in Chapter 3); Chapter 4, pp. 46–56: "Choral Interpretation"; Appendix E, pp. 108–134: Interpretative Analyses.

MARSHALL, MADELEINE, *The Singer's Manual of English Diction.* A comprehensive and very complete manual of this important aspect of singing.

15 Applied Musicianship: Band, Orchestra, Chorus

The conductor's musicianship is on display as the baton is raised to start the rehearsal. The rehearsal is where creation begins. The skeleton of the written notes puts on its living garment, transforms itself into living sound, and becomes live music. Just what kind of a life it has depends upon *your* musicianship—your imagination, your technique and that of your musicians.

Band or Orchestra?

Are different conducting techniques used for band and orchestra? Fundamentally, the technique is the same. But in its application it leans a bit toward one or the other organization. H. Robert Reynolds expresses the band approach this way:

> Two Principles of Band Conducting: (1) The way you move through space [gestures] is the same as the air moves through the instrument. It can be with intensity, or with breadth, or with depth of sound. Or it can be loud with intensity, or soft with great intensity. Show the resistance of the air in your gestures! (2) The way the conductor shows the beat-point is the way the player attacks the sound. How you conduct the beat is the way the attack sounds. In fermatas keep the baton moving to show the progress of the sound.*

*Used by Permission

Orchestrally, the actual technique is the same, but the conductor is conscious of the sweep of the bow across the strings and of the variety of staccatos possible in the various bow techniques. The bow, not the breath, is the phrasing. Also serious attention is paid to similarity of attack and style of execution among the several string sections and the winds—that they correlate to produce one interpretation, not two different interpretations proceeding simultaneously in the one performance.

Musicianship Factors: Orchestra, Band, Chorus

Tessitura of the Melody Line

The melody is clearest heard when it occupies a place in the score-range not cluttered up by accompanying instruments in the same octave.*

Danger: When the melody is written in octaves for flute and oboe, the tessitura lies in the oboe octave. When both instruments are played perfectly in tune, the oboe tends to blot out the flute and also a soprano voice in unison.

Projecting the Melody

When the melody does not sound clearly, the **first** temptation is to ask the soloist to play louder—to project more. Far better, first, would be to **temper down the accompaniment**—a thing the conductor has every right to insist upon. If the melody cannot be heard, it is probably the conductor's fault. The conductor's ear, not the composer's dynamic markings, must be the judge.

The Melody Accompanied by Sustained Tones

A soloist may be accorded certain expressive liberties when the accompaniment is in the form of sustained tones. A slight rubato in the phrasing will not upset anything. But when the reiterated-note accompaniment exists, the soloist must hew to the line rhythmically. Any lack of total precision in the rhythmic accompaniment, to accommodate the soloist, will be instantly noticed by the audience. Composers know these things and write accordingly.

Balance

The interpretation of the dynamic markings in the score for the large ensemble is something quite different from their significance in solo music. In the latter, one can accept the dynamic at its face value. In the orchestra or the

---

*One remembers a band competition where the melody disappeared for some eight measures in rendition after rendition. The melody was scored in the flutes on the five lines of the staff, undoubled, with thirteen instruments accompanying! An impossible situation! A bit of rewriting was warranted.

band the **marked dynamics are only guidelines,** open to all kinds of variations and interpretations in performance. The underlying reason for this is that no composer can predict the musical prowess of every organization that may play his or her music. Therefore the marked dynamic becomes a variable quantity to be intelligently interpreted by the conductor and the performers. The conductor should have a mental concept of what he or she wants to hear in performance. The conductor then works with the instrumental balance to achieve the desired sound.

The Two Systems of Marking Dynamics

There are two generally accepted systems of marking dynamics. The earliest one, historically, is the block dynamic, wherein all instruments (or voices) in the score are marked *forte* at the same time; all are marked *piano* simultaneously. If a crescendo or a diminuendo is desired, it is identically marked for all parts. The composer has given a general indication of his or her ideas. Today, however, many composers make an attempt to balance the score by marking varied dynamics among the several sections of the ensemble. This gives a clue as to what the composer considers important.

Interpretation of the Block Dynamic   A generally accepted principle in dealing with the block dynamic is to **play the melody one degree louder than marked, the accompaniment one degree softer.** There is also one other consideration: A *forte* played on a French horn will be much more powerful than it would be on an alto clarinet. This means that the instruments have to adjust until a uniform *forte* results. Further, it takes four violins to double the power of two and sixteen to double the power of four. Note that it proceeds by the square of the number in the violins. In studying score, try to imagine the sound as played by *your* ensemble.*

The Second Type of Dynamic Marking   The marking of a special dynamic for each section of the ensemble also has a historical basis. In Dvořák's orchestral score for the *Slavonic Dance,* Op. 46, No. 1, in C major, at measure 99, the violas and bassoons (melody line) are marked *forte.* The other strings together with the third and fourth horns are marked *double piano,* while the first horn and clarinet have a *piano* indication. What a struggle it is for the conductor of the less-than-professional group to get the accompanying players to "shush down" when they hear the *forte* in the bassoons and violas!

Continuity of Dynamic

There are many places in the orchestral scores of Haydn, Mozart, Beethoven, and others where a small motif is played in succession by different instruments (for example, flute, oboe, clarinet, bassoon, or cello). Such places

---

*Rimski-Korsakov, in his *Principles of Orchestration,* pp. 33–35, has attempted to compare the relative strengths of the various instruments.

need careful dynamic rehearsing. **The given dynamic should sound with equal loudness as the motif bounces around from instrument to instrument.** If the dynamic continuity is not preserved, the musical result is ragged. Each player should temper his or her sound to preserve the overall line of the passage.

A second type of dynamic continuity has to do with crescendos and diminuendos. These should progress smoothly, not by leaps and bounds. Beethoven particularly is fond of adding instruments to the ensemble as the crescendo builds. Instruments entering should do so softly and then gradually build up their own dynamic so that the crescendo does not suddenly take a great leap forward. In a long diminuendo, each instrument should soften before disappearing. Crescendos and diminuendos are smooth lines not interrupted by peaks and valleys.*

Customary Adjustments in Dynamic Markings

There are certain things that the fine professional musician does as a matter of course when performing in the large ensemble. The first of these concerns a passage in which the whole ensemble arrives at a *double forte* climax and then all instruments drop out except for one section, usually marked *piano.* (In the orchestra, the section that remains is often the violas.) In this circumstance the composer's marked *piano* does *not* apply to the remaining section. The composer's *piano* dynamic has occurred automatically simply because most of the instruments have suddenly ceased to play. If the remaining section actually performs *piano,* the audience hears nothing for a moment. There is a hole in the music. The section that continues should play *forte* for an extra beat or two, establishing itself, and then diminuendo rapidly to the required *piano.* In this way the continuity of the music is preserved. The remaining section has to have strength enough to carry the weight of the whole ensemble on its shoulders momentarily when the other instruments cease to play.

Another dynamic variation concerns passages in which a certain note is repeated continuously, interrupted here and there by a single note of a different pitch. This odd note should be subtly projected above the surrounding reiterated notes. Such adjustments are too delicate for the composer to mark.

Repeated notes (or sustained tones) leading into a melodic line should crescendo slightly just before taking over the melody. In this way the attention of the audience is guided to hear the *first* note of the melody.

To enrich the sound of a chord, strengthen the third of the chord. This effect can add greatly to a long diminuendo from sound to silence at the end of a piece, but it must be done with finesse.

When the **brasses have a sustained *double forte* chord,** it is very easy for them to blot out the rest of the ensemble. In both band and orchestra, such sustained *forte*s **should be attacked at the marked dynamic and then immediately tempered down so that the moving voices are clearly heard.** It is the moving

*The reader will find information from professional performers on the interpretation of marked dynamics in the first chapter of *The Dynamic Orchestra* (Green). See the Bibliography.

voices that carry the music forward, and they must not be covered up by the less interesting static chord.

Note: This does not apply when the tutti ensemble has the sustained sound. In that case a simple balancing of the harmony is all that is needed.

Sustained tones tend to drag. Be sure that they are synchronized precisely with the change of note in the florid or moving parts.

Two Performance Customs: Band and Orchestra

In music of all periods, when a note is tied over, *in fast tempo*, to a sixteenth of the same pitch, and that sixteenth is the first of a group of sixteenths, it is customary to replace the tied sixteenth with a rest (Examples 119 and 120). Without the moment of rest, the following sixteenths usually lack precision of ensemble. This custom is followed in both band and orchestra. In the orchestra, the bows must stop still for that instant, thus ensuring uniformity of attack as they continue.

Example 119. Beethoven, Symphony No. 3 in E-flat major, Op. 55 *(Eroica)*. Finale (measure 1).

Example 120. Mozart, *Don Giovanni*. Overture (measure 56).

The second custom concerns the eighth note followed by two sixteenths. Marked *allegro,* it is often notated thus: ♪♬ . Here we come to a discrepancy between band and orchestra. In the band, in fast tempo, the simple act of tonguing the sixteenths will ensure the staccatos. The discrepancy occurs in the orchestra. When each note is given its own bow-stroke in fast tempo, obviously there is not time to stop the bow and start it again after each sixteenth note. Therefore the staccato dot does not mean staccato here. It means only separate bows. In performance, the spacing or separation comes after the eighth note. The sixteenths are played broadly, without stops, unless . . . read on!

Closely related is Example 121a, b, and c. In (a), the staccato dots again do not mean staccato. They are used only to show that the following notes are not slurred, but bowed separately, and on the string. When the tempo is fast enough to permit the use of the "staccato volante" (the bow coming off the string after each sixteenth note), the bowing given in (b) and (c) becomes practical.

Example 121.

Example 121d places the two sixteenths ON the beat, followed by the eighth note. Here the bow is dropped onto the string, down-bow. It rebounds naturally, performing the second note without effort. The eighth note comes up-bow.

All the facets of large-ensemble performance should be taught as young musicians are progressing through high school. When they know the "professional tricks," the end result is most gratifying. **Train the players to recognize the visual difference on the page between a melody line and an accompanying passage.** Sustained tones, repeated notes, recurrent rhythmic figures are probably accompaniment and should be played softer than marked. Measures filled with varied pitches, coupled to notes of differing values, are likely to be melodic. Project them. Musicians who are trained to make these dynamic adjustments automatically are invaluable just in saving rehearsal time.

A Few Words on "Style"

Style deals with three facets of score interpretation: the musical customs in vogue when the composition was created, the personal stamp of the artistic individuality of the composer, and the inner emotional drive of the composition itself. (Here brevity must be considered. We can only indicate the direction.)

The most obvious characteristics of the four basic historic periods are shown in Example 122.

Example 122.

The Early Classical Style

See Example 122a. This style is contrapuntal in nature, dealing with concomitant horizontal lines rather than vertical harmonies. Interpretatively, the faster, running notes (measure 1 in the example) are performed broadly and closely connected tonally. The longer notes (measure 2) are spaced but not staccato. The strings will use the broad détaché bowing.

Note: *Détaché* is a French word. It does not mean "detached"; it simply means "unslurred." Winds might experiment with a ta or du tonguing seeking breadth and continuity in the sixteenths.

An ostinato bass line (a constantly repeated figure), used in the passacaglia, requires perfect rhythmic execution of the parts written above it so that it does not "stagger." **Band:** See the *First Suite in F* by Fauchet, first movement.

Embellishments

Linking the early Classical and the later Classical periods we find the entire category of embellishments.

The Appoggiatura   During Mozart's lifetime, the appoggiatura and the grace note were undergoing a change. The appoggiatura, written as a small note but showing exactly half the rhythmic value of the following note (Figure 61a), is played *on* the beat and becomes the first (and accented) note of a group of notes of equal value (Figure 61b). Notice that the slur is retained. This type is known as the "long appoggiatura," and it usually indicates that the small note is not part of the prevailing harmony.

The appoggiatura also appears as a link, melodically, in the interval of the third, thus producing a scalewise progression. In this case it becomes the "short appoggiatura" and is played on the beat (Figure 61c). It is often played simultaneously with the chord, which is then sustained.

Figure 61.

Figure 62.   Figure 63.

The Mordent   The mordent is typically a three-note figure. It is accented—played on the beat—and it takes its time from the note over which it is placed (Figure 62).*

The Trill   In a stepwise progression, the trill starts on the upper note and ends on the lower note. In intervals of the third, its first note fills in the missing scale tone. See Figure 63.

The Turn   The turn follows the contour shown by the shape of the sign. Usually it proceeds upward first (Figure 64a), but the upside-down form is used in performances of Wagner's *Rienzi* (b). When the turn is written in conjunction with a dotted note, it is performed so that it terminates on the dot (c). The main melody line is therefore reestablished before the music proceeds.

Figure 64.

The Later Classical Style

See Example 122b. This is the style that culminated in the works of Haydn and Mozart. Here the big word is *clarity*. Every note sparkles. Crisp articulations are called for. Staccatos are functioning. Spiccato bowing has fully entered the picture, aided by the advent of the Tourte† bow. In slow compositions, beauty of melodic line and depth of emotion are maturing. Dynamics (block style) move immediately from loud to soft and soft to loud. All parts are marked the same, but in performance the melody is played one degree louder than indicated, the accompaniment one degree softer than notated. Vertical harmony is apparent.

*See Frederick Neumann, *Ornamentation in Baroque and Post-Baroque Music: With Special Emphasis on J. S. Bach* (Princeton: Princeton University Press, 1978).

†François Tourte (1747–1836), a French violin-bow maker, changed the shape of the bow from its early upward-curving stick to the modern shape known today.

The Romantic Period

See Example 122c. The romantic style develops the long, steady crescendo leading to intense climaxes, as witness Beethoven's writings. Beethoven marks his staccato dots carefully. Schubert is a link in lyricism. During this period there is a constant expanding of brilliance and emotion leading to Berlioz and accompanied by the emergence of the Russian School: Glinka, Glazounov, Tchaikovsky, Rimski-Korsakov.

The Contemporary Period

See Example 122d. The twentieth century goes down in history as the time of the greatest scientific development since the world began. And music followed the same path. Here we have experimentation in harmonic relationships, rhythmic independence of voicing, beats that stutter instead of flow, requiring lopsided time-beating (the Russian revolutionary spirit bursting forth in Stravinsky!), all of this leading finally to the exploration of the minds of the performers themselves through the "chance" or aleatoric score. The "nationalistic" schools have fully emerged: Bartók with his irregular dance and folksong rhythms; Sibelius with his "northern" flavor; Debussy and Ravel presenting the French image; in Germany the stretching in length of everything that had gone before—Wagner, Mahler, Bruckner, and Richard Strauss; in Russia, Stravinsky, Prokofiev, and Shostakovich, all uniquely individual reflections of Rimski-Korsakov's teaching.

The atomic bomb itself affected our music. See Krzysztof Penderecki's *Threnody to the Victims of Hiroshima* (1959–61). Its scoring is for "fifty-two strings," featuring "'controlled aleatoricism,' extremes of pitch, novel instrumental effects, microtonal glissandi, quarter-tone writing, stereophonically distributed bands of sound, and vibrating 'tone areas.'" It is an amazing work. The recording is by EMI Records, Ltd., Hayes, Middlesex, England. (The quotation is used by permission.)

In line with this, the band has come into its own. Karlheinz Stockhausen used only wind instruments to accompany his opera *Samstag aux Licht,* which has its first performance in Milan, Italy, in May of 1984.

Orchestral Bowing Principles

This chapter ends with the basic bowing principles in their simplest form. Complete discussions are found in *The Dynamic Orchestra* (Green, Prentice-Hall, Inc., 1987) and in *Orchestral Bowings and Routines.* (See the Bibliography.)

Uniformity of bowing deals with the *direction* of the bowing motions. In general, the down-bow synchronizes with the conductor's downbeat, but there are many exceptions to this principle.*

*The exceptions to the basic bowing principles presented in this outline are to be found in Green, *Orchestral Bowings and Routines,* and in Green, *The Dynamic Orchestra.*

The Basic Bowing Principles in Their Simplest Form*

1. The note on the first beat of a measure is taken down-bow. (Exceptions)
2. The unslurred note before the barline is taken up-bow.
3. A note slurred over the barline is taken down-bow.
4. After a rest, the entrance is made on *up-bow* if an *odd number* of bows is needed before the barline is reached.
5. The entrance is made *down-bow* if an *even number* of bows is needed before the barline is reached.
6. In rhythmic figures interspersed with rests, the note present with the greatest accent takes the down-bow:

7. In passage work, four even, unslurred notes starting ON the beat take down-bow on the first note of the group. (Not always pertinent in Bach and polyphonic writing.)
8. Link the dotted-eighth and sixteenth:

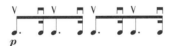

9. In continuous passages of dotted-eighth-plus-sixteenth marked *piano,* this bowing may be used at the point of the bow:

10. In $\frac{6}{8}$ time, link the quarter and the eighth:

11. Chords are played down-bow, all notes attacked simultaneously.
12. An ending note preceded by a very short note is played at the frog of the bow:

*Adapted from Green, *Orchestral Bowings.* Used by permission. Available through Theodore Presser Co., Bryn Mawr, Pa.

13. In $\frac{4}{4}$ time marked *forte,* an accented half note on beat Two is taken on a *new* down-bow:

14. In continuous, unslurred string-crossings, fast tempo: (a) violins-violas, up-bow on upper string, (b) cellos-basses, down-bow on upper string:

15. The last note of a crescendo is up-bow, the climax note is down-bow.

Exercises for Practice: Score Interpretation—Band, Orchestra, Chorus

1. Compare recordings of the same composition, one played by the band, the other played by the orchestra: for example, Bernstein, *Candide;* Shostakovich, *Festival Overture;* Wagner, "Liebestod" (from *Tristan und Isolde*); J. Strauss, Overture to *Die Fledermaus.* Listen particularly for balance problems.

2. Look through the scores in Chapter 13. Decide what clues are present to help you place them in their correct setting and style historically.

3. In soft pencil, mark the bowings in Chapter 13, applying the principles given in this chapter.

4. Study the scores in Chapter 13. Apply to them the knowledge you have gained thus far regarding building your own interpretation.

Recommended Reference Readings

AUSTIN, WILLIAM A., *Music in the Twentieth Century: Debussy Through Stravinsky.* The music of each composer is dealt with individually and at some length. Contains 110 pages of bibliography!

BERRY, WALLACE, *Form in Music.* The whole book is applicable.

CHRISTIANI, ADOLF F., *Principles of Expression in Pianoforte Playing.* This book is probably the greatest treatise available to the English-speaking student on expression in music. Starting with the section on "Melodic Accents" (p. 138) and reading to the end of the book, one can pick up information not obtainable from other sources. In reading the book for uses other than pianoforte playing, one may interpret the word *accent* simply as "stress" or "swell" in the tone.

COPE, DAVID, *New Directions in Music.* Information on twentieth-century writing.

CROCKER, RICHARD L., *A History of Musical Style*. A very complete history of music approached through the music itself; pp. 355–526, the development of the orchestra via composition.

FARKAS, PHILIP, *The Art of Musicianship*. Farkas (for many years solo French horn of the Chicago Symphony) gives an authoritative analysis of the many facets of musicianship. Highly recommended.

GALAMIAN, IVAN, *Principles of Violin Playing and Teaching*. Bowing styles dealt with in detail.

GREEN, ELIZABETH A. H., *The Dynamic Orchestra*. For the conductor/performer outside the teaching field. Professional.

HEFFERNAN, CHARLES W., *Choral Music: Technique and Artistry*.

NEIDIG, KENNETH L., *The Band Director's Guide*. A compendium of articles by various authors covering all phases of band performance.

RABIN, MARVIN, and PRISCILLA SMITH, *Guide to Orchestral Bowings Through Musical Styles*.

VAN ESS, DONALD H., *The Heritage of Musical Styles*.

WENNERSTROM, MARY H., *Anthology of Musical Structure and Style*.

Recommended Videotape

Celibidache Conducts Bruchner (No. 8). Munich Philharmonic Orchestra. VHS Hi-Fi Stereo NTSC No. 41-048317-82. © 1992 Sony Classical GMBH. Celibidache is unique. His dictum: "Every performance is a first performance." This magnificent tape shows his intensity of concentration on the **sound of the music** as it unrolls in the performance. The music speaks its own language in its own way without superimposed human interference. Celibidache lets the music sound. Note his showing of the "and" in the baton just before an important entry-beat or a change of character, thus preparing the musicians for security of ensemble. Marvelous **left hand.**

16 Memorizing the Score; Performing the Score

There is no set rule, universally recognized, for memorizing a score; no surefire, cut-and-dried method guaranteeing foolproof results. Charles Munch stated in his book (see the Bibliography) that he did not require his students in conducting classes in Paris to work from memory at the outset of their training. He felt that the security of having the score present helped the young conductor. Hermann Scherchen, on the other hand, required absolute memorization and intense mental concentration before he permitted the student to conduct the work. However, Scherchen may have geared his approach to those who had some previous experience.

Perhaps the most often asked question is "Just what is meant by '**memorizing the score**'?" The answer is interesting. It varies with the convictions of the conductor. Some say that one must know every single note of every single part, and be able to write out every part from memory. Others contend that it is sufficient to know how the melody sounds and the sequence throughout, to know the harmony and what the accompanying instruments do, but not necessarily to know how each note of each accompanying chord is distributed among the various instruments. This latter approach is akin to memorizing a solo with piano accompaniment. The player knows how the parts fit together, and whether they sound right or whether wrong notes are being played by the accompanist, but has not learned the piano part so that he or she could perform it alone. There are still other conductors who contend that it is sufficient to know the number of measures and conduct accordingly.

Obviously this last approach is the product of the "time-beater" who is doing only that. (One wonders about the emotional appeal of those performances!)

Toscanini, when asked, said that he did not know how he memorized. Chotzinoff (see the Bibliography) tells that Toscanini remarked that he had always had a facility for knowing how a score would sound by looking at it. "Sometimes I tell myself a story about a beautiful girl. This melody depicts the forest. This melody is an evil man . . . ," and so on. One can see why his performances were so often described as having great imagination and great appeal for the audiences. He lived them in his mind.

The author has been told that Guido Cantelli* memorized the part for each instrument *in toto* first, starting with the first flute and working right down through the score. When he finished an individual part, he would ask his wife to give him an examination on it. She would ask such questions as "What note is played by the second clarinet on the first beat of the second measure after A?" After memorizing the several parts Cantelli would group them by families, working with the four or five lines of the family in the score. Last he would correlate the whole score.

It is probably safe to say that *a score is memorized when one can think it through accurately in tempo (cues included) without stumbling and without recourse to the printed page or to audible sound.*

The Memorizing Process

How Do We Memorize?

By paying attention to what is transpiring as the music progresses. By noticing similarities and differences while studying. By keeping the mind alert. That is how we memorize.

In music, the ear comes first. We must know how the music sounds. Then, during the study process, the mind works hard as a conscious force. Subtly, there are many facets of the memory that help.

Some people are endowed with a strong visual memory. They remember how the music looked on the page, reading it from their inner mental picture as they perform.

All of us remember some things by comparison and contrast. Suppose that there are two passages that are similar but lead to different sequels. We locate the first note that is different. It acts as the switch in the tracks and tells us where to go.

Here is a passage of difficult beat-sequences: $\frac{3}{4}, \frac{2}{4}, \frac{3}{8}, \frac{1}{4}, \frac{3}{16}, \frac{2}{4}$. We think in sixteenths throughout. Direction of beats is indicated by arrows.

$$\downarrow \quad \rightarrow \quad \uparrow \quad \downarrow \quad \uparrow \quad \downarrow \; \uparrow \; \downarrow \quad \downarrow \quad \downarrow \quad \uparrow$$
In sixteenths 1234 1234 1234/ 1234 1234/ 123412/ 1234/ 123/ 1234 1234

*Guido Cantelli, a protégé of Toscanini, had begun to make a name for himself when he was killed in a plane crash in the 1950s.

Each number 1 signifies a beat. And then we practice. This is a process of analysis, synthesis, and **mental-physical habit-formation** until the passage is conquered.

Charting   This deals with the mental side of the study. Charting clarifies structure—how things hang together. It consists of writing out, in your own variety of musical shorthand, a synopsis of the composition. It is a good initial step in memorizing. You will write in detail at first. Then you will find where you can condense, and the outline will gradually become shorter and shorter as you assimilate the music. Eventually you will find that you can write the outline rapidly, carrying the music in your inner ear throughout. Still later you will discard the pencil and perform the whole piece in your mind from memory. Allow no outside interruptions when you give yourself the final test.

Safety Checks   Locate **audible clues** before difficult passages so that you will be prepared when they occur: a distinctive note, rhythm, or instrumental phrase several measures ahead of time. Also, use the switch in the track.

Fast, Sequential Cues   Notice the **geometric design** of where the players are sitting. See Figure 65.

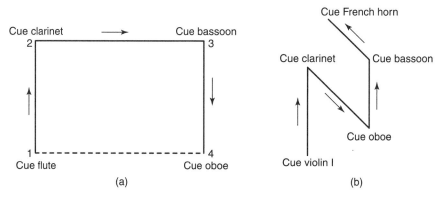

Figure 65. Geometric *design* for cues.

Counting Measures   This can be a good idea when the phrasing is very irregular or is varied among several instruments.

Interlocking Phrases   When the new phrase starts on the ending note of the preceding phrase (Mozart!), be ready to conduct the new phrase.

Sometimes it helps with cues to have certain words highlighted in your mind (Malko). "After the trumpets . . ." or "Oboe to cellos . . ."

Important: Also locate places in the music where everything is so safe that your mind can snatch a few measures of release from is intensive concentration during a performance. These moments of rest are very precious and very necessary. Set an audible cue to realert your mind.

Performing the Score: Rehearsing

From Podium to Players

Every rehearsal is a "performance" for the conductor. The conductor must be secure in his or her own mind as to what to produce and how to achieve it.

The purpose of the rehearsal is to bridge the gap from conductor to performers, to give the players an opportunity to fit their own individual part into the unified whole. The conductor is the unifying agent.

How you rehearse depends upon the quality of your players. With top-notch performers, conduct! Play the music, listen with all your powers, fix the spots where the players misunderstand, and do as much playing-through as the time allows. Be prepared beforehand with the places that can be skipped safely if time runs short.

Regardless of the level of your players, poise is a requisite. The conductor's authority is respected if he or she is organized and working toward definite musical goals.

Student Orchestras and Bands

1. *The Warm-up:* Important for the winds. Slower scales for tone and intonation. But use this time also to warm up the minds! Try Figure 66 on the scale.

Figure 66.

During the long fermata, the student prepares to play the next TWO notes. Then, on the conductor's signal to play, the two notes are played as fast as humanly possible. The students really begin to think. When this rhythm functions well, try the reverse rhythm, which creates the speed between the first and second notes. See Galamian, pages 96–97, for other suggestions (Bibliography herein).

2. *New Music:* Play the "prettiest parts" first, before the students can dislike the difficult parts. Play through somehow. In the next rehearsal, begin to solve the hard places.

3. *Formerly Rehearsed Music:* Drill the places that need it; then play through. There are cases where the only time the students have ever played through without stopping is in the public performance. (Not recommended!) **Stopping:** Regardless of the skill of your players, **do not stop unless you can remedy something immediately and with few words.** If you are puzzled, mark the spot with red pencil and bring the solutions to the next rehearsal.

Every time a stop is made, the forward motion of the rhythm is destroyed, the emotional involvement of the players with the music is interrupted, and everything has to be rebuilt again to continue. The longer the halt, the harder it is to recapture the music.*

The Public Performance

The public performance is the final test. During the short interval after the orchestra is on stage and tuned, take time to relax and collect your thoughts. They cannot start without you. You are in control.

Walk onto the stage with confidence and authority. Create a feeling of friendliness, within yourself, toward the audience and their welcoming applause. Smile when you make your bow, stage front. Bow, preferably before stepping on the podium. The act of ascending the podium is a command for attention, addressed both to the musicians and to the audience. During all of this, be thinking your tempo and the first notes of the music you are about to conduct. Do not pick up the baton until you feel that you yourself are ready to begin. *You* are in control.

Be patient if the audience is restless and not yet settled down. Almost any audience will eventually quiet itself if you just wait. (Moments can seem very long.) There is no point in starting before the audience is ready to listen. A *piano* gesture in the left hand—fingers together, pointing upward, palm facing the players—can help.

If things begin to slip, muddle through somehow, but *don't stop!* Everything exaggerates its importance in your mind when you are performing. Things that seem completely tragic may not even be noticed by the audience—unless you stop!

In performance your own musical intensity is felt vitally by players and listeners. The professional performer, whether actor or musician, recognizes this magic of the theater. One "feels" the intensity of the audience response.

Stage Etiquette

There is a formalized stage etiquette that should be observed. Before stepping onto the podium, it is always permissible at the beginning of the concert to shake hands with the concertmaster. This is almost invariably done in "guest" performances.

The conductor's handshake at the end of the concert is his or her formal thank-you to the entire membership of the orchestra. It should not be interpreted as a "pat on the back" for the concertmaster alone. (In the band, the solo clarinet becomes the concertmaster—first chair to the conductor's left as he or she faces the band.)

---

*From *The Dynamic Orchestra,* Green, © 1987 by Prentice-Hall, Inc., a division of Simon & Schuster. Used by permission.

When you leave the stage, do not delay your reentrance after your first exit. Return almost immediately. A hesitation may kill the applause. Modesty at this time is not good showmanship. And applause is "money in the pocket" for your musicians as well as yourself.

When the conductor motions the orchestra to rise, they stand up simultaneously with the concertmaster. When the conductor leaves the stage, the players again watch the concertmaster and resume their chairs as he or she sits down.

Soloists precede the conductor going on and off stage. If the conductor is a woman, a male soloist may step aside for her to precede him going off stage—or he can lead the way and step aside at the exit, permitting her to go out first. This applies only to going off stage.

At the end of a solo rendition, the soloist thanks the conductor (and through him or her, the orchestra) by shaking hands. *The soloist, not the conductor, makes the first move toward the handshake.* If the soloist is unhappy with the accompaniment, the handshake may be omitted—and may leave the conductor stranded with outstretched paw and no response.

The soloist may also shake hands with the concertmaster if desiring to do so. But **under no circumstances does the soloist motion for the orchestra to stand.** The soloist has no authority over the players. They obey only the conductor. The soloist can ask the conductor to have the players stand.

Building the Program

Think "**interest**" when setting up the concert program. Think "**contrast**" to guard against monotony. One slow number following another slow number is usually not effective.

Consider "**sequence**"—how one composition leads to the next. Some conductors are key-conscious, taking key relationship into consideration for continuity. Too great a difference between key sequences may have a disruptive effect. Live the concert in your mind. Imagine yourself as a member of the audience. Will you be interested throughout the concert, or will you fall asleep? Careful planning can "sell" the program regardless of the maturity of the players.

See that your performers keep the vitality going through to the very end of the very last note of a composition. There is nothing worse than a final note that sags. The rendition is not finished until *after* the applause starts.

Final Words

And so the final words arrive.

Be sincere and honest in your musicianship. Work to describe, with the tip of the stick, the music and the spirit underlying it. In this way the conducting can become as varied as the music itself.

Feel the texture of the tone as you call it forth. Sense that the hands and baton are molding, shaping, sculpturing a living thing, for **music is an art that exists and breathes only while it is being performed.**

Remember that certain gestures in conducting are for the purpose of guiding the listeners to what you want them to hear. The audience itself is the ultimate reason for your public performance. Respond to their intensity as they respond to yours. Listen to the music yourself, and be not unmindful that *it* is speaking to *you*.

Finally, above all, be sincere and honest in your approach to the creative element in conducting. Keep modest, work hard, and do not forget the composer. "After all," as Efrem Zimbalist, Senior, the magnificent violinist, so beautifully remarked on one occasion, "the greater genius is the one who put the notes on paper in the first place. All we, as interpretive artists, can do, is do the best we can."

Recommended Reference Reading

MEMORIZING

BERRY, WALLACE, *Form in Music.*

GREEN, ELIZABETH A. H., and NICOLAI MALKO, *The Conductor's Score.* Phrasal analysis for memorizing.

WENNERSTROM, MARY, *Anthology of Musical Structure and Style.*

REHEARSING VS. PERFORMANCE

BARRA, DONALD, *The Dynamic Performance.*

GREEN, ELIZABETH A. H., *The Dynamic Orchestra.*

KOHUT, DANIEL L., and JOE W. GRANT, *Learning to Conduct and Rehearse.* Chapter 8 deals with rehearsing.

LEINSDORF, ERICH, *The Composer's Advocate.*

PETERS, THOMAS J., and ROBERT H. WATERMAN, *In Search of Excellence.* Advice on handling people, Chapter 8, and on leadership, Chapter 9.

APPENDIX A

Seating Charts

Choral Groups

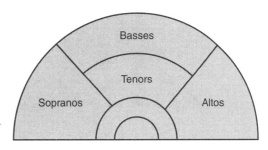

Figure A-1. This arrangement is good when the tenors and basses are strong and the sopranos and altos fully adequate.

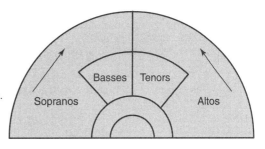

Figure A-2. A highly recommended setup is given here. Unified strength is given to the sopranos and altos in their joining behind the men's voices. This setup is also good when boys' voices are timid in school groups. The centering of tenors and basses together in front gives them confidence through proximity to the conductor.

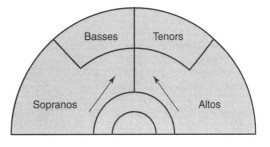

Figure A-3. A good arrangement for unity between sopranos and altos, since their voices are not split by the intervention of the men's voices.

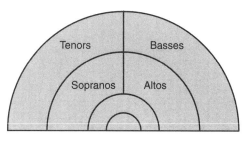

Figure A-4. This is good when tenors and basses are strong. Note that it shows the tenors on the same side as the sopranos, which is preferred by some conductors. This placement of the tenors is feasible in the preceding chart, also, if desired.

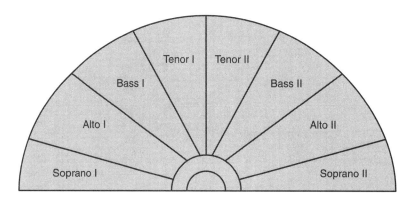

Figure A-5. The large double choir is shown here in one of the standard setups. This formation is often used in large auditoriums where the strength of the soprano sound needs to come from both sides of the stage. Otherwise, the setups of Figures A-1 through A-4 may be used with each section split into first and second parts.

   Note: In all the foregoing arrangements, the sopranos are located at the conductor's left, comparable in position to the first violins in the orchestra or to the leading clarinets in the band. Customarily, the lead melodies come from the conductor's left. However, there are instances in which conductors have experimented with the sopranos on the right, and a few prefer that setup.

Special Choral Groups

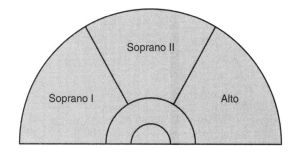

Figure A-6. Three Women's Voices.
This is the standard setup for this type of vocal ensemble, owing to the usual close correlation between the first and second sopranos in vocal composition. The other choice would be to place the altos in the middle.

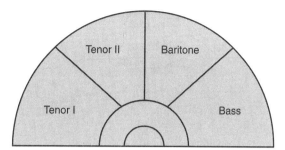

Figure A-7. Men's Chorus. The most common arrangement is given here.

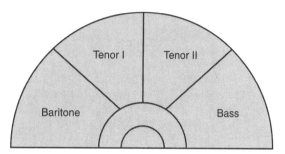

Figure A-8. Men's Chorus. This formation is also standard and may be used if desired or whenever it is necessary for acoustical purposes.

Orchestra

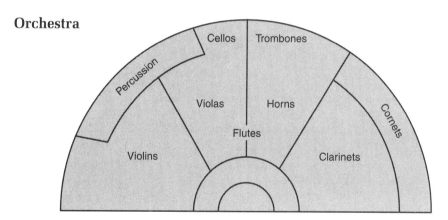

Figure A-9. Grade School Ensemble. The present trend is to use only one violin part in the young orchestra, that is, "first" violins only. It is not wise to split a weak section into two parts. When all children play first violin, strength is confidently adequate. Most grade school orchestras have a surplus of clarinets and cornets. These should be seated at the right, blowing *toward* the strings. This helps to soften their tone for the audience and to hold the group together. The location of the percussion behind the strings also helps to produce good rhythm in the ensemble. Furthermore, when the percussion is too close to the young brass section, the latter usually plays much too loudly. The violins must *always* be seated at the conductor's left so that their F-holes face the audience for maximum sound.

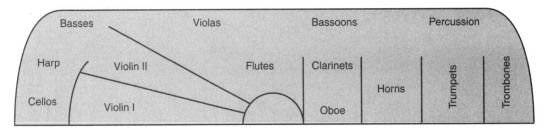

Figure A-10. Pit Orchestra. Customarily, the pit orchestra also groups the strings on the conductor's left with the winds in the center and on the right, blowing toward the strings. This helps the balance against the stage voices. The shape of the pit has to be considered in any setup of this type. In school performances, if the pit is shallow (from audience to stage) and very extended (left and right), it helps to seat the trumpets near the front on the conductor's right. Their strength holds the group together.

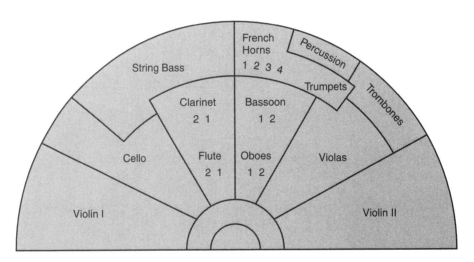

Figure A-11. Traditional Symphony Arrangement. The difference between traditional and modern arrangements for symphony orchestras lies in the positions of the second violins, the cellos, and the basses. Compare this setup with that in Figure A-12. Four things must be observed in all orchestral setups: (1) The first violins must be on the conductor's left. (2) The first chairs in the woodwinds are grouped in the center with the sections spreading outward from them; this is for efficiency when only solo winds are called for in the score. (3) The trumpets are usually seated so that they blow somewhat across the orchestra, not directly toward the audience. (4) The basses should stand behind the cellos, since they double the cello line an octave lower almost constantly. A unified bass line results.

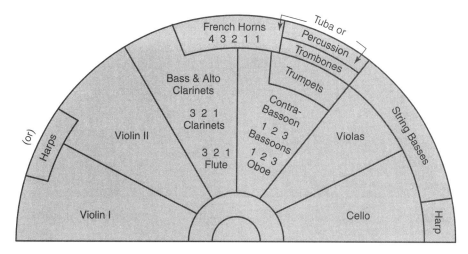

Figure A-12. Modern Symphony Arrangement. This arrangement has evolved largely during the twentieth century, and many orchestras use it as standard now. Sometimes violas are on the outside.

Band

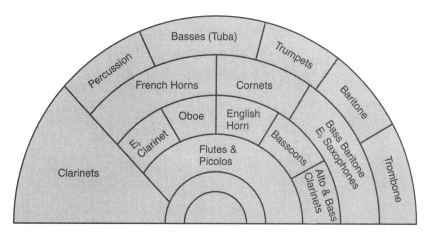

Figure A-13. School Bands, General Setup. As in the orchestra, the instruments that play the lead melody line (the clarinets) are placed on the conductor's left as he or she faces the band. The trumpets and cornets are generally located so that they do not blow directly toward the audience. Sometimes two rows of clarinets replace the flutes at the conductor's right. In that case the flutes and piccolos are grouped in the center, the alto and bass clarinets are moved back a row, and the saxophones slide to their own right or are placed behind the English horn. When there are too many trombones, the baritones may be moved ahead a row, between the saxophones and the cornets. Within the clarinet section, the first clarinets are grouped near the front with the seconds and thirds filling the back part of the section—a decided difference from the seating of the second violin section in the orchestra.

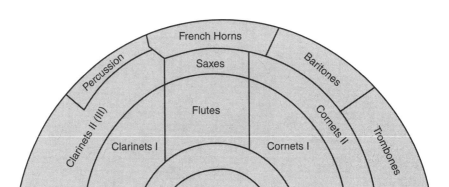

Figure A-14. Young Band, Incomplete Instrumentation. This is a typical adaptation of the larger band setup for a grade school band.

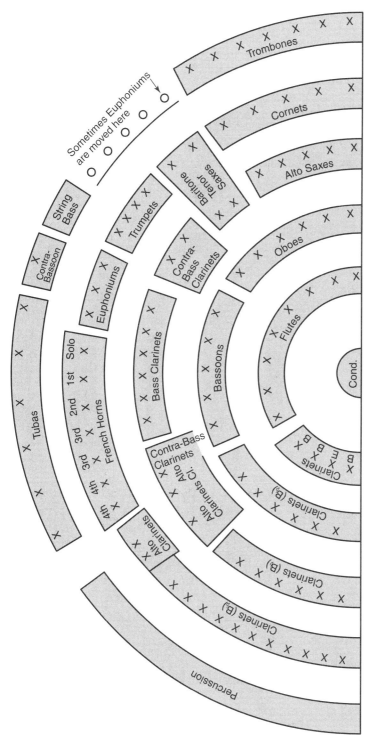

Figure A-15. Symphonic Band. The setup given here is subject to variations, among which are: Bassoons move from row two, center, to row three, outside right; bass clarinets and saxophones move to row four, outside right; cornets move toward the center; baritones move to back row as indicated in the figure; flutes in front of clarinets on conductor's left, completing their circle or adding oboes. Many variations exist.

255

_____
_____
_____
_____
_____

APPENDIX B

Instrumentation

ORDER OF INSTRUMENTS IN THE SCORE

Orchestra	Band
Piccolo	Piccolo in C (and/or D♭)
Flutes I, II	Flutes I, II
Flute III (sometimes plus Piccolo)	Oboe, I, II
Oboes I, II	E♭ Clarinet
English horn	Clarinets I
Clarinets I, II	Clarinets II
Alto Clarinet	Clarinets III
Bass Clarinet	E♭ Alto Clarinet
Bassoons I, II	B♭ Bass Clarinet
Contrabassoon	E♭ Alto Saxophones I, II
French horns I, II	B♭ Tenor Saxophone
French horns III, IV	E♭ Baritone Saxophone
Trumpets I, II, III	Bassoons I, II
(Cornets)	Cornets I
Trombones I, II	Cornets II, III
Trombone III and Tuba	Trumpets I, II
Timpani	French horns I, III
Percussion	French horns II, IV
Harp	Trombones I, II
Violins I	Trombones III
Violins II	B♭ Baritone horns (treble clef)
Violas	Euphoniums (bass clef)
Cellos	Basses (Tubas)
Basses	String Basses
To balance such an orchestra the strings would number, from violins to basses, respectively, approximately 20, 18, 12, 10, 8.	Timpani
Percussion	

LANGUAGE CHART: GENERAL TERMS

English	German	French	Italian
Major	Dur	Majeur	Maggiore
Minor	Moll	Mineur	Minore
B-sharp	Bis, His (Kreuz)	si dièse	si diesis
B-natural (ti)	H	si	si
B-flat	B (Be)	si bémol	si bémolle
A-sharp	Ais	la dièse	la diesis
A-natural	A	la	la
A-flat	As	la bémol	la bémolle
G-sharp	Gis	sol dièse	sol diesis
G-natural	G	sol	sol
G-flat	Ges	sol bémol	sol bémolle
F-sharp	Fis	fa dièse	fa diesis
F-natural	F	fa	fa
F-flat	Fes	fa bémol	fa bémolle
E-sharp	Eis	mi dièse	mi diesis
E-natural	E	mi	mi
E-flat	Es	mi bémol	mi bémolle
D-sharp	Dis	re dièse	re diesis
D-natural	D	re	re
D-flat	Des	re bémol	re bémolle
C-sharp	Cis	ut dièse	do diesis
C-natural	C	ut	do
C-flat	Ces	ut bémol	do bémolle

NOTATION TERMINOLOGY

United States	British
double whole note (eight counts)	breve
whole note	semibreve
half note	minim
quarter note	crotchet
eighth note	quaver
sixteenth note	semiquaver
thirty-second note	demisemiquaver
sixty-fourth note	hemidemisemiquaver

LANGUAGE CHART: ORCHESTRAL INSTRUMENTS

Abbreviation	English	German
Fl.	Flute(s)	Flöte, Flöten
Ob., Hb.	Oboe(s)	(H) oboe, (H) oboen
E. H.	English horn	Englisch Horn
Cl., Kl.	Clarinet(s)	Klarinette(n)
B. Cl., Bkl.	Bass clarinet	Bassklarinette(n)
Bn., Fg.	Bassoon(s)	Fagott(e)
C. Bssn., Con. Bn., C. Fag., C. Bon	Contrabassoon	Kontrafagott(e)
Hn., Cor.	French horn(s)	Horn, Hörner
Tr., Tbe. (pl.)	Trumpet(s)	Trompete(n)
Crnt., Kor.	Cornet(s)	Kornett(e)
Trb., Tbn., Tbni. (pl.) Pos.	Trombone(s)	Posaune(n)
Tuba, Btb.	Bass Tuba	Basstuba
Timp., Pk.	Timpani (pl.)	Pauke(n)
*Sn. Dr., Tr., C. C.	Snare (side) Drum	Trommel
B. Dr., Gr. Tr., C., Gr. Cassa	Bass Drum	Grosse Trommel
Cymb., Bck., Ptti.	Cymbals (pl.)	Becken (pl.)
Trgl.	Triangle	Triangel
Tmbn., Tamb.	Tambourine	Tamburin, Schellen Trommel
Ch., Glk., Cloch., Camp.	Chimes	Glocken
Harp, Hpe., Arp.	Harp(s)	Harfe(n)
V., Vn.	Violin(s)	Violine(n)
Vla., Va., Br.	Viola(s)	Bratsche(n)
Vlc., Vc.	Cello(s)	Violoncello(-e)
Cb., Kb.	Double bass(es)	Kontrabass(-bässe)

The following instruments are occasionally used in the orchestra:

Sax.	Saxophone(s)	Saxophon(e)
Bar., Eph.	Baritone horn(s) Euphonium(s)	Euphonion Baryton
Xyl.	Xylophone	Strohfiedel (Holz und Strohinstrument)
Cas., Kas.	Castanettes	Kastagnetten
Glck., Glsp.	Orchestra bells	Glockenspiel

Note: Cel., Celesta; Caisse sourde, tom-tom

---

*The term *tamburo* is a general term meaning *drum;* tabor, small drum. For complete and detailed percussion information, the reader is referred to *Modern School for Snare Drum,* by Morris Goldenberg (New York: Chappell & Co., 1955).

LANGUAGE CHART: ORCHESTRAL INSTRUMENTS (continued)

Abbreviation	French	Italian
Fl.	Flûte(s)	Flauto(-i)
Ob., Hb.	Hautbois	Oboe, Oboi
E. H.	Cor anglais	Corno Inglese
Cl., Kl.	Clarinette(s)	Clarinetto(-i)
B. Cl., Bkl.	Clarinette-basse	Clarione, Clarinetto basso
Bn., Fg.	Basson(s)	Fagotto(-i)
C. Bssn., Con. Bn., C. Fag., C. Bon.	Contre-basson(s)	Contrafagotto(-i)
Hn., Cor.	Cor(s)	Corno(-i)
Tr., Tbe. (pl).	Trompette(s)	Tromba, Trombe
Crnt., Kor.	Cornet(s)	Cornetto(-i)
Trb., Tbn., Tbni. (pl.)	Trombone(s)	Trombone(-i)
Tuba, Btb.	Tuba basse	Tuba di basso
Timp., Pk.	Timbale(s)	Timpano(-i)
*Sn. Dr., Tr., C. C.,	Caisse claire	Piccola Cassa Tamburo
C., Gr. Cassa	Grosse caisse	Gran cassa Tamburone
Cymb., Bck., Ptti.	Cymbales (pl.)	Piatti (pl.) (Cinelli)
Trgl.	Triangle	Triangolo
Tmbn., Tamb.	Tambour de Basque	Tamburin
Ch., Glk., Cloch., Camp.	Cloches	Campane
Harp, Hpe., Arp.	Harpe(s)	Arpa, Arpe
V., Vn.	Violon(s)	Violino(-i)
Vla., Va., Br.	Alto(s)	Viola, Viole
Vlc., Vc.	Violoncelle(s)	Violoncello(-i)
Cb., Kb.	Contrebasse(s)	Contrabasso(i)

The following instruments are occasionally used in the orchestra:

Sax.	Saxophone(s)	Sassofono(-i)
Bar., Eph.	Baryton	Bombarda
Xyl.	Claquebois	Gigelira (Silofono)
Cas., Kas.	Castagnettes	Castagnette, Nacchere
Glck., Glsp.	Jeu de timbre(s) Jeu di clochette	Campanelli Strumento d'acciaio Carillon

---

*See also *Dictionary of Percussion Terms,* by Morris Lang and Harry Spivack (New York: Lang Percussion Company, 1977).

Classification of Bowings

ON-THE-STRING BOWINGS—LEGATO

Name of Bowing	Section of Bow Used	How Performed	Notation	Typical Use
Whole bow Smoothly	Entire length of bow from frog to point ⊓ or any part thereof.	Bow must remain parallel with the bridge through-out its length of stroke. Requires bow-arm to reach forward as bow moves from middle to tip, and pull inward as motion goes from tip to middle.		Any slow passages where breadth or length of tone is important.
Slurs	May be performed in any section of the bow ⊓ and ∨.	The bow moves smoothly in one direction while the fingers change the notes on the string or strings.		Used wherever the slur-line indicates in the music. Used in legato melodic passages, in short motifs, and in scales and arpeggios where indicated.

Name of Bowing	Section of Bow Used	How Performed	Notation	Typical Use
Détaché	Middle or middle to point ⊓ ∨.	Short separate bows played smoothly: *not* slurred, *not* staccato.	(fast tempo)	In passage work where the notes are of equal length and are *not* marked with staccato dots. Also used in broad figures of this type on the eighth notes. Used in fast *fortes* for notes with staccato dots among slurred notes.
Louré	Any section of the bow is feasible ⊓ and ∨.	The bow *continues its motion* as in any slur, but releases pressure slightly between notes so that the notes become somewhat articulated.		Used for expressiveness in slurs where the notes need emotional individuality and in slurred bowings on the *same pitch* to distinguish rhythm.
Tremolo (bowed)	Middle and middle to point ⊓ ∨.	Very short separate bows, very fast. Actually a speeded-up détaché bowing. Motion centers in flexibility of the wrist. Not necessary to count the number of notes per beat. Usually indefinite.	(Adagio) trem.	For the excitement of a fast shimmering effect in chordal accompaniments or in melodic playing. Softer effects are played near the point of the bow. Louder at the middle. If very loud, inside players on each stand broaden to détaché instead of tremolo.
Tremolo (fingered)	Any section of the bow is practical ⊓ and ∨.	The bow plays smoothly as in a slurred bowing. Fingers alternate rapidly on a pair of notes on *one string*—as rapidly as a trill.		Wherever a trill-effect is desired on notes more than the interval of a second apart.

ON-THE-STRING BOWINGS—STACCATO

Name of Bowing	Section of Bow Used	How Performed	Notation	Typical Use
"Staccatos"	Any section of the bow ⊓ and ∨.	Any note with a stop at the end of it may fall under the generic term "staccato" on the stringed instruments.	Invariably printed with a dot above or below the note, but not all dots mean on-the-string staccatos. See Spiccato, Sautillé, Staccato volante, Ricochet below.	Anywhere a stop is desired after a note. The note may be long or short, but if followed by a momentary stop it is some variety of staccato.
Martelé	Any section of the bow is practical from whole bow to half an inch of bow ⊓ ∨.	The bow applies pressure to the string while standing still before moving. The pressure is sufficiently released, at the instant the bow starts to move, to produce a good sound. The bow stops still at the end of the stroke, and again sets pressure preparatory to the next stroke. This bowing is the underlying foundation on which ultimate clarity of attack is built.	Sometimes: Sometimes:	This bowing cannot be used in fast passage work. The tempo must be slow enough to provide time for the stopping and the setting of the bow between notes. It is used for all types of on-the-string staccatos from *pp* to *ff*. Used wherever heavy ictus is needed in the sound. Also for accents.
Slurred staccatos	Any section of the bow is good ⊓ and ∨, most often ∨. Not used in orchestra	A series of martelé strokes moving in one direction of the bow. The bow does not leave the strings between notes.		Most often written, when written, on long runs. is practical in Moderato or slower, and *f* or heavy.

OFF-THE-STRING BOWINGS

Name of Bowing	Section of Bow Used	How Performed	Notation	Typical Use
Spiccato (controlled)	Anywhere between frog and middle, including middle ⊓ ∨.	The bow is dropped on the strings and rebounds of its own accord. Must be held very lightly by hand and allowed to recoil of its own volition.	Fairly fast tempo with staccato dots on the notes **molto allegro**	From *pp* to *f* in passage work where lightness and sparkling character is desired.
"Chopped"	At the frog ⊓ ∨.	Similar to spiccato, but heavier, with less finesse.	Moderate tempos and loud dynamics. *ff*	When a spiccato effect is called for but the dynamic is too loud for a real spiccato.
Sautillé (Uncontrolled spiccato)	Middle, and very slightly above and below the middle ⊓ ∨.	A very fast détaché that is so rapid that it flies off the string each time the bow changes its direction from ⊓ to ∨, and ∨ to ⊓. The hand moves in a more perpendicular swing in the wrist joint than for tremolo.	**Presto** **and Prestissimo**	In very fast, continuous passage work where lightness and speed are the requisite.
Staccato volante (Flying staccato)	A series of spiccatos in one direction of bow, ∨-bow only.	The bow is dropped on the strings, rebounds and drops again without changing its direction, continuing in this manner.	(volante)	For lightness on scale passages usually. For the two-note-bow slurred-staccato in very fast passages.

263

OFF-THE-STRING BOWINGS (continued)

Name of Bowing	Section of Bow Used	How Performed	Notation	Typical Use
Ricochet	A series of spiccatos in one direction of the bow, ⊓-bow only.	The bow is dropped on the strings going down-bow and allowed to bounce the requisite number of times.		Short, light, sputtering runs and "galloping" rhythms as in the *William Tell* Overture.
Ricochet tremolo	Middle ⊓ v.	Two down-bow bounces followed by two up-bow bounces (spiccato).	**Presto**	To replace the single spiccato on repeated notes, especially in fast tremolos of long duration.

From *Orchestral Bowings and Routines* by Elizabeth A. H. Green. Used by permission. (See the Bibliography.)

APPENDIX D

Synopsis of Musical Form

Musical form deals with the patterns underlying the construction of our many types of musical composition. A composer desiring to write a simple Minuet will use a small two-part song form. If the Minuet is to have an added Trio, the composer will build around the pattern of the three-part song form. If the aim is to write the first movement of a symphony, the form adopted will usually be the large sonata form. Such forms are subject to variation just as patterns for clothing are subject to variation. There is, therefore, a certain amount of flexibility to be found in the application of these forms to individual compositions.

The experienced conductor knows that one of the greatest aids to score memorization is a thorough acquaintance with the form of the particular composition being studied. Many conductors make this a point of departure. Since musical form is quickest grasped through the medium of the worked-out example, the following very simple development may be of assistance to the student who has not yet had formalized instruction in this branch of music theory.

The **germ** of the musical thought is a basic rhythmic figure or a simple grouping of several notes:

(a) Monometer: One major accent

(b) Bimeter: Two major accents

It is important to recognize the germ in Beethoven's works especially. It helps in balancing the parts dynamically. Perhaps the best-known germ in all of music is the opening notes of Beethoven's Fifth Symphony:

The germ may be *developed* in many ways to lend variety and interest while preserving the feeling of unity within the work. The conductor should be alert to recognize the composer's cleverness in the handling of motifs. Development may take place through the following means:

1. Transposition of the notes (letter a above):

2. Expansion of the intervals between the notes:

3. Contraction of the intervals between the notes:

4. Diminution of the note time-values:

5. Repetition of the members of the motif:

6. Omission of members of the motif:

7. Irregular changes in the order of the notes, rhythm unchanged:

8. Retrograde motion of 1, rhythm unchanged:

9. Combinations of members of the germ:

10. Inversion: turning the intervals upside-down:

11. Various combinations of the foregoing, used simultaneously; for example, Inversion and Repetition:

The development of the germ often results in the **motif,** the basic thought of the composition. In the case of our example, it might be stated as follows:

Example D-1, on page 268, presents (1) the motif (first two measures), (2) the phrase (second two measures), (3) the period, ending on the eighth measure, (4) the second theme of a two-part song form, ending on the sixteenth measure. This simple form may be enlarged greatly by the composer by doubling the length of each section as given here in the small form.

When the second theme of a two-part song form is followed by the first theme again, the three-part song form results. Retain similarity of style in conducting parts I and III. This is shown in Example D-2 (page 268).

In a real musical composition, the length could be doubled by marking repeat dots at the double bars. The composition may further be lengthened by the addition of Introduction and Coda, each of which may assume quite some proportion in the larger compositions.

Example D-1.   The Two-Part Song Form

Example D-2.   The Completed Three-Part Song Form

The gradual expansion of form proceeds as follows. (Refer to the preceding examples.)

The **phrase:** Four or eight measures ending with a cadence or a half cadence. Mark phrases not from the upbeat but from the first full measure following the upbeat.

The **period:** Eight or sixteen measures. If it is eight measures, it is then four plus four with a cadence separating it from the next section; or if sixteen, then eight measures ending on the dominant plus another eight measures ending on the tonic. (The shorter form was used in the tune developed herein.) Vary size and speed of gestures to show these divisions.

The **two-part song form** (A-B): Eight measures ending on the dominant (Section A) and eight measures ending on the tonic (Section B). In the long form, each section is sixteen measures instead of eight.

The **three-part song form** (A-B-A): Short form, eight measures (A), eight measures (B), eight measures of (A) used as a *D.C.* Long form, sixteen measures each.

The **rondo** forms: A rondo is like a layer cake where the cake is always the same but the filling between each layer is different. Technical names are theme and episode. The theme, either in its original form or embellished, occurs more than twice in the rondo form. For specialized details, the reader is referred to one of the books on musical form in the Bibliography. Retain similar conducting style for the theme.

The **theme and variations:** The theme usually consists of four or more measures. It can be followed by any number of variations the composer may wish to write. These variations may take the form of embellishments of the melody, changing meters and rhythms, changes in mode, developments of germs drawn from the principal theme, and clever adaptations of the various devices numbered 1 to 11 in the forepart of this discussion. In the Classical period, these transformations adhered rather closely to the original harmonic structure, but this is not true in the subsequent writings. Classed as types of theme and variation are the often-encountered **chaconne** and **passacaglia.** Adjust the conducting style for the variations.

The **fugue** concerns itself with a principal theme called the *subject.* As each instrument enters, it plays the subject, previously stated in another instrument. Once having stated the subject, the instrument continues with counterpoint to the subject, which counterpoint may be called the countersubject when it has an individual character of its own and recurs repeatedly. The first instrument states the subject in the tonic key; the second instrument renders the subject either a fifth higher or a fourth lower than the original instrument. Such a statement is called the *answer.* The third instrument usually states the theme an octave higher or lower than the original instrument, and it, in turn, is followed by a fourth instrument on the subject—this in the case of a four-voice fugue. The conductor's job is to see that each statement of the theme is clearly heard as such. When the third voice enters, balance requires the two voices already playing to be toned down. Most fugues have a stretto section where the subject and answer are brought as close together as possible. Many fugues include a coda.

The (early) **Classical sonata form:** Part I is usually somewhat in excess of a sixteen-measure unit. It starts in the tonic key and modulates to the dominant, in which key the first part ends at the double bar. Part II starts again with the first theme, but this time in the key of the dominant and gradually moves back into the tonic for the ending of the movement. If the first part is in a minor key, then the modulation before the double bar may go to the major with the section following the bar in the major.

The **large sonata form** is used almost invariably for the first movement of the multiple-movement works such as symphonies, quartets, solo sonatas of the Romantic and post-Romantic periods, and solo concertos after the early Classic period. (In the last-named; a lengthy orchestral exposition precedes that of the solo instrument.) Part I of this form is called the *exposition*. It comprises two themes of contrasting character, the first in the tonic key, the second in the dominant. Part II, the *development*, is to be found after the double bar in the Classic and Romantic symphonies. This concerns itself with the rather exhaustive treatment or "development" of motifs drawn from the first two themes. Part III is called the *recapitulation*. It brings in the material of the exposition once again. In the Classical use of this form, the second theme is in the tonic key in the recapitulation. This form is often expanded by a lengthy introduction (usually slow) and a closing theme or codetta, which is present (if not of major importance) in Mozart and Haydn symphonies and sometimes assumes the proportions of another major theme in the works of the Romantic period (Brahms symphonies, for example). A facile recognition of form aids memorization.

The **modern sonata form** in use today is far freer than its predecessors in its motion, its key relationship, and its general structure. The double bar, which is an almost ever-present adjunct of the large sonata form, is most often missing in the modern version.

Let us emphasize again that this short summary gives only the obvious and most generalized structures. In actual composition, each work has its own idiosyncrasies and the work states its form rather than the form stating the work.

Any of the forms discussed herein, except the fugue and the modern sonata form, may be found lengthened by the composer through the addition of repeat dots at the double bars.

Terminology for the Conductor

The following list of one hundred terms comprises foreign-language designations that the young conductor should know. Common words such as *legato* and *allegro* are not included in the list. It is taken for granted that the college student in music will know such customary markings. The terms given here are frequently encountered in conducting the standard repertoire and the school music of a training nature. A lack of knowledge of these words can cause the conductor to make bad mistakes rhythmically, musically, and in handling the instrumentation and routines generally. Since the lists are limited to the more common terms, the student will have to resort to the large musical dictionary for further help when needed.

Classification is made alphabetically under three headings: (1) Terms of a General Nature, (2) Terms Affecting the Tempo and Time-Beating, (3) Terms Affecting the Handling of the Instruments Themselves.

Terms of a General Nature

A due (a 2)   To be played by both, as by first and second flute.

Colla parte   With the other part; often refers to accommodating the soloist at that place in the score.

Come prima   Like the first time.

Come sta   Exactly as written; do not change anything.

Con   With; seen in other forms as a contraction with the article in Italian, thus: *col, coi, colle, cogli, colla* (depending upon the gender and number).

En dehors   Out in front of; means the part so marked should be projected through the ensemble; it must be heard.

Erstes Mal   The first time.

Etwas   Somewhat.

Forte possibile   As loud as possible.

Frappe; frapper   The downbeat; to beat time.

Gleich   Quickly.

Glissez; glisser   Slide; to slide.

Immer   Always.

L'istesso (lo stesso)   The same; used usually with the word *tempo*, meaning that the new part should be in the same tempo as the preceding part.

Marcato   Marked, accented.

Meno   Less.

Mezzo   Half; usually *mezza voce*, softly, as if whispered.

Modo   Style, manner.

Morendo   Dying away.

Moto   Motion.

Murkey bass   Broken octaves, lower note coming first.

Muta   Change; usually reads *muta in_____*, meaning change the instrument to the pitch designated. Most often seen in timpani and French horn parts.

Ohne   Without; usually *ohne Dämpfer*, without mute.

Ossia   Otherwise; often refers to a simplified part—otherwise do it so.

Partitur   The score.

Petit   Little.

Peu   A little.

Piacere, a piacere   At pleasure.

Pieno   Full.

Più   *More;* most often seen with *mosso*, meaning more motion, slightly quicken the tempo. Also, PLUS.

Pult   Desk, a music stand. Usually refers to number of stands that are to play the part.

Ripieno   Similar to *tutti*, it distinguishes the accompanying instruments from the soloist.

Ruhig   Tranquil.

Sans   Without.

Schnell   Quick, rapid, *presto*.

Sciolto   Fluently.

Scordatura   Tuning contrary to the normal, addressed to the strings.

Sec, secco   Dry, very short, no after-ring.

Segue   Follow, continue in the same manner.

Sehr   Very.

Senza   Without; usually *senza sordini*, without mutes.

Smorzando   Suddenly dying away.

Sotto voce   In an undertone, soft voice.

Spianar la voce   With smooth voice.

Stentato   Labored.

Stimme   A single voice or part in the score.

Strepitoso   Noisily.

Strisciando, strisciato   Legato motion, smooth.

Subito   Suddenly; usually with a *piano* marking.

Troppo   Too much.

Tutti   The whole ensemble, everybody.

Unisoni   In unison; as *violini unisoni*, all violins in unison.

Vide   A cut; VI is printed where the cut starts and DE is shown at the end of the cut, thus: VI . . . DE.

Virgula   The old terminology for the baton.

Voci pari   Equal voices.

Terms Affecting the Tempo and Time-Beating

Accelerando   Gradually increasing the tempo.

Ad libitum   At liberty; take time, permit liberties here.

Affrettando   Excitedly, increasing the tempo.

A punto   Exactly in rhythm.

Con alcuna licenza   With some license; not perfectly rhythmic.

Etwas langsamer   Somewhat slower.

Im Takt   In tempo.

Langsam, Langsamer   Slow, slower.

Mässig   Moderato.

Pressando   Hurrying, pressing forward.

Rhythmé   Rhythmic feeling emphasized.

Rubato   Varying the note values within the rhythm, not strictly as written.

Stretto   Condensing, accelerating the tempo. (Do not confuse with the stretto of the fugue form, which is only a condensing of the distance between subject and answer.)

Stringendo   Accelerating the tempo.

Suivez   Follow; usually refers to following the soloist who may take some liberties with the tempo for expression.

Tacet   Silent; usually means the particular instrument does not play in that movement of the work.

Taglio   A cut.

Takt   The time, the measure, rhythmically; sometimes, an accenting of the first beat in the measure.

Tempo perdito   Unsteady tempo.

Tempo reggiato   Regulate the tempo, usually to accommodate the soloist.

Tempo rubato   Not strictly on the beat.

Zurückhalten   Ritard.

   Note: the term *agogic* is a general classification for the modifying of the tempo in favor of the expression.

Terms Affecting the Handling of the Instruments Themselves

Am Steg   Played with a light bow-stroke very close to the bridge so that the quality of the tone is shimmering, sounding the component harmonics of the fundamental tone (*ponticello*).

A punta d'arco   At the point of the bow.

Archet   Bow, with the bow.

Arco   Bow, with the bow.

Col legno   With the stick of the bow; usually performed by striking the strings with the stick of the bow.

Con sordini   With mutes.

Dämpfer   Mute; usually *mit Dämpfer*, with mute, or *ohne Dämpfer*, without mute. Often seen as *gedämpft* (stopped) in horn parts. Also means without snares.

First treble; second treble   First soprano; second soprano.

Legno   Wood (of the bow).

Otez   Remove (the mute).

Paukenschlägel   The timpani stick.

Ponticello   Light tone near the bridge so upper partials sound in the tone.

Sordino   Mute; also *sourdine.*

Spitze   Point of the bow.

Steg   Bridge.

Stimmung   The tuning.

Sulla tastiera; sul tasto   On the fingerboard; a command to bow the string just over the end of the fingerboard for a light, flutelike tone.

Sur la touche   On the fingerboard, same as *sulla tastiera.*

Sur le chevalet   Literally, "on the little (wooden) horse," bowed very close to the bridge, *ponticello.*

Sur une corde   On one string; the melody to be played entirely on one string. The German word for string is *Saite.*

Ton bouché   Stopped tone in French horn playing.

+   Refers to plucking the string with the *left* hand when used in string music, and to playing the notes so marked as stopped tones on the French horns when given in their parts.

Regarding abbreviated writing:

One bar on the stem = play eighths:

Two bars on the stem = play sixteenths:

Three bars on the stem usually means tremolo, free, fast reiteration:

But in Adagio and Largo, it may mean play thirty-second notes, rhythmically.

Some Specialized Percussion Terms

Coperti   Covered, muffled.

Étouffé   Dampened.

Laisser vibrer; lasciare vibrare   To let it ring.

Nadel   Mit dem = played with a knitting needle.

Schwam   Aus = made of sponge, soft stick.

Scordate   Tuned, no snares.

Secoué   Rubbed, struck.

Skin   Membrana, peau, fell, parche.

Snares   With = con, mit, avec. Without = sans, ohne, senza. Snares = timbres, cordes, Schnarren.

Wire brush   Spazzole, brosso, scavolo di ferro, spazzola di ferro, balais, ballai mettalique, cepillos metal, rute, and verga or verghe (as in *Peter and the Wolf*).

Played where

>   *On the rim:* au ribord, al cerchio.

>   *On the edge:* au bord, am Rand.

>   *Close to the rim:* près du rebord.

>   *At the center:* au centre, au milieu.

Played how

>   *With the thumb:* Avec la pouce, mit dem Daumen.

With the knuckles: colla nocce, mit dem Knöcheln.

With the fist: mit der Faust.

On the knee (tambourine): Sur la genou.

Cymbals

Antique: crotales.

Attached: befestigt.

Crash: tellern, platos.

Suspended: cymbale sospendue, frei, hangend, sospeso.

Caution: *Schlitten* means tuned sleighbells, as in Mozart's *Sleighride.* ***Tambourine di basque,*** as in the *Farandole* by Bizet, is played on drum without snares.

The Training Exercises in Sequence

Note: These exercises can be taught consecutively: first two weeks, grouping 1 and 2; thereafter, one a week. It takes only ten minutes *each day* to build a good, readable hand technique. Remember: The right half of the brain controls the left hand; the left brain controls the right hand. These exercises are *imperative* if real independence of the two hands is to be achieved. Each hand has its own language to speak. *The neurons in the brain must be trained as independence slowly becomes habitual.*

1. The straight *horizontal* line. See pages 5–6.

2. The straight *perpendicular* line. See page 6.

3. Left hand moves UP while right hand goes DOWN, and vice versa. *The first step in independence of the two hands.* See pages 48–49.

4. Add *staccato* to Training Exercises 1 and 2. Use fast motion ending in a complete *stop* at the end of each line. See that hands are still in the starting position when the stop is made. During the stop, flip hands into position for the next line of motion. See page 123.

5. Make the *perpendicular* gesture with one arm while the other arm is performing the *horizontal* gesture. Check hand positions at end of each stroke. Further independence. See page 49.

6. Preparation for cuing: Fist gesture. See page 91.

7. Time-beating in right hand, cuing gestures with left hand. TWO WAYS: (a) Cue suddenly ON THE BEAT. (b) Activate the left hand *one beat ahead of the cue and make a preparatory gesture leading to the cue.* See pages 94–95.

8. Right hand beats time ($\frac{2}{4}$, $\frac{3}{4}$, or $\frac{4}{4}$). For *crescendo*, left hand starts at bottom of *perpendicular* gesture and rises slowly (*palm upward*) *carrying the sound to* forte *during several measures. Hand reverses, comes downward, showing the* diminuendo. See page 93.

9. Lower arm forms a right angle at elbow. Freeze upper arm, shoulder to elbow, tight against the side of the body. Perform the *perpendicular* exercises of numbers 2, 3, and 4 using lower arm up and down only from the right-angle position. See page 143.

10. Arms bent at elbows to form a right angle. Lower arm static. Repeat Exercises 2, 3, 4 with just the hands moving in the wrist joint. See pages 143–144.

11. Controlling the *speed of motion* during the line of connection between beat-points. Right hand only: Baton in hand, time-beating in FOUR. Start with a quarter-inch square—all four beats to be within that tiny square. Gradually enlarge to a half-inch square, to a 1-inch square, a 2-inch square, etc., to a 10-inch square. Then a 12-inch square and upward by three-inch additions: 15 inches, 18 inches, 21 inches, 24 inches. Return downward, unit by unit, to the quarter-inch square.

Bibliography

The following works are specifically mentioned in the Recommended Reference Readings at the ends of the chapters.

ADLER, SAMUEL, *Choral Conducting: An Anthology*. New York: Holt, Rinehart & Winston, 1971.

AUSTIN, WILLIAM A., *Music in the Twentieth Century*. New York: W. W. Norton & Co., Inc., 1966.

BALK, WESLEY, *The Complete Singer-Actor*. Minneapolis: University of Minnesota Press, 1977.

BAMBERGER, CARL, *The Conductor's Art*. New York: McGraw-Hill, 1965.

BARRA, DONALD, *The Dynamic Performance: A Performer's Guide to Musical Expression and Interpretation*. Englewood Cliffs, N.J.: Prentice Hall, 1983.

BATTISTI, FRANK, and ROBERT GAROFALO, *Guide to Score Study for Wind Band Conductors*. Fort Lauderdale, Fla.: Meredith Music Publications, 1990.

BERRY, WALLACE, *Form in Music* (2nd ed.). Englewood Cliffs, N.J.: Prentice-Hall, 1986.

BLACKMAN, CHARLES, *Behind the Baton*. New York: Charos Enterprises, 1964.

BOULT, ADRIAN C., *A Handbook of Conducting*. Oxford: Hall the Printer, 1936.

BOWLES, MICHAEL, *The Art of Conducting*. Garden City, N.Y.: Doubleday, 1959.

BRAITHWAITE, WARWICK, *The Conductor's Art*. London: Williams and Norgate, 1952.

BUSCH, BRIAN R., *The Complete Choral Conductor: Gesture and Method*. New York: Schirmer Books, 1964.

CALVIN, WILLIAM H., and GEORGE A. OJEMANN, *Conversations with Neil's Brain*. Reading, Mass.: Addison-Wesley, 1994.

CHESTERMAN, ROBERT, *Conversations with Conductors*. Totowa, Conn.: Rowman and Littlefield; Copyright Canadian Broadcasting Corp. and R. Chesterman, 1976.

CHOTZINOFF, SAMUEL, *Toscanini: An Intimate Portrait*. New York: Knopf, 1956.

CHRISTIANI, ADOLF F., *Principles of Expression in Pianoforte Playing*. New York: Harper Brothers, 1886.

COOPER, G. W., and L. B. MEYER, *The Rhythmic Structure of Music*. Chicago: The University of Chicago Press, 1960.

COPE, DAVID, *New Directions in Music*. Dubuque, Iowa: Wm. C. Brown, 1971.

COWARD, HENRY, *Choral Technique and Interpretation*. London: Novello and Co., n.d.

CROCKER, RICHARD L., *A History of Musical Style*. New York: McGraw-Hill, 1966.

DANNREUTHER, EDWARD, *Musical Ornamentation*. London: Novello and Company, n.d.

DAVISON, ARCHIBALD T., *Choral Conducting*. Cambridge: Harvard University Press, 1940.

DECKER, HAROLD A., and JULIUS HERFORD, *Choral Conducting, A Symposium* (2nd ed.). Englewood Cliffs, N.J.: Prentice Hall, 1988.

DECKER, HAROLD A., and COLLEEN J. KIRK, *Choral Conducting: Focus on Communication*. Englewood Cliffs, N.J.: Prentice Hall, 1988.

DEMAREE, ROBERT W., JR., and DON V MOSES, *The Complete Conductor*. Englewood Cliffs, N.J.: Prentice Hall, 1995.

EARHART, WILL, *The Eloquent Baton*. New York: M. Witmark and Sons, 1931.

FARKAS, PHILIP, *The Art of Musicianship*. Bloomington, Ind.: Musical Publications, 1976.

FUCHS, PETER PAUL, *The Psychology of Conducting*. New York: MCA Publications, A Division of MCA, Inc., 1969.

GALAMIAN, IVAN, *Principles of Violin Playing and Teaching* (2nd ed.). Englewood Cliffs, N.J.: Prentice Hall, 1985.

GOLDMAN, RICHARD FRANKO, *The Concert Band*. New York: Rinehart and Co., 1946.

———, *The Wind Band: Its Literature and Technique*. Boston: Allyn & Bacon, 1962.

GREEN, ELIZABETH A. H., *The Dynamic Orchestra: Principles of Orchestral Performance for Instrumentalists, Conductors, and Audiences*. Englewood Cliffs, N.J.: Prentice Hall, 1987.

———, *Orchestral Bowings and Routines*. Ann Arbor, Mich.: Campus Publishers, Ed. 2, 1957, renewed, 1985. Theodore Presser Co., selling agent.

———, and NICOLAI MALKO, *The Conductor's Score*. (Formerly *The Conductor and His Score*.) Englewood Cliffs, N.J.: Prentice Hall, 1985.

GRIFFITHS, PAUL, *A Concise History of Avant-Garde Music*. New York: Oxford University Press, 1978.

GROSBAYNE, BENJAMIN, *Techniques of Modern Orchestral Conducting*. Cambridge: Harvard University Press, 1956.

HANSEN, PETER, *An Introduction to Twentieth-Century Music* (3rd ed.). Boston: Allyn & Bacon, 1971.

HEFFERNAN, CHARLES W., *Choral Music: Technique and Artistry*. Englewood Cliffs, N.J.: Prentice Hall, 1982.

HOWERTON, GEORGE, *Technique and Style in Choral Singing*. New York: Carl Fisher, 1957.

HUNSBERGER, DONALD, and ROXY ERNST, *The Art of Conducting*. New York: Knopf, 1983.

HYLTON, JOHN B., *Comprehensive Choral Music Education*. Englewood Cliffs, N.J.: Prentice Hall, 1995.

JACOB, GORDON, *How to Read a Score*. London: Hawkes and Son, 1944.

JACOBSON, BERNARD, *Conductors on Conducting*. Frenchtown, N.J.: Columbia Publishing Co., Inc., 1979.

JONES, ARCHIE M., *Techniques of Choral Conducting*. New York: Carl Fisher, 1948.

KAHN, EMIL, *Conducting*. New York: Macmillan, 1965.

KAPLAN, ABRAHAM, *Choral Conducting*. New York: W. W. Norton & Co., Inc., 1985.

KELLER, HERMAN, *Phrasing and Articulation*. New York: W. W. Norton & Co., Inc., 1965.

KENNAN, KENT, and DONALD GRANTHAM, *The Technique of Orchestration* (4th ed.). Englewood Cliffs, N.J.: Prentice Hall, 1990.

KJELSON, LEE, and JAMES MCCRAY, *The Conductor's Manual of Choral Music Literature*. Melville, N.Y.: Belwin-Mills, 1973.

KOHUT, DANIEL L., *Instrumental Music Pedagogy: Teaching Techniques for School Band and Orchestra*. Englewood Cliffs, N.J.: Prentice Hall, 1973.

————, and JOE W. GRANT, *Learning to Conduct and Rehearse*. Englewood Cliffs, N.J.: Prentice Hall, 1990.

LABUTA, JOSEPH, *Teaching Musicianship in the High School Band*. West Nyack, N.Y.: Parker Publishing Co., 1972.

LANG, PHILIP J., *Scoring for the Band*. New York: Mills Music, 1950.

LEIDZÉN, ERIK, *An Invitation to Band Arranging*. Philadelphia: Oliver Ditson Co., 1950.

LEINSDORF, ERICH, *The Composer's Advocate*. New Haven: Yale University Press, 1981.

LOEBEL, KURT, "A Symphony Player Looks at Conductors," *The Instrumentalist*, 29, no. 7, (February 1975), 30–34.

MALKO, NICOLAI, *The Conductor and His Baton*. Copenhagen: Wilhelm Hansen, 1950.

MARSHALL, MADELEINE, *The Singer's Manual of English Diction*. New York: G. Schirmer, 1951, 1953, 1956, 1957.

MARTIN, WILLIAM A., and JULIUS DROSSIN, *Music of the Twentieth Century*. Englewood Cliffs, N.J.: Prentice Hall, 1980.

MCELHERAN, BROCK, *Conducting Technique, for Beginners and Professionals*. New York: Oxford University Press, 1966.

MORRIS, R. O., and HOWARD FERGUSON, *Preparatory Exercises in Score Reading*. London: Oxford University Press, 1931.

MOSES, DON V, ROBERT W. DEMAREE, JR., and ALLEN F. OHMES, *Face to Face with an Orchestra*. Princeton: Prestige, 1987.

MUNCH, CHARLES, *I Am a Conductor.* New York: Oxford University Press, 1955.

NEIDIG, KENNETH L., *The Band Director's Guide.* Englewood Cliffs, N.J.: Prentice Hall, 1964.

PETERS, GORDON B., *The Drummer: Man.* Wilmette, Ill.: Kemper-Peters Publications, 1975.

PETERS, THOMAS J., and ROBERT H. WATERMAN, JR., *In Search of Excellence.* New York: Warner Books, Inc., Harper and Row, 1982.

PIETZSCH, HERMANN, *Die Trompete,* ed. Clifford Lillya and Renold Schilke. Ann Arbor, Mich.: University Music Press, n.d.

PRAUSNITZ, FREDERIK, *Score and Podium.* New York: W. W. Norton & Co., Inc., 1983.

POE, FRANCES, *Teaching and Performing Renaissance Choral Music.* Metuchen, N.J.: Scarecrow Press, 1994.

RABIN, MARVIN, and PRISCILLA SMITH, *Guide to Orchestral Bowings Through Musical Styles.* Madison: University of Wisconsin Press, Extension Arts, 1984.

READ, GARDNER, *Modern Rhythmic Notation.* Bloomington: Indiana University Press, 1979.

———, *Thesaurus of Orchestral Devices.* New York: Pitman Publishing Co., 1953.

RESTAK, RICHARD M., *The Brain: The Last Frontier.* Garden City, N.Y.: Doubleday, 1979.

RIMSKI-KORSAKOV, NICOLAI, *Principles of Orchestration.* London: Russian Music Agency, n.d.

ROOD, LOUISE, *How to Read a Score.* New York: Edwin Kalmus, 1948.

ROSS, ALLAN, *Techniques for Beginning Conductors.* Belmont, Calif.: Wadsworth, 1976.

RUDOLF, MAX, *The Grammar of Conducting.* New York: G. Schirmer, 1980.

SALZMAN, ERIC, *Twentieth-Century Music: An Introduction.* (3rd ed.). Englewood Cliffs, N.J.: Prentice Hall, 1988.

SCHONBERG, HAROLD C., *The Great Conductors.* New York: Simon & Schuster, 1967.

SLOBODA, JOHN A., *The Musical Mind: A Cognitive Psychology of Music.* Oxford (England): Science Publications (Univ. of Keele), 1985; New York: Oxford University Press, Clarendon Press (paperback), 1985/1993.

TAYLOR, CHARLES, *Exploring Music: The Science and Technology of Tones and Tunes.* Bristol (England) and Philadelphia: IOP Press (Institute of Physics, Inc.), 1992.

VAN ESS, DONALD H., *The Heritage of Musical Styles.* New York: Holt, Rinehart & Winston, 1970.

WAGNER, JOSEPH, *Band Scoring.* New York: McGraw-Hill, 1960.

———. *Orchestration: A Practical Handbook.* New York: McGraw-Hill, 1959.

WEERTS, RICHARD K., *Developing Individual Skills for the High School Band.* West Nyack, N.Y.: Parker Publishing Co., 1969.

WEINGARTNER, FELIX, *On the Performance of the Beethoven Symphonies,* trans. Jessie Crosland. New York: Edwin F. Kalmus, n.d.

WEISBERG, ARTHUR, *Performing Twentieth-Century Music.* New Haven: Yale University Press, 1993.

WENNERSTROM, MARY H., *Anthology of Musical Structure and Style.* Englewood Cliffs, N.J.: Prentice-Hall, 1983.

Reference Works

Index of New Music Notation. New York Public Library at Lincoln Center. 111 Amsterdam Avenue, New York, NY 10023.

Music Industry Directory, Seventh Edition, 1983. Marquis Professional Publications, Marquis Who's Who, 200 Ohio Street, Chicago, IL 60611.

The Norton Manual of Music Notation. Heussenstamm, George. New York: W. W. Norton & Co., Inc., 1985.

Prospectus of New Music. Box 270, Yardley, PA 19067.

Terminorum Musicae Index Septum Linguis Redactus (Polyglot Dictionary of Musical Terms). Akademiai Kiado-Budapest.//Bärenreiter Kassel-Basel Tours—London, 1978.

Indexes

Topical Index

Index of Musical Examples

Index of Music for Performance